Queer Theory and the Prophetic Marriage Metaphor in the
Hebrew Bible

BibleWorld

Series Editors: Philip R. Davies and James G. Crossley, University of Sheffield

BibleWorld shares the fruits of modern (and postmodern) biblical scholarship not only among practitioners and students, but also with anyone interested in what academic study of the Bible means in the twenty-first century. It explores our ever-increasing knowledge and understanding of the social world that produced the biblical texts, but also analyses aspects of the Bible's role in the history of our civilization and the many perspectives—not just religious and theological, but also cultural, political and aesthetic—which drive modern biblical scholarship.

Recently Published:

Linguistic Dating of Biblical Texts: An Introduction to Approaches and Problems
Ian Young and Robert Rezetko

Sex Working and the Bible
Avaren Ipsen

Jesus in an Age of Terror: Scholarly Projects for a New American Century
James G. Crossley

On the Origins of Judaism
Philip R. Davies

The Bible Says So!: From Simple Answers to Insightful Understanding
Edwin D. Freed and Jane F. Roberts

From Babylon to Eternity: The Exile Remembered and Constructed in Text and Tradition
Bob Becking, Alex Cannegieter, Wilfred van der Poll and Anne-Mareike Wetter

Judaism, Jewish Identities and the Gospel Tradition: Essays in Honour of Maurice Casey
Edited by James G. Crossley

A Compendium of Musical Instruments and Instrumental Terminology in the Bible
Yelena Kolyada

Secularism and Biblical Studies
Edited by Roland Boer

Jesus beyond Nationalism: Constructing the Historical Jesus in a Period of Cultural Complexity
Edited by Halvor Moxnes, Ward Blanton and James G. Crossley

The Production of Prophecy: Constructing Prophecy and Prophets in Yehud
Edited by Diana V. Edelman and Ehud Ben Zvi

The Social History of Achaemenid Phoenicia: Being a Phoenician, Negotiating Empires
Vadim S. Jigoulov

Biblical Resistance Hermeneutics within a Caribbean Context
Oral A. W. Thomas

Three Versions of Judas
Richard G. Walsh

The Archaeology of Myth: Papers on Old Testament Tradition
N. Wyatt

Edward Said, Contrapuntal Hermeneutics and the Book of Job: Power, Subjectivity and Responsibility in Biblical Interpretation
Alissa Jones Nelson

Bible and Justice: Ancient Texts, Modern Challenges
Edited by Matthew J.M. Coomber

Simulating Jesus: Reality Effects in the Gospels
George Aichele

An Introduction to the Bible (Third Edition)
J.W. Rogerson

The Joy of Kierkegaard: Essays on Kierkegaard as a Biblical Reader
Hugh Pyper

Queer Theory and the Prophetic Marriage Metaphor in the Hebrew Bible

Stuart Macwilliam

SHEFFIELD OAKVILLE

Published by Equinox Publishing Ltd.
UK: Unit S3, Kelham House, 3, Lancaster Street, Sheffield S3 8AF
USA: DBBC, 28 Main Street, Oakville, CT 06779

www.equinoxpub.com

First published 2011

British Library Cataloguing-in-Publication Data

A catalogue record for this book is available from the British Library.

ISBN-13   978 1 84553 672 5   (hardback)
          978 1 84553 673 2   (paperback)

Library of Congress Cataloging-in-Publication Data

Macwilliam, Stuart. Queer theory and the prophetic marriage metaphor in the Hebrew Bible.
    p. cm.—(BibleWorld)
  Includes bibliographical references (p.   ) and index.
   ISBN 978-1-84553-672-5 (hb)—ISBN 978-1-84553-673-2 (pb) 1. Bible. O.T. Prophets–Gay interpretations. 2. Marriage in the Bible. 3. Metaphor in the Bible. I. Title.
BS1505.6.M3M33 2011
224'.0608664—dc22

                              2010039816

Typeset by S.J.I. Services, New Delhi
Printed and bound in Great Britain by Lightning Source, Milton Keynes, UK

MJM

ut te postremo donarem munera mortis
et mutam nequiqam alloquerer cinerem

Contents

Tables and Figures   xi

Acknowledgments   xiii

Abbreviations   xv

Introduction   1

Section I: Methodological Foundations

Chapter 1: Queer Theory   9

  1.1   Understanding Queer Theory   9

  1.2   Sedgwick: Proto-Queer Theorist   10

  1.3   Butler: The (im)Practicality of Performativity   13

      1.3.1 Butler and *Gender Trouble*: Introduction   13

      1.3.2 The well-known Butler: Gender Performativity
            and Drag   13

      1.3.3 Perfecting Performativity: Butler and her Sources   14

      1.3.4 Self and the Sexed Body   16

      1.3.5 "Necessary Failures": Butler's Gender Politics   18

  1.4   Conclusions   22

Chapter 2: Feminist and Queer Biblical Encounters   27

  2.1   Introduction   27

  2.2   Feminist Forebears and Queer Anticipations   27

      2.2.1 Reception Criticism   30

      2.2.2 Inception Criticism   32

      2.2.3 Queer Anticipations 1: Gender Play   34

      2.2.4 Queer Anticipations 2: "Raped Men As Well"   36

      2.2.5 Dilemmas of Masculinity   40

2.3   Queering the Biblical Texts   45
2.4   Queer Convictions   50
2.5   A Note on Nomenclature   55

Section II Queer and Metaphor

Chapter 3: A Queer Theory of Metaphor   63
3.1   Introduction   63
3.2   Definitions   63
3.3   Metaphorical Attributes: Non-Substitution and
       Interaction   65
3.4   Metaphor and Ideology   67

Chapter 4: Are the Israelites Male?   70
4.1   Introduction   70
4.2   Examples of Gender Inclusivity   72
4.3   Examples of Gender Exclusivity   75
4.4   Discussion: Soldiers and Censuses   79

Chapter 5: Queering Jeremiah   84
5.1   Introduction: Two Questions   84
5.2   Question 1: Gender Polarities   85
5.3   Question 2: Identifying   92
5.4   A Suite in Three Movements   94
5.5   Conclusions   95

Chapter 6: Queering Hosea   97
6.1   Introduction: The Complexities of Hosea   97
6.2   The Anti-schema and Hosea   98
6.3   Yhwh's So-Called Feminine Qualities   100
6.4   Linearity in Hosea   103
       6.4.1 Linearity: The Thematic Sequence of
              Chs. 1–3 Stage 1   105
       6.4.2 Linearity: The Thematic Sequence of
              Chs. 1–3 Stage 2   107
       6.4.3 Linearity: The Thematic Sequence of
              Chs. 1–3 Stage 3   109
       6.4.4 Linearity: The Thematic Sequence of
              Chs. 1–3 Stage 4   110

6.5	The Unmanning of Hosea	111
6.6	The Three-Movement Model	114
	6.6.1 Where Does the Third Movement Begin?	117
	6.6.2 The Content of the Third Movement	119
	6.6.3 Hos.2.22(20): יָדַע	122
	6.6.4 Hos.2.25(23): וּזְרַעְתִּיהָ לִּי בָּאָרֶץ	123
	6.6.5 Third Movement: Conclusion	124
6.7	Queering Hosea: Conclusions	125
6.8	Postscript: Methodological Reflections	129

Chapter 7: Queering Ezekiel, Part 1 — 135

7.1	Introduction	135
7.2	The Case of Masculine for Feminine Forms	136
7.3	Chance or Design? Rooker and the M for F Forms in Ezekiel	137
7.4	Chance or Design? Case Study 1: Living Creatures	139
7.5	Chance or Design? Case Study 2: Sheep & Shepherds	142
7.6	Chance or Design? Case Study 3: Dry Bones	145
7.7	Chance or Design in Ezekiel's *Marriage Metaphor*: The Two Women	146
7.8	Re-reading Jeremiah and Hosea	150
	7.8.1 Jeremiah	150
	7.8.2 Hosea	153
7.9	Conclusions	154

Entr'Acte: An Orgy of the Ego: Reflections on the Methodology of Section III — 157

Section III Queer and Camp

Chapter 8: The Methodological Potential of Camp — 167

8.1	Introduction: A Telephone Conversation	167
8.2	Resolute Frivolity: Some Features of Camp	169
	8.2.1 Camp, Gays and Effeminacy: Who Owns Camp?	169
	8.2.2 Camp Stylistics	172
	8.2.3 The Functions of Camp	173

8.3   A Camp Application   177
   8.3.1 Introduction   177
   8.3.2 'Reading' Ezekiel   180

Chapter 9: Queering Ezekiel, Part 2   184
9.1   Strange Flesh   184
9.2   Dirty Words?   184
9.3   Monstrous Meanings   186
9.4   Drastic Metaphor: Big Dicks in the Bible?   189
9.5   Broadening Out   190
9.6   First Performance: Sex Addicted   192
9.7   Second Performance: He knows the Secrets of the Heart   198
9.8   Conclusions   203
9.9   Excursus One: The Hidden Penis   205
9.10   Excursus Two: Oholibah's Disgust   206

Chapter 10: Conclusions   210
10.1   Introduction   210
10.2   Gender Slippages in Jeremiah   211
10.3   The Prophets Unmanned   212
10.4   The Third Movement   213
10.5   The Anti-Schema and Ezekiel: M for F forms   213
10.6   The Significance of the Subverted Metaphor   215
10.7   Ezekiel, Camp and Mae West   215

Schedule of Antischemas   219

Bibliography   225

Index of Biblical References   239

Index of Modern Authors   242

Subject Index   246

Tables and Figures

Table 1: Schmitt's Chiastic Structuring in Jeremiah 2   87

Table 2: Another Alleged Chiastic Structuring in Jeremiah 2   87

Table 3: Diamond and O'Connor's Pattern of Reversed Themes   88

Table 4: Jerusalem versus Israel   89

Table 5: Textual Levels for Jeremiah 2–3   92

Figure 1: Photograph that accompanies Cummings 2004   195

Figure 2: 'Semen Volumiser': *Gay Times*, 307 (Ap. 2004, p. 114)   196

Figure 3: Dickie Collier's Hardcore Review: *Gay Times*, 307
    (Apr. 2004, p. 116)   197

Figure 4: Mae West (1892?–1980)   201

ACKNOWLEDGMENTS

This book began life as a PhD thesis submitted to the University of Exeter in 2006. It remains substantially the same, apart from minor corrections and some amendments that take account of more recent literature.

It is a pleasure to acknowledge all the support given by colleagues in the Department of Theology and Religion both during my time as an MA and PhD candidate, and since then as a Teaching Fellow. I am particularly grateful to Dr Francesca Stavrakopoulou who supervised the later stages of my thesis and who has encouraged and nagged me ever since.

Dr Gareth Owen first introduced me to the complex of ideas called queer theory. The telephone conversation that sparked Section III in this book was just one of the many ways in which he helped me to arrive at an understanding of what I was doing, and he continues to inspire both invaluable self-criticism and new ideas.

It is a pleasure, too, to record my thanks to Equinox Publishing, and especially to Professor Philip Davies for encouraging the publication of this book and for his helpful advice; and to Valerie Hall for her practical and refreshingly relaxed support.

I am grateful to the following for permission to reproduce the illustrations in Chapter 9:

> For Figure 1 (page 195): Mr James Stafford
> For Figure 2 (page 196): A.L.L. Studios
> For Figure 3 (page 197): Falcon Studios, Conwest Resources, Inc.
> For Figure 4 (page 201): TopFoto, Topham Partners LLP.

I am grateful to BibleWorks for the use of their Hebrew and Greek fonts:

> BWHEBB [Hebrew] and BWGRKL [Greek] PostScript© Type 1 and TrueType™ fonts. Copyright© 1994–2002, BibleWorks, LLC. All rights reserved. These Biblical Greek and Hebrew fonts are used with

permission and are from BibleWorks, software for Biblical exegesis and research.

Finally, thank you, Gareth and Tony, beloved friends; and thank you, Francesca and Geoff for gently and persistently guiding me in my befuddlement through the hallowed doors of the Hour Glass, the Fat Pig, the Rusty Bike and the Old Fire House.

Abbreviations

AB	Anchor Bible
ABR	Australian Biblical Review
AV	Authorized Version
BI	Biblical Interpretation
BRev	Biblical Review
CB	Century Bible
CBQ	Catholic Biblical Quarterly
EvT	Evangelische Theologie
GLQ	Gay and Lesbian Quarterly
HALOT	The Hebrew and Aramaic Lexicon of the Old Testament (see Bibliography *sub* Koehler, Ludwig and Baumgartner, Walter)
Herm	Hermeneia
HUCA	Hebrew Union College Annual
ICC	International Critical Commentary
JAAR	*Journal of the American Academy of Religion*
JBL	*Journal of Biblical Literature*
JFSR	*Journal of Feminist Studies in Religion*
JJS	*Journal of Jewish Studies*
JNSL	*Journal of Northwest Semitic Languages*
JSOT	*Journal for the Study of the Old Testament*
JSOTSup	*Journal for the Study of the Old Testament*, Supplement Series
LXX	Septuagint
MT	Masoretic Text
NRSV	New Revised Standard Version
OTG	Old Testament Guides
OTL	Old Testament Library
PMLA	Publications of the Modern Language Association of America
SJOT	*Scandinavian Journal of the Old Testament*

TDNT   *Theological Dictionary of the New Testament* (see Bibliography
        sub Kittel, Gerhard)
TDOT   *Theological Dictionary of the Old Testament* (see Bibliography
        sub Botterwick, G. Johannes and Ringgren, Helmer)
VT   Vetus Testamentum
WBC   Word Biblical Commentary

Introduction

The object of this book is to subject the so-called *marriage metaphor* in Jeremiah, Hosea and Ezekiel to queer scrutiny.

It is easy enough to explain what is meant by *marriage metaphor:* it is a conceptual shorthand for the sexual imagery used in the description of the relationship between Yhwh and Judah/Israel in Jeremiah 2–3, Hosea 1–3 and Ezekiel 16 and 23.[1] Sarah Moughtin-Mumby has cogently objected to the use of this phrase on the grounds that, amongst other things, it "gives the impression that there is a story-line lying behind sexual and marital language which progresses along similar lines in various prophetic books" (2008: 7–8). But although her study amply demonstrates the remarkable variety with which the metaphor is treated in the Hebrew Bible I have decided to retain the phrase, if only for the sake of convenience, and in the hope that readers will be reminded of Moughtin-Mumby's objection, like some large warning label, every time they see the two words.[2]

It is less easy to explain what is involved in the proposal to "subject" these texts to "queer scrutiny"; indeed much of Section I will be taken up with a discussion of what I understand by the word "queer"; but, in order to provide a context to that discussion, I should first like to outline the various meanings offered in recent scholarship – and in the process to make clear what I do *not* mean by queer.

One could make no better choice for a companion on this first part of the journey than Ken Stone, who in his Introduction to *Queer Commentary and the Hebrew Bible* teases out the "possible connotations of 'queer' in biblical commentary'" (2001a: 14). He first distinguishes a cluster of variations on an understanding of queer as a holdall label for gay, lesbian and bisexual. Such an understanding may be used simply as a self-appellation reclaimed from the use of the word queer as a term of abuse. But by understanding "queers" as an identifiable group located in a particular way within society, some scholars go on to place "'queer readings of the Bible' within the framework of conversations already taking place among biblical scholars about 'social location and biblical interpretation'" (Stone 2001a: 16). Stone links this understanding of queer to reception theory, so that queer readings of the Bible are those that in effect use the biblical texts as a resource for a particular group within society. He cites as an example of this use of queer West's paper in *Queer Commentary and Biblical Interpretation*; she suggests that the "poetry of Lamentations provides those in the Queer community who are in 'mute despair' words to order and articulate their experience of AIDS" (West 2001: 141).

Stone is right to argue that this use of queer has the advantage of getting away from "the handful of texts that are endlessly analyzed in discussions of 'the Bible and homosexuality'" (2001a: 18).[3] Those readings that seek to express and defend non-heterosexual desires and practices as authentic and legitimate might be described as inward-looking – the voices of a minority speaking for a minority.

Stone goes on to discuss what might be termed a more outward-looking use of queer, one that looks beyond the ghetto in order to invest the insights of those on the margins with generic transformative value. By what I call this outward-looking understanding I mean queer theory, the methodological stance that Stone himself uses in his own paper in *Queer Commentary and the Hebrew Bible*;[4] which indeed is the methodological stance used in this book.

I should like to emphasize two important qualifications. First, it is not my wish to disparage an inward-looking understanding of queer. Both inward- and outward-looking understandings can produce valuable work – something proven by the polychromatic picture of queer presented by Stone's contributors to *Queer Commentary*.[5] Second, it is worth remembering that queer theory challenges the naturalness of the binaries heterosexuality/homosexuality and female/male, and one might add that, in line with other poststructuralist projects, it is suspicious of binaries in general. On closer study, then, the distinction between inward- and outward-looking understandings of queer may well prove to be not as sharp as the binary framework implies. So, for example, Stone associates reception theory with what I have just described as inward-looking queer; he reports the criticism that reception theory is often accused of saying more about the interpreter than about the text. Yet that is not an inevitable outcome. Reception criticism necessarily describes how the text has been approached – that is, from the point of view of a particular reader who brings his/her (community's) insights and experiences to bear upon the text. But it does not necessarily govern *to* whom the interpreter speaks. The implications of what s/he finds in the text may ripple far beyond his/her particular centre. It is in this hope of further-reaching ripples that I use reception theory in Section III.

Section I begins with my understanding of queer theory (chapter 1). I go on to discuss in chapter 2 how the theory can be applied to biblical texts. Section II offers a linguistic/literary approach to Jeremiah 2–3, Hosea 1–3 and Ezekiel 16 and 23. It starts by articulating in chapter 3 a queer understanding of how metaphor can (fail to) work as a means of expressing an ideological message. In chapter 4 I set out to demonstrate from textual evidence drawn from the wider Hebrew Bible that one part of the tenor of the metaphor, the inhabitants of Israel/Judah/Jerusalem, are to be understood as male. In chapters 5–7 I apply these theoretical arguments to the texts of Jeremiah, Hosea and Ezekiel, respectively.[6] In chapter 5, a schematic device (dubbed an anti-schema), which exploits features of grammatical gender in biblical Hebrew in order to explicate the gender structure of the *marriage metaphor*, is applied to Jeremiah 2–3.[7] The purpose of chapters 6 and 7 is to see whether the findings of chapter 5 can be replicated in the texts of Hosea and Ezekiel. The handling of the metaphor in those books, very different from that in Jeremiah, results in only partial success in the application of the anti-schema, and so I turn to other literary means of queering the metaphor, pointing out the way, for instance, that Hosea is unmanned by the text, and, in the case of Ezekiel, offering a discussion of the significance of a specific feature of biblical Hebrew. It will be noticed that in a methodological approach that exploits grammatical features of the Hebrew language, little help can be gained from the Greek of the Septuagint, where the grammatical structure is different.[8] The limitations of the anti-schema are accepted in Section III, where a move away from the methodology of Section II, heralded in chapters 6 and 7, is fully embraced. The general approach remains firmly literary but the focus shifts from the text to the reader, and the methodology adopted owes much to reception criticism. The point of view is still queer, but the emphasis is now on a reader who experiences the text of Ezekiel 23 as a camp performance. Camp is, to say the least, an unusual adjunct to biblical scholarship, and the theoretical exploration that begins Section III, chapter 8, offers an account of the complex of ideas and nuances that camp, an otherwise lightly regarded twentieth-century Western cultural phenomenon, is capable of bringing to Ezekiel. But beyond this, as it were, contrastive intertextuality, I set out to show in chapter 9 that there is a sense in which camp and Ezekiel 23 are made for each other, in that they share a penchant for extravagance and outrageousness, and that they can reveal truths in an entirely unexpected, and very queer, manner.

Two important sub-themes will receive attention along the way: first, I explore the debt I owe to feminist biblical criticism; second I hope to convey my fascination with the controversial question of queer theory as a socio-politically engaged methodological tool. But what need is there to apply an engaged methodological tool to the *marriage metaphor* at all? For an answer I could offer the conclusion drawn by Raymond C. Ortlund in his study of the metaphor. In a remark that neatly exemplifies the phenomenon of metaphorical interaction,[9] he describes what he sees as the theological and ethical consequences of a metaphorical theme that begins in the Hebrew Bible and reaches its "ultimate reality of a Saviour with his Bride, which the biblical story will eventually unveil as the mystery revealed through human marriage" (Ortlund 1996: 19):

> Among all men and women, married and single, the institution of marriage is to be honoured and its sexual parameters carefully observed. Why? Because marriage bespeaks a higher reality – the love of Christ for his Church and her joyful deference to him – and is itself enriched by what it bespeaks. (Ortlund 1996: 173)

He concludes that the ethical consequences of the biblical use of marriage to illustrate the divine/human relationship are that premarital sex, extramarital sex and same-sex marriages are wrong (the first "toys with" the second "violates" and the third "perverts" the 'biblical mystery').[10] For Ortlund, then, the *marriage metaphor* conveys a powerful ideological message.

And as a more recent indication of the need for such an engaged approach, I should like to offer a remark reported while I was in the process of re-considering what I had to say about the socio-political relevance of queer theory. The Rev. David Anderson, President of the conservative American Anglican Council, responded to a homily given by Katharine Jefferts Schori on 21 June 2006, the day before her election as Presiding Bishop of the Episcopal Church of the USA. Schori had included the remark, "Our mother Jesus gives birth to a new creation, and you and I are his children." Anderson commented:

> If Jesus is our mother and the Church is the Bride of Christ what kind of a relationship does mother Jesus and the Bride of Christ have? It would suggest that somehow this is a lesbian relationship.[11]

Anderson's comment was meant as a severe criticism of Schori; for him, it is unthinkable that the metaphor of the Church as the Bride of Christ can be compromised into suggesting forbidden gender relationships. What I set out to show in Section II is that the *marriage metaphor* is compromised within the biblical text itself, and that "forbidden" gender relationships are implicit in the deep structures of its language. And in Section III I argue that a reading of the text from the vantage point of someone within the world of "forbidden" gender relationships can provide fresh insights which may be of interest to the wider readership of the Hebrew Bible.

Notes

1. I have confined this study to these texts, on the grounds that they represent the most sustained use of the metaphor; I leave aside less-extended examples, for instance Isa. 1:21; 50:1; 54:1–6; 57:6–13; 62:4–5.
2. With this hope in mind, I have italicized the phrase throughout the book. In retaining it, I keep company with Gerlinde Baumann, who comments that "since it has become customary usage among scholars I have adopted it" (2003: 1).
3. Stone condemns the sterility of such analysis: it pushes, he comments, "some lesbian, gay or bisexual readers into an unfortunate false alternative where one's only options appear to be a denial that the Bible condemns homoeroticism or a rejection of the value of biblical interpretation altogether" (Stone 2001a: 18).
4. Stone (2001b).
5. Vigorous work on "inward" preoccupations continues to be produced; Michael Carden's excellent study of the Sodom and Gibeah texts is evidence of this vigour (2004).
6. I offer a study of Jeremiah before that of Hosea, the "primal text", as Baumann calls it (2003: 85), because Jeremiah is less complicated in terms of interpretative questions.
7. A version of this chapter has been published elsewhere (Macwilliam 2002).
8. It is as if the maternal imagery used by Schori (see below, page 211; the remark is "Our mother Jesus gives birth to a new creation, and you and I are his children") had found its way into the French-language media; the gender instability, the contrast between "our mother Jesus" and "*his* children", would become "notre mère Jésus" and "*ses* enfants", and, although in general French uses grammatical gender far more than English, the possessive adjective happens not to reflect the gender of the referent, and the gender contrast of the English original is lost.
9. Black sums up what is meant by metaphorical interaction: "If to call a man a wolf is to put him in a special light, we must not forget that the metaphor makes the wolf seem more human than he otherwise would" (Black: 1962: 44). See also below, pages 65–67.
10. Ortlund 1996: 173.

11. These remarks by Schori and Anderson were taken from the BBC Radio 4 programme *Profile: Katharine Jefferts Schori*, broadcast on Saturday 24 June 2006. Anderson fails to comment, understandably enough, on the unstable gender of Schori's Jesus, who not only is a mother, but also retains a masculine possessive adjective ('*his* children').

Section I

Methodological Foundations

Chapter 1

Queer Theory

Undoubtedly, a lot of queer theory is little more than linguistic or historical pedantry that is far more irritating than it is "challenging".
(Simpson 1996: xvii)

1.1 Understanding Queer Theory

If queer activism has met with only limited success,[1] queer as a methodological tool maintains a strong presence in anglophone academic literature.[2] Yet, although there is a growing body of commentaries on what has come to be known as queer theory,[3] it is notoriously difficult to arrive at a definition of the phrase. Annamarie Jagose insists that "part of queer's semantic clout, part of its political efficacy, depends on its resistance to definition" (1996: 1). If she is right, and definitions are certainly hard to find in other commentators on queer theory,[4] is it possible, nevertheless, to arrive at some understanding of queer theory?

A suggestion made by Arlene Stein and Ken Plummer may provide an answer. Writing in a collection of essays that both bemoans and seeks to redress the dearth of sociological contributions to queer theory, they comment:

> Clues as to what queer theory looks like can be glimpsed through some of its (emerging) canonical works, which come mainly from philosophy, literature, and cultural studies. (Stein and Plummer 1996: 133)

Who makes up this canon?[5] Stein and Plummer single out Butler and Sedgwick (1996: 13–14). Nikki Sullivan (2003: 66) uses the phrase "canonical lists", on which appear the names "Sedgwick, Butler, de Lauretis, Bersani, Califia, Warner, Watney, and so on". On the other hand, Tamsin Spargo emphasizes such precursors of queer theory as Lacan and Derrida (1999: 40–41). Similarly Jagose is interested in "the post-structuralist context in which queer emerges", provided by Freud, Althusser, Lacan and Saussure (1996: 79), and she adds Michel Foucault, with the result that her list, like Spargo's, is not so much a canon as a remote Pantheon. But both Jagose and Spargo single out Judith Butler for special discussion; in Spargo's words *Gender Trouble* is "arguably the most influential text in queer theory" (Spargo 1999: 52).

After looking first at the part played in the formation of queer theory by Sedgwick, who anticipated some of its more important elements, I shall focus attention upon the influence exerted by *Gender Trouble* and some of Butler's other work. Was this influence wholly positive or can one also attribute to it the reputation for socio-political quietism that queer theory has earned from some of its critics? In asking this question I am conscious that I may be trying the patience of those readers who would prefer an immediate dip into biblical waters. But it is important first to clarify my understanding of queer theory, and also to begin a justification of its use as an ethical biblical tool.

1.2 Eve Kosofsky Sedgwick: Proto-Queer Theorist

If Butler is the obvious choice as a prophet of queer theory, she is not without rivals. The strongest is Sedgwick. First published in 1991, the same year as *Gender Trouble*, her *Epistemology of the Closet* (1994) attracts much attention in the literature of queer theory. By means of detailed analyses of certain nineteeth- and twentieth-century literary texts (the authors of which include Melville, Wilde, Nietzsche, James and Proust), in a style that at times equals Butler's in convolution,[6] Sedgwick sets out to demonstrate that the "open secret" of homosexual concealment, the "closet", has been a crucial factor for same-sex desire, but, far more than that, has influenced the formation of many twentieth-century cultural binaries, "crucial sites for the contestation of meaning".[7]

As an important corollary to this central theme, Sedgwick observes ambiguities in modern conceptualizations of same-sex desire; she uses them to reveal how the apparent confidence with which reality is generally conceptually organized along binary lines is in fact troubled and undermined by incoherence and contradiction. It is this running motto theme that makes a claim for *The Epistemology of the Closet* to be called foundational for queer theory. A significant feature of her book – and something that is particularly significant in my own application of queer theory to biblical texts – is that it is not another study of same-sex desire *per se*. She does not place same-sex desire under the microscope in order to understand its origins, to reveal to the "normal" audience the odd behaviour of a minority species, let alone to advocate means of ameliorating their condition. Rather, her concern is to show how the conceptualization of same-sex desire provides a way of understanding how sexuality in general is organized, and to contextualize this organizing process in gender politics and the struggles for power in society.

She introduces her book with two pairs of contrasting views of homosexuality. The first pair is a minoritizing versus a universalizing view of homosexual/heterosexual definitions.[8] Although queer theorists and Sedgwick herself favour the latter view, her point is that both views exist side by side in society, and, to show the confusion produced by this symbiosis, she observes how the minoritizing view has been held both by those gay liberationists who champion the cause of a gay-identified minority, and by those heterosexists who oppose it.[9] Sedgwick dubs her second pair of contrasting views of homosexuality, transitive (or liminal)[10] versus separatist. Again, these contrasting views of homosexuality continue to exist side by side. Sedgwick's model of binaries with coalescent tendencies consolidates my own model of outward- and inward-looking interpretations of queer.[11] A common perception may be that what I have termed an inward-looking view of queer is more concerned with socio-political engagement than its binary partner. But I shall argue – in a tactic that moves towards a breakdown of the binary – that an outward-view of queer, the one most often associated with academic queer theory, does have a potential for such engagement.

It is this rich profusion/confusion of ideas about same-sex desire, a confusion shared by both sides in the homo/heterosexual "divide" that is mapped so powerfully in *The Epistemology of the Closet*, a confusion that pervades much of the material laid out in Sedgwick's well known seven Axioms (pp. 22–63). I do not intend to examine the Axioms, except to use one of them, Axiom 5 (pp. 44–48),[12] along with a later brief passage (pp. 82–85) as convenient pegs to hang a picture of queer theory's emergence in the late twentieth century. For Sedgwick takes up the now classic account of how "Foucault among other historians locates in about the nineteenth century a shift in European thought from viewing same-sex sexuality as a matter of prohibited ... *acts* ... to viewing it as a function of stable definitions of *identity*" (pp. 82–83; emphases original). She takes for granted her readers' familiarity with the way this classic account further proceeds: how, that is, homosexual identity, emerging pathologized and proscribed from nineteenth-century medical, legal and psychological discourses is gradually appropriated by reformist and, later, liberationist homosexual lobbies. Now, this last sentence is admittedly a highly conflated and simplistic summary; for instance, it takes no notice of a homosexual input into the original nineteenth-century discourses[13] and ignores proto-homosexual identities in early modern European urban communities as observed in the pioneering work of Bray (1982).[14]

However imperfect, this summary is nevertheless adequate to describe the process whereby the conceptualization of same-sex desire developed by the 1970s. After that time, the model became embroiled in the tug of war between social construction and essentialism. Sedgwick herself avoids such embroilment, partly on the grounds that the terms in which the debate has been conducted involve political dangers,[15] and partly because she wishes to use the minoritizing/universalizing axis to extricate her from what she regards the theoretical stalemate reached by the constructionist/essentialist debate.[16] Sedgwick's own treatment of the classic account goes beyond the constructionist/essentialist debate and takes us into queer territory. Axiom 5 challenges what she calls 'supersession': she criticizes both Foucault and David Halperin[17] for arguing that the identity model of homosexuality *replaced* the older view of homosexuality as isolated acts to which all human beings are potentially prone. On the contrary, she argues, both models continue to exist concurrently – her position obviously has a close relationship with her minoritizing/universalizing binary. What she is criticizing is the view that the conceptualization of (same-sex) desire has developed in an orderly, even progressive, fashion. Rather one should regard it not even as multi-layered but as a jumble of mutually contradictory ideas. This insight, as well as her insistence that a study of same-sex desire tells us something about all sexual desire, marks Sedgwick out as a queer theorist *avant la lettre*.

But it is clear too that the theoretical underpinning of queer theory is not thoroughly worked out in *The Epistemology of the Closet* (indications of this are that she devotes two-thirds of the book to her literary analysis, not to mention the fact that I have been able to tag an historical mini-account of queer's origins to my discussion of her book). To explore in more depth, for instance, the nature, or, rather, process, of gender identity, I need to turn at last to Butler.

1.3 Judith Butler: The (im)Practicality of Performativity

1.3.1 *Butler and* Gender Trouble: *Introduction*

In the 1999 preface to *Gender Trouble,* Butler reveals her failure to anticipate that the book "would be cited as one of the foundational texts of queer theory" (p. viii).[18] Such has indeed been its fate. But *Gender Trouble* has been more cited than read. Some responsibility for this must lie with the author's writing style, although I remain undecided as to whether this is the inevitable result of the difficult contents or simply authorial idiosyncrasy.[19] Whatever the case, Butler has expended much energy since the writing of *Gender Trouble* in "clarifying and revising the theory of performativity" (p. xiv), not only because she has altered her views since its publication, but also because "so many others have taken it up and given it their own formulations" (p. xiv).

1.3.2 *The Well-Known Butler: Gender Performativity and Drag*

First, it would be as well to rehearse those passages most often quoted when queer theorists summarize what they see as Butler's main position. She sets out to show how the apparatus of "compulsory heterosexuality"[20] contrives to "naturalize"[21] not only (biological) sex, gender (behaviour) and sexuality, but also effects a seamless continuity between the three. The means whereby the apparatus works, particularly in relation to gender, is termed "performativity". The best-known quotation in *Gender Trouble* describes how performativity produces an appearance of stable gender:

> Gender is the repeated stylization of the body, a set of repeated acts within a highly rigid regulatory frame that congeals over time to produce the appearance of substance, of a natural sort of being. (pp. 43–44)

This formula is repeated in a shorter version towards the end of the work:

> [G]ender is an identity, tenuously constituted in time, instituted in an exterior space through a *stylized repetition of acts.* (p. 179; original emphasis)

Another brace of quotations focuses on Butler's placing of lesbian and gay sexuality *vis-à-vis* this framework and the related question of how the apparatus of compulsory heterosexuality can be resisted. During a discussion of the status of "so-called heterosexual conventions within homosexual contexts" (p. 41), which she claims "cannot be explained as chimerical representations of originally heterosexual identities ... [nor] as the pernicious insistence of heterosexual constructs with gay sexuality and identity",[22] Butler declares:

> The replication of heterosexual constructs in non-heterosexual frames brings into relief the utterly constructed status of the so-called heterosexual original. Thus gay is to straight not as copy is to original, but, rather, as copy is to copy. The parodic representation of the "original" ... reveals the original to be nothing other than a parody of the *idea* of the natural and the original. (p. 41; original emphasis)

The mention of parody here is taken up in Butler's discussion of drag, which she interprets as a practice that shows up the naturalizing process of compulsory heterosexuality:

> *In imitating gender, drag implicitly reveals the imitative structure of gender itself – as well as its contingency.* (p. 175; original emphasis)

Butler's discussion of drag has been controversial; should it be interpreted as descriptive or prescriptive? And this leads to the wider question of the efficacy of *Gender Trouble* for sexual politics: is the book purely theoretical or is it a text book for action? This crucial question is implicit in much of the book, and it is closely linked to Butler's view of identity.

1.3.3 Perfecting Performativity: Butler and Her Sources

Moving from the bare bones of Butler's arguments as received by queer theorists (very much an incomplete and disarticulated skeleton), I should like to consider some aspects of *Gender Trouble* in a little more detail, for the way in which she uses her sources is particularly striking.[23] According to her 1999 preface, *Gender Trouble* "tends to read together, in a syncretic vein, various French intellectuals (Lévi-Strauss, Foucault, Lacan, Kristeva, Wittig) who had few alliances with each other" (p. x), and one can add to this pantheon Freud, Gayle Rubin, Esther Newton and Mary Douglas, amongst others. Her preoccupations are reflected in the elements of her sources that she appropriates, but they are also underlined by other elements that she explicitly rejects: throughout the book, and especially in chapters 2 and 3 she energetically quashes any challenge to her thoroughgoing materialist view of identity, a view which lies at the heart of the suspicion, articulated by Martha C. Nussbaum (1999), Deryn Guest (2005) and others, that queer theory has a tendency towards socio-political disengagement.

At the core of Butler's theory of performativity is the idea of gender regulatory processes. She derives these from a number of sources. She draws, for instance, from Lévi-Strauss's structural anthropological work (1969) on the exogamic incest taboo. Psychoanalysis, too, is particularly important: for instance, Lacan's theory (1985) of the pre-Symbolic state helps her to understand the subject as individuated only after its emergence from that primary experience, and, what is more, individuated through language (p. 57). Again, Riviere's theory of masquerade (1929) serves as an anticipation of the regulatory process of compulsory heterosexuality that underlies Butler's own articulation of gender performativity. The third psychoanalytical contribution to Butler's thinking is provided by Kristeva's claim (1980 and 1984) to find in human language not only the means whereby the Lacanian Law of the Father exerts its authority, but also the very element that subverts that same Law.

Two other writers are worth consideration. First, Wittig (1992) has much to offer Butler; her view of sex (as distinct from gender), for instance, comes close to Butler's own: for Wittig "the category of sex is neither invariant nor natural, but is a specifically political use of nature that serves the purpose of reproductive sexuality" (p. 143). Moreover, Butler is influenced by Wittig's argument that "sex" is produced by language, "a system of significations oppressive to women, gays, and lesbians" (p. 144), and that the operation of language is effected by insistent repetitions "that produce reality-effects that are eventually misperceived as 'facts'" (p. 147). The last writer who demands consideration here is Foucault (1977 and 1990). He occupies a pivotal position in the production of Butler's gender theory (p. 119). She appeals to his reversal of the traditional view that the naturally sexed body is the cause of sexuality; Butler sees in Foucault's work a claim that sexuality "is an historically specific organization of power, discourse, bodies, and affectivity" (p. 117). The work of Foucault is crucial to Butler, then, in her argument against pre-discursive subjectivity. It helps her to provide a satisfyingly coherent account of the construction of personal identity; on a practical level, too, it aids her demonstration of how an identitarian political position, based on an appeal to an authentic "inner" or "original" gender or sexuality, derives from a false premise; moreover, the theory of "naturalization", which she owes to him, helps to explain why the idea of a pre-discursive ontology is something to which it is so tempting to appeal.

The debt owed by Butler to her predecessors is considerable, but what is in some ways equally prominent is her vigilance in criticizing them for any suggestion that (gender) identity is evident in the pre-discursive state. Nearly all her predecessors mentioned above are taken to task for making such suggestions; Lévi-Strauss (p. 53), Lacan (p. 60), Kristeva (p. 112), Wittig (p. 149 and p. 154), and even Foucault (pp 123–127) are found guilty on this count.[24]

These repeated criticisms and Butler's insistence on the facticity of sex as well as gender, leave two impressions in the reader's mind. One is the questionable status of the sexed body; in other words, what connexion, if any, does she see between sex/gender and the biological facts of the human body? The other impression or, rather, question, which stems from this apparent distancing of the body from sex, is that if the conventional concepts of sex and gender are undermined, is identitarian politics bereft of identity?

1.3.4 Self and the Sexed Body

Butler's apparent denial of the sexed body is the element in her model that has caused perhaps the most controversy, and it was the fear that she had been misunderstood in what she said about it that led to the publication of *Bodies That Matter* (1993). For her, the 'indisputable' biological given of sex allows a space for at least a partial notion of essentialism to take hold: that the fact of the sexed body dictates the course of gender formation. Consider the following characterization by Butler of older sociological discourse:

> Sociological discussions have conventionally sought to understand the notion of the person in terms of an agency that claims ontological priority to the various roles and functions through which it assumes social visibility and meaning. (p. 22)

And one crucial ingredient of personhood is biological sex; "the moment in which an infant becomes humanized", remarks Butler in another context, "is when the question, 'is it a boy or girl?' is answered". "Sex," she continues a little later, "qualifies the human as a necessary attribute" (p. 142). So bodily features define sex, as conventional thinking has it, and lead in turn to desires and gender behaviour.

I have already mentioned Butler's use of Foucault to contest this causal sequence. In her critique of Kristeva, Butler exploits Foucault's contention that "the body is not 'sexed' in any significant sense prior to its determination within a discourse through which it becomes invested with an 'idea' of natural or essential sex" (p. 117). But how does this work in practice? What are the mechanics of the process? First, Butler disassociates herself from a view of the body as a "mute facticity, anticipating some meaning that can be attributed only by a transcendent consciousness" (p. 164). Even Foucault's famous dictum that "the body is the inscribed surface of events" (quoted at p. 165), implies, in her view, a stable body prior to discourse (it is destroyed, she admits, in the process of inscription, but it is still nevertheless implied). Her next step is a familiar one: she calls upon the work of a predecessor, on this occasion the structuralist anthropological model proposed by Douglas (1969), to explain the imposition of order by culture upon nature. Douglas argued that order is imposed by the creation of taboos, which in their turn are created by the discursive process of defining the boundaries of the body, "by exaggerating", as she put it, "the differences between within and without, above and below, male and female, with and against" (Douglas 1969: 4). Butler proposes a poststructural reordering of Douglas's model. She replaces its binary notion of culture-ruling-nature with an understanding of "the boundaries of the body as the limits of the socially *hegemonic*" (p. 167; original emphasis).

Butler introduces the final development of her re-ordered model by recalling Foucault's discussion of inscription in *Discipline and Punish* (1977); there he famously used the example of the treatment of criminals to challenge the notion of interiority; he argued that the prohibitive law, to use Butler's gloss, "is not literally internalized, but incorporated, with the consequence that bodies are produced which signify that law on and through the body" (p. 171). Butler applies this notion to gender:

> [A]cts, gestures, and desire produce the effect of an internal core or substance, but produce this on the surface of the body, through the play of signifying absences that suggest, but never reveal, the organizing principle of identity as a cause. (p. 173; original emphasis)

She is thus safely back on the familiar ground of performativity, but where exactly has she left the body? Is she saying that it does not exist? My understanding is that this is certainly not the case. In her discussion of Douglas, she remarks:

> Her [i.e. Douglas's] analysis suggests that what constitutes the limit of the body is never merely material, but that the surface, the skin, is systematically signified by taboos and anticipated transgressions. (p. 167)

In *Bodies That Matter*, Butler makes her position somewhat clearer. In arguing that "there is no reference to a pure body which is not at the same time a further formation of that body" (Butler 1993: 10–11), she is reducing J. L. Austin's binary of constative versus performative statements, so that the performative function,[25] clearly observable in statements like "I now pronounce you man and wife" where the words effect a deed or state, also attaches to constative statements, which in a common sense view merely describe an existent deed or state. To say *anything*, then, about a body, is to (re)form it. Not that the body has disappeared; Butler is not denying "an array of 'materialities' that pertain to the body, that which is signified by the domains of biology, illness, age, weight, metabolism, life and death" (p. 6). But, as she argues at length in chapter 2, although the body might be thought to be a fixed given, in fact there is a complicated, mutually dependent, ongoing relationship between language and the material body:

> The linguistic categories that are understood to "denote" the materiality of the body are themselves troubled by a referent that is never fully or permanently resolved or contained by a given signified. (Butler 1993: 6)

This later refinement, then, may go some way to clarify Butler's view that identity is formed solely by the process of performativity.

1.3.5 "Necessary Failures": Butler's Gender Politics

This discussion of Butler ends with some thoughts on her understanding of gender politics, and since this feature of the book has proved as controversial as its treatment of the body, I should also like to move towards a discussion of the critical reaction to *Gender Trouble*. At the outset of the book, Butler makes clear her belief that the usual basis for identitarian politics, the represented subject, has been destabilized beyond repair. The subject is a naturalized fiction:

> In effect, the law produces and then conceals the notion of "a subject before the law" ... in order to invoke that discursive formation as a naturalized premise that subsequently legitimates that law's own regulatory hegemony. (p. 6)

And I have argued that her treatment of her sources bears witness to a determination to insist on this destabilization. Any programme that seeks fairer representation for "women" needs to take into account how that category (and, it is reasonable to add, other categories such as "lesbian" or "gay") "is produced and restrained by the very structures of power through which emancipation is sought" (p. 5). But if the pre-discursive subject is abolished, if there is no "doer behind the deed", and therefore no agency, what resistance is possible? Butler's answer is given in her conclusion (pp. 181–190). It has to be said that it is, in terms of practicality, vague. Perhaps a fairer way of expressing it would be to say that in "this theoretical inquiry" (p. 188), Butler is laying the philosophical foundations for others to add levels of strategic thinking. There are indeed some pregnant remarks. In arguing against a half-way house view of construction, for instance, which considers the subject's agency "to be intact regardless of its cultural embeddedness", Butler significantly rejects the fatalistic notion "that to be *constituted* by discourse is to be *determined* by discourse" (p. 182; original emphasis).

For Butler, the possibility of resistance lies not outside but within the normative apparatus of discourse. It is clear from earlier passages in *Gender Trouble* that she owes this optimistic view of discourse to Foucault's theory of power; her interpretation of his theory emphasizes the double-edged effect of power:

> Power, rather than the law, encompasses both the juridical (prohibitive and regulatory) and the productive (inadvertently generative) functions of differential relations. (p. 182)

The normative apparatus of discourse can produce unexpected results, and *keeps on* producing new possibilities:

> The theories of feminist identity that elaborate predicates of color, sexuality, ethnicity, class, and able-bodiedness invariably close with an embarrassed "etc." at the end of the list. (p. 182)

The "subject" is never complete; the "etc." is a sign of "the illimitable process of signification itself" and "and a new departure for feminist political theorizing" (p. 182). For the performative process does not always produce the result that one might expect:

> The injunction *to be* a given gender produces necessary failures, a variety of incoherent configurations that in their multiplicity exceed and defy the injunction by which they are generated. (p.185; original emphasis)

Why exactly these failures are "necessary" is never fully explained (necessary for Butler's own theory to work at all?). One must assume some individual slippages, perhaps during the complex operation of the paternal law. Whatever the case, according to Butler such "failures" do occur, and allow for the emergence of "new possibilities for gender that contest the rigid codes of hierarchical binarism" (p. 185). It seems, then, that the subversion of the otherwise seemingly inevitable formation of heterosexual gender identity is to be found only in these "necessary failures".

But where exactly is the site of resistance, or, as Butler puts it, what "constitutes a subversive repetition within signifying practices of gender" (p. 185)? The answer she gives is where vagueness sets in, a series of inconclusive dicta, inconclusive, that is, if *Gender Trouble* is expected to provide a prescriptive political programme. To take two of them:

> Practices of parody can serve to re-engage and reconsolidate the very distinction between a privileged and naturalized gender configuration and one that appears as derived, phantasmatic, and mimetic – a failed copy as it were. (p. 186)

and

> There is a subversive laughter in the pastiche-effect of parodic practice in which the original, the authentic, and the real are themselves constituted as effects. (pp. 186–187)

If at the end of *Gender Trouble* the reader is left uncertain about the practical nature of resistance, Martha C. Nussbaum, in a vigorous overview of both this and three subsequent books by Butler, has no doubt about Butler's message. In summarizing the "feminist thinkers of the new symbolic type", of whom Butler is the leader, she concludes:

> We are all, more or less, prisoners of the structures of power that have defined our identity as women; we can never change those structures in a large-scale way, and we can never escape from them. All that we can hope to do is to find spaces within the structures of power in which to parody them, to poke fun at them, to transgress them in speech. (Nussbaum 1999: 38)

According to Nussbaum, Butler is responsible for inducing "so many to adopt a stance that looks very much like quietism and retreat" (p. 38). This is a devastating criticism, if true. One immediate reaction is that Butler does not seem to dismiss the traditional struggle to effect practical change for women, and by extension for lesbians and gay men amongst others, as utterly ineffectual, only as limited:

> It is *not enough* to inquire into how women might become more fully represented in language and politics. Feminist critique ought also to understand how the category of "women", the subject of feminism is produced. (p. 5; emphasis added)

Gender Troubles led to a common belief that Butler was prescribing parody, especially in drag, as a way of subverting the normative process of performativity. In *Bodies that Matter*, Butler seems hesitant to dismiss altogether the potential of drag to express the artificiality of gender:

> [D]rag exposes or allegorizes the mundane psychic and performative practices by which heterosexualized genders form themselves through the renunciation of the *possibility* of homosexuality. (Butler 1993: 235; original emphasis)

On the other hand, in discussing the film *Paris is Burning* (a study of drag), Butler says that it "calls into question whether parodying the dominant forms is enough to displace them" (Butler 1993: 125). She adds, unequivocally:

> Although many readers understood *Gender Trouble* to be arguing for the proliferation of drag performances as a way of subverting dominant gender norms, I want to underscore that there is no necessary relation between drag and subversion, and that drag may well be used in the service of both the denaturalization and reidealization of hyperbolic heterosexual gender norms. At best it seems drag is a site of a certain ambivalence, one which reflects the more general situation of being implicated in the very regimes of power that one opposes. (Butler 1993: 125)

On Butler's own terms, drag (in the sense of a drag performance rather than transvestism in general) neither casts much light on the operations of performativity nor can act as a satisfactorily subversive tactic. The drag performer is not a person whose aim is to deceive the onlooker: s/he is a person of identifiable original gender who chooses to perform as though of the opposite gender. Drag gives the impression that gender is a rôle that one can assume at will;[26] here one recalls Butler's ironic comment in her preface to *Bodies That Matter*:

> For if I were to argue that genders are performative, that could mean that I thought that one woke in the morning, perused the closet or some more open space for the gender of choice, donned that gender for the day, and then restored the garment to its place at night. (Butler 1993: x)

Butler cannot be blamed for another confusion which is similar to the misplaced attention paid to drag and has similar consequences. This is the assumption that performativity is synonymous with performance. The mistake is made by both supporters and critics of Butler; consider this statement from Nussbaum:

> The idea of gender as performance is Butler's most famous idea, and so it is worth pausing to scrutinize it more closely. (Nussbaum 1999: 40)

Performance, however, requires a performer, with a pre-existing identity. Performativity, as Butler describes it, is very different. It *creates* identity and does so by repetition.[27] It is significant that in *Bodies that Matter* she further empties the "performer" of any initializing power by invoking the notion of citationality. She argues, after Derrida, that despite the first-person grammatical structure, the authority for the speech enactment does not derive from the speaker, but depends on the repetition, or "citing", of an already-established formula or norm. She extends this idea of citationality to the performative process of gender formation (1993: 224–225); just as the official at a marriage ceremony effects the marriage not with his/her own words or will but by means of an already established, authoritative formula, so what is repeated in gender performativity is a set of established norms, out of which emerges the gendered subject, though the citational process disguises its own operation and gives the impression that a pre-existing subject develops its own natural gender identity.

If we are still undecided about whether to don or destroy those wigs/moustaches, Butler seems to assure us that she is not denying the efficacy of more traditional resistance practices of gender politics. She does this by a further extension of performativity:

> They do not represent pregiven constituencies, but are empty signs which come to bear phantasmatic investments of various kinds. (Butler 1993: 191)

There is a possibility of resignifying terms such as "woman" or "democracy" so that a political organization or movement that "represents" "gays" does not do so in the sense that it speaks or acts on behalf of an already existing, coherent group, but collects a set of free-floating elements and performatively creates a new political reality out of them. With this manoeuvre, Butler tries to solve the problem of how you can represent unstable identities; it is now all right to pick up those banners again. But where does that leave the parodic potential; where does queer theory go?

1.4 Conclusions

Gender Trouble (supplemented by *Bodies That Matter* and *The Epistemology of the Closet*) helps to find "clues as to what queer theory looks like", the task I undertook at the start of chapter 1. The very vagueness of the phrase is eloquent of queer theory's elusiveness and suits my own version of it. There is a certain wry amusement to be gained from looking back at queer theory's rapid development out of a misunderstanding of *Gender Trouble*;[28] it is this misunderstanding that led to a certain self-distancing from queer theory on Butler's part.[29] The original impetus behind queer theory, then, may have been based on a mistake – in this sense queer theory began by accident. Moreover, theatrical performances feature prominently in its practitioners' literature. Yet Butler's work lies at the heart of queer theory; for, in her synthesis of previous work, as I have argued, queer theory has inherited a solid theoretical framework to explain the regulatory process whereby sex, gender and sexuality are formed. By means of her model queer theorists have a clearer idea of the task before them: to expose the artificiality of this process, to subvert the idea of the naturalness of gender. But it is at this point that Butler's legacy becomes problematic: how is this exposure, this subversion, to be effected? Butler has left indications, but not a coherent programme, and this is not exactly because she is concerned with theory rather than application, but rather because there are some facets of her theoretical structure that make its application obscure. These cluster round her treatment of identity. She pushes to the extreme the denial of essential identity; in contrast to the moderate social constructionist, she will not allow even biological sex as some sort of basic given.[30] Such a diminution of the subject's inaugurative capability precludes any possibility of voluntarist interference in the inexorable mechanism of performativity. If there is no subject, who is there to subvert the regulatory process? It is this conundrum that underlies Nussbaum's accusations of quietism and such feminist attacks upon Butler and queer theory as those launched by Jeffreys (for a discussion of which see Jagose 1996: 50–51, 87–88 and 117). There is a danger in Butler's model that it might conflate, in Steven Seidman's words, "identity as a disciplining force with domination[,] and a politics of subversion with a politics against identity" (1993: 132). But he qualifies this criticism with an "at times", and in the same sentence concedes that Butler "often elaborates complex understandings of identity as both enabling and self-limiting" (1993: 132). Despite her attempts in *Bodies That Matter* to articulate more clearly the subversive potential of her theoretical model, it is the idea of "necessary failures", as described in *Gender Trouble* (especially pp. 185–190) – very much the double-edged "enabling and self-limiting" sword as described by Seidman – that has provided queer theory with its subversive opportunity.

It is also perhaps to Butler, and to Sedgwick, that queer theory owes the *milieu* in which it has largely operated, that is, discourse – not discourse in the wider sense of the whole field of human communication, but the narrower one of texts, literary and visual. Despite its roots in the theoretical work of Butler and Sedgwick, not to mention its growing corpus of secondary literature, queer theory has been less interested in theoretical perspectives than in a practical work with texts, and it is with this work, I believe, that it makes its best contribution to gender politics.

Notes

1. See, e.g., Halperin (1995: 62–66) and Jagose (1996: 106–110) for an assessment, especially of the organization Queer Nation.
2. A search in the bibliographical database ISI Web of Science (in the Social Sciences and Arts & Humanities sections) shows that interest in queer theory has been maintained consistently. In June 2010 the term *queer**, where the asterisk is a truncation operator, produced 637 articles for the period up till December 1999, 798 for the period 2000–2005, and 1098 for 2006 onwards. The more narrowly-focused term *"queer theory"*, where the inverted commas act as a phrase restrictor, produced 86, 114 and 172 articles for the same periods.
3. For example, Warner (1993, esp. pp. vii–xxxi), Jagose (1996), Seidman (1996), Spargo (1999), Sullivan (2003).
4. Michael Warner suggests that "we might think of queer theory as the project of elaborating, in ways that cannot be predicted in advance, this question: What do queers want?" (Warner 1993: vii) – not so much a definition as a begging of the question.
5. "Canon" is not the word one might most expect in the context of queer theory; it has overtones of the fixed, the authentic and the exclusive, notions that run counter to the fluidity of queer.
6. My favourite, if not particularly serious, example is: "Socrates within the life of the Greeks, like the individual vessel of same-sex desire within the homoerotic tradition of homophobic Western high culture, depends for his survival on the very misrecognitions that his prestige comes from having the power to demystify" (p. 57).
7. These include not only expected ones such as secrecy/disclosure and private/ public, but also those less obviously associated with closet/coming out: masculine/feminine, for example, or growth/decadence, cognition/paranoia, art/kitsch and sincerity/sentimentality. See Sedgwick 1994: 72.
8. The minoritizing view sees homosexuality "as an issue of active importance primarily for a small, distinct, relatively fixed homosexual minority" (p. 1), while the universalizing view "sees it as an issue of continuing, determinative importance in the lives of people across the spectrum of sexualities" (p. 1). In this section, Sedgwick's book (1994) will be cited simply by its page number.
9. One might add that the universalizing view has been held not only by queer theorists and Sedgwick but also, for example, by those Christian fundamentalists who see homosexuality not as an identity but as a curable disorder of those who are essentially heterosexual.
10. By transitive she means seeing sexuality in a "trope of inversion, *anima muliebris in corpore virili inclusa* ... and vice versa" (p. 87), a view introduced in the nineteenth-century medical literature on homosexuality and surviving

in popular imagination; she observes that in an odd way this view preserves the integrity of heterosexuality, since it is the female soul in a homosexual man that desires another man. She exemplifies what she calls "the trope of gender separation", on the other hand, by the second-wave feminist phrase "woman-identified woman", which she glosses with the remark that "it is ... the most natural thing in the world that people of the same gender ..., people whose economic, institutional, emotional, physical needs and knowledges [*sic*] may have so much in common, should bond together also on the axis of sexual desire" (p. 87).

11. See above, pages 2–3.
12. Axiom 5 states 'The historical search for a Great Paradigm shift may obscure the present conditions of sexuality today' and the opening sentence of the section may serve as a gloss on the shift: "Since 1976, when Michel Foucault, in an act of polemical bravado, offered 1870 as the date of birth of modern homosexuality ..., the most sophisticated historically oriented work in gay studies has been offering ever more precise datings, ever more nuanced narratives of the development of homosexuality 'as we know it today'" (p. 44).
13. See Weeks (1990: 26–27) for a discussion of this point.
14. For considered accounts of the development of homosexual identity in the nineteenth and twentieth centuries, see, for instance, Weeks (1990) and Sinfield (1994).
15. One danger is posed by a misunderstanding of social construction, that it entails malleability, so that gay and lesbian sexuality is considered to be "only" constructed and therefore alterable; another danger, in this case caused by a belief in essentialism, lurks in the idea that homosexuality represents some deficiency in a body's genetic make-up, which will be at some time in the future subject to medical avoidance or correction (pp. 41–44).
16. Sedgwick argues that the constructionist/essentialist debate has conflated two opposing ideas: "phylogeny" (the interrelationship of sexual identity and other social variables in society as a whole) and "ontogeny" (the aetiology of an individual's sexuality).
17. Foucault (1990) and Halperin (1989); for Halperin's response to and partial acceptance of Sedgwick's criticism, see Halperin (2002: 10–13).
18. In this section, Butler's book (1999) will be cited simply by its page number.
19. Butler herself, mildly if not completely convincingly, defends herself against criticism of her style in the 1999 Preface to *Gender Trouble* (pp. xviii–xix); Nussbaum's sharp words on the subject will be discussed later. In a robust and fascinating defense of Butler's opacity, Sara Salih argues that "the way she writes is a self-conscious struggle with serious ethical and political aims" (Salih 2003: 44). Ordinary language and grammar "shape and limit our thinking ..." (Salih 2003: 45). Butler uses a performative language with the aim of not feeding readers with the author's own thought, but forcing them to struggle with a new language and thus break out of the grip of orthodox language and thought processes.
20. A key term in *Gender Trouble*, for instance, p. 24.
21. Another key term; it means "to make to appear natural", a process that requires the concealment of its own operation.

22. An example of such "so-called heterosexual conventions" might be the apparent mimicry of male/female partnerships by a butch/femme binary relationship in a lesbian context.
23. I mean by her sources those she explicitly discusses, and I leave aside such implicit influences as Hegel and Derrida.
24. Riviere, on the other hand, is criticized for relying on a problematic case study (p. 67).
25. Austin (1962), who is an important but unnamed source of performativity in *Gender Trouble*, at last makes an acknowledged appearance in *Bodies that Matter*.
26. Camp may offer more potential for subverting the heteronormative gender system; for such an application of camp, see chapter 9 below.
27. I am not saying that performativity does not involve an element of performance, but that the two are not synonymous or coterminous. Performativity may be thought of as performance plus citationality but without an independent performer.
28. The mistake lay in confusing performativity with performance; in the former the subject is constituted by the process, whereas the latter implies the opposite. It is a further, if minor, irony that the interview with Butler referred to here is entitled *"Gender as Performance"*.
29. For instance, in the interview quoted at the start of this section, she begins with the remark "I would say that I'm a feminist theorist before I'm a queer theorist or a gay and lesbian theorist"; the chapter "Critically Queer" of *Bodies That Matter* (1993: 27–55) may represent a certain rapprochement.
30. This is in contrast to Sedgwick, who does seem to make such an assumption; for example, Sedgwick 1994: 27–30; see especially her table "Some Mappings of Sex, Gender and Sexuality", p. 30.

Chapter 2

FEMINIST AND QUEER BIBLICAL ENCOUNTERS

They write to promote a new gender reality. (Greenberg 1997: 494)

We also want to frustrate the already audible assertions that queer theory has only academic – which is to say, dead – politics. (Berlant and Warner 1995: 344)

2.1 Introduction

In chapter 1, I sought to articulate my own understanding of queer theory in the context of Butler's *Gender Trouble*. Since I concluded with the observation that most queer theorists engage in a practical encounter with texts, this seems the appropriate place to discuss the implications of a practical application of queer theory to the Hebrew Bible. Three themes will dominate such a discussion. First, how does a queer encounter with the marriage metaphor relate to previous work on the subject, in particular that of feminist biblical criticism? Second, what does a queer encounter with the biblical text actually look like? The third theme has already threaded its way through the previous chapter: there I discussed the implications of Butler's articulation of gender performativity for political engagement. The third theme in this chapter, then, will be that of the ethical potential of queer theory. Will my application of queer theory to biblical texts have any point other than a theoretical exercise?

2.2 Feminist Forebears and Queer Anticipations

Just as queer theory itself has emerged to a great extent from feminist thought, so my own queer approach to the *marriage metaphor* owes an overwhelming debt to the feminist debate on that subject. As Stone points out, "the central concerns of queer theory often (though not always) overlap with central concerns of feminist studies, inasmuch as feminism, too, is devoted to the critical analysis of sex and gender" (Stone 2001a: 25). This section, then, is in part a tribute to the complex of ideas and methodologies that has accumulated in the last 25 years; it is also intended to provide a clearer context to my own approaches to the texts than would have emerged from a wider review.[1]

Occasionally I have had some difficulty in deciding whom exactly I should designate as "feminist", a label that in consequence I have chosen to interpret loosely.[2] A related problem is that of classification, that is, how we should understand and place the various feminist writings in relation to each other. Moshe Greenberg implies that that particular problem does not exist:

> At bottom, what feminists criticize is not what the text meant to those who composed and received them in their historical context, but what the text means in today's context. (Greenberg 1997: 494)

The feminist approach to the *marriage metaphor*, then, is opposed to the traditional "historical-philological search for the primary, context-bound sense of Scripture" (Greenberg 1997: 494); it uses reader-response theory to find, presumably, a "secondary" sense in the biblical texts. Yvonne Sherwood, in noting that "very few critics make reference to other feminist articles and they never engage in dispute", finds an apparent aggregating tendency, which she relates to a wider context:

> Ironically, as biblical feminists, like all feminists try to counter the idea of woman as the eternal feminine, or a "universal unified simplistic abstract", they inadvertently create another seeming monolith called Feminist Biblical Criticism. (Sherwood 1996: 267)

But despite such perceptions, feminist criticism of the *marriage metaphor* is not monolithic, nor is the feminist position monopolized by reader-response critics. They are certainly well represented, yet they too employ a variety of tactics.

There have been some attempts to understand the various strategies involved. In his Introduction to *Troubling Jeremiah* (1999), to take one example, A. R. Pete Diamond identifies what he calls the "subtext of contemporary hermeneutic debate – namely where does the privilege of meaning lie in the interpretation of a text: in the author, the text, or the reader?" (1999: 16). His map, then, traces three lines: author-centred (the historical-critical method); text-centred (literary readings) and reader-oriented (which include reader-response). As a means of capturing a flavour of the feminist writings on the *marriage metaphor*,

I should like to consider them in two broad categories, reception and inception criticism, which bear a marked resemblance to the third and second of Diamond's three lines. I understand reception criticism as a focus on the impact of the text upon the reader in his or her context, and inception criticism as an attempt to reconstruct the historical, social and/or religious setting of the biblical text in order to create an understanding of the *Sitz im Leben* and the role of women pictured within it. The use of two very different categories invites the charge of introducing a polarizing binary into the debate; in defence, I should emphasize that many practitioners use a mixture of the two categories, and that indeed there is a third approach to the text, which sits easily in neither (though I have included its practitioners in the first): this is that close reading of the text from which there emerges an understanding that undercuts conventional readings (Derridean deconstruction being the outstanding, though not the only, example of this methodology).[3]

In "placing" these writings, however, consideration has to be paid to not only the broad methodological approach to the text, but also the hermeneutical conclusions, which are often the criteria by which feminist writers on the *marriage metaphor* are categorized. It is commonly assumed that reception critics, enraged by what they see in the text, reject its authority, while inception critics try to find some accommodation with it. T. Drorah Setel, for example, argued that "contemporary religious feminists" must "either believe that an understanding of the historical setting of prophetic texts may provide a perspective of 'moral realism' which allows them to be read as sacred scripture" or "the 'pornographic' nature of female objectification may demand that such texts not be declared 'the word of God' in a public setting" (1985: 95). Corrine L. Patton, in an article in which she distances her work from feminist criticism of Ezekiel, has a slightly different perspective:

> One response to the offensiveness of God's actions in this text would be similar to that of Dinah's brothers: slaughter this god and all of his followers, declare this god no god, or this text not revelatory. Another response is to use a "trickster" hermeneutic, that is, to allow the text to unravel its own meaning. (Patton 2000: 221–222)

Patton agrees with Setel in linking rejectionism to reception critics, but contrasts their position not with "regular" inception critics, but with that third methodological approach, which I associated with deconstruction. Athalya Brenner (1996), on the other hand, whose own position is rejectionist, sees the situation as more complicated; she discusses a number of strategies, not all of which fit into a receptionist model. I shall return to some of these strategies in due course, when I pick out features of the feminist critiques of the *marriage metaphor* that are particularly helpful to my own approach. Before that I should like to give a very brief discussion of those critiques in the broad methodological categories outlined above.

2.2.1 Reception Criticism

Kathleen O'Connor most succinctly summarizes why the *marriage metaphor* produces such a strong reaction in some readers:

> The marriage metaphor exalts men because it uses them alone as appropriate symbols of the divine. It brands women because it uses them and their sexuality as symbols of wickedness and treachery. (O'Connor 1992: 171)

O'Connor was writing about Jeremiah, but her remarks could apply equally well to Hosea and Ezekiel. In fact it is Hosea who preoccupied many feminist biblical scholars in the 1980s. Setel was indeed the first to make a sustained attack on Hosea's handling of the *marriage metaphor* from a woman reader's point of view (1985). That she partly situates her critique in the biblical view of female sexuality and attempts to relate Hosean sexual imagery to the political events of Hosea's time shows that one should be wary of making too absolute a distinction between inception and reception criticism. But Setel's major concern is to relate the *marriage metaphor* to twentieth-century feminist theory on the objectification of women, and in particular on the objectification of female sexuality as a function of pornography. Despite its title, her literary study of the text concentrates on aspects of objectification rather than of pornography, and concludes that the text contains "indications of an objectified view of the female experience as separate from and negative in relationship to male experience" (Setel 1985: 94).

Setel's work was continued with vigour in the 1980s and 1990s. Marie-Theres Wacker (1987) attempted to "depatriarchalize" Hosea's version of the *marriage metaphor* by arguing that, since women were excluded by the covenant, Hosea's strictures do not apply to them. Fokkelien van Dijk-Hemmes (1989) regards the Hosean version as a male repackaging of Songs of Songs, the focus of which is a plea for the authority of the male figure; a later paper (1993) further explores the idea of male propaganda (and includes Ezekiel in her study). Renita J. Weems (1989) emphasizes the sexual violence of the *marriage metaphor*: such is the power of the vehicle of the metaphor that it overwhelms the tenor. From

1990 onwards, the receptionist debate widened to include Jeremiah and Ezekiel,[4] from which emerged two major (and related) themes. Setel's application of the current feminist theory of pornography to the *marriage metaphor* was developed by, in particular, Cheryl Exum (1993, 1995 and 1996) and Brenner (especially 1995b and 1996, in which she coined the term pornoprophetics); my own discussion of gay pornography (in chapter 9) can be regarded as a response to their work. The second major theme emerges from a reaction to the sexual violence expressed in the *marriage metaphor*, as introduced by such earlier writers as Weems (1989): it is the view that in depicting Yhwh himself as the perpetrator of marital violence the *marriage metaphor* necessarily condones or even promotes its human equivalent. Among those who take up this theme are, in addition to Weems (1989 and 1995), Gale A. Yee (1992), Naomi Graetz (1995) and Tristanne J. Connolly (1998). Weems is interesting as an example of someone who attempts a synthesis of text-affirming and text-negating approaches. Indeed Sherwood criticizes her for doing exactly this; Weems, Sherwood says, accepts the tenor (Yhwh's right to punish), but rejects the vehicle (sexual or spousal abuse) (Sherwood 1996: 282–286). Weems' ambivalence is certainly fascinating. She is firm about the danger of divinizing violence:

> To the extent that God's covenant with Israel is like a marriage between a man and a woman, then a husband's punishment against his wife is as warranted as God's punishment of Israel. (Weems 1989: 100)

On the other hand, she accepts the genuineness of and justification for the reconciliation.

Other feminist scholars would go much further in their criticism of the text. Connolly, for instance, argues that:

> On the tail of numerous threats of stripping, starving and imprisonment, the phrase "I am going to seduce her" (2.16) gives the reader a shudder rather than a glimmer of hope ... It [the "sudden gentleness" of the words "I will speak to her heart"] sounds like the cycle of abuse in which, when the abuser apologizes and shows love, the abused is made to forget the violence. (Connolly 1998: 62)

2.2.2 Inception Criticism

If the emphasis of reception criticism, as described above, is on the effect of the *marriage metaphor* on readers today, inception criticism focuses on the setting of the text at the time of its (implied) composition.

Inception critics may not deny the harm done by these texts, but they seek to use methodological tools borrowed from such disciplines as history and anthropology as a means of finding an alternative – and more acceptable – view of the *marriage metaphor*. One ploy is to (re) construct the Female Counter-Voice, a procedure fraught with danger, and a version of which I offer in chapter 9. Sometimes the process works by appealing to alleged historical evidence, most often, since evidence external to the text is hard to come by, from elsewhere within the text. Thus, Helgard Balz-Cochois interprets Gomer as a member of the cult focused on Asherah, the Great Mother (1982); as such Gomer is a free agent carrying out an established role of cultic קְדֵשָׁה, and embodying the erotic power of goddess worship. One problem of Balz-Cochois' approach was that the theory of cultic prostitution was losing its credibility among biblical scholars. It is an irony that the theory was based, in J. R. Hackett's words not on "ancient goddesses, ancient religions, and ancient women, but rather the fears and fantasies of modern Western scholars" (1989: 68).

Another way of creating the Counter-Voice is by an imaginative reconstruction of the intrinsic evidence of the text. At least this is how I view Teresa J. Hornsby's reading of Gomer "as a formally prosperous business woman who is finally [i.e. in Hosea 3] compromised and controlled through the wealth of an outsider" (Hornsby 1999: 116). The danger in creating such female Counter-Voices is that they may not subvert the androcentric tradition overtly reflected in the text; indeed they may serve to underscore the gender division, that polarizing binary where the male is dominant and the female dominated. Sherwood compellingly argues that Balz-Cochois "writes in the shadow of androcentric scholarship and is intimidated by the force of a tradition which she ostensibly aims to resist" (1996: 271). And this is no less the case with Hornsby's prostitute, who tries to live off the privileged male system that finally destroys her.

Of other methodological tools brought to bear upon the *marriage metaphor*, Phyllis Bird's socio-philological analysis of Hosea's use of זנה (1989) displays a connotative complexity which contrasts strongly with Hornsby's comparatively simplistic account and exerted a considerable influence on subsequent feminist critiques. Sherwood, for instance, comments that in demonstrating how the text blurs the distinction between prostitution, promiscuity and sexual betrayal, Bird (1989) furthers an appreciation of how this reflects a marked patriarchal trait.

Hosea made another appearance in the collection of essays that contained Bird's, this time as the object of an anthropological approach made by Mary Joan Winn Leith. She saw the transformation of Israel from condemnation to re-creation "as a mythic journey that conforms closely to a rite of passage" (Leith 1989: 95).

Various attempts have been made to understand the historical contexts which the texts may reflect. In a study of Ezekiel 23, for instance, Patton argued that the female imaging of Israel should be seen in the context of the humiliation experienced in invasion and defeat, where the defeated were "unmanned"; Ezekiel and his audience would have been aware of, or indeed, would have shared such an experience. Patton says of her examination of the historical setting that it was "more central to the meaning of the text than previous analyses have been" (Patton 2000: 322). But she ignores the fact that two of her predecessors have used a similar historical approach.

In 2001, Yee and Alice A. Keefe produced two notable examples of inception theory. Yee's earlier attempt (1992) to reconcile text-affirming and text-negating critical positions was brushed aside in her later article (2001), in which it is evident that she has digested the work of, among others, Gottwald (1991), Hopkins (1983), Premnath (1988) and Keefe (1995); using their reconstruction of the socio-political situation in eighth-century Israel, she pictures Hosea as a "polemical monoculturist" denouncing the religious and political elite that was damaging the land through its foreign tributary means of production, and through its official cult, which shared popular religion's syncretizing tendencies. Hosea's attack, though not helpful to women (whose religious feelings found expression in popular cultic practices), was not aimed specifically at them. The female aspect of the *marriage metaphor* was part of its "ideological dynamic" whose purpose was to belittle the male elite by feminizing them.

The outstanding example of inception criticism of Hosea, Keefe's *Woman's Body and the Social Body in Hosea* (2001), an expansion and development of an earlier work (1995), is underpinned by a historical reconstruction similar to that of Yee's (2001) article; that is, she situates Hosea 1–2 in the socio-economic conditions of eighth-century Israel. One example of Keefe's feminist contributions is of particular interest. Although, she owes much of her reconstruction of eighth-century Israel to the work of other (mainly male) scholars, she offers her own feminist slant on it, but a slant that is very different to the outlook of feminist scholars who favour reception criticism. For she argues that their thought "is rooted in the Enlightenment's redefinition of the human in terms of individual autonomy and rationality" (Keefe 2001: 156); but in eighth-century Israel "the basic social unit was not the individual but the kinship group, and personhood was defined in terms of one's place within the corporate structure and by one's contributions to those corporate structures" (Keefe 2001: 158). To understand the *marriage metaphor* one has to be clear about the place of women in an ancient society. Her own complex interpretation of the metaphor involves the highlighting of woman's body as a symbol of fecundity, and, by extension, the well-being and continuity of the social body; transgression in the *marriage metaphor* symbolizes the traumatic disturbances in the community. Keefe presents a powerful case, though it must be said that it is a case that depends on a particular cultural interpretation of ancient Israel; it also depends to an extent on redaction-critical decisions about the reliability of the text.[5] Moreover, Keefe's position, however attractive from an historian's point of view, leaves us with a hermeneutical blank. What can today's readers bring from it, beyond interesting evidence from a particular social situation, unless, as Stone suggests, they are content to view it "as a protest against unjust land policies" (Stone: 2001b: 122)?

2.2.3 Queer Anticipations 1: Gender Play

I mentioned earlier that there was another approach to the *marriage metaphor* that is neither reception nor inception criticism, though it is related to the latter in that it focuses upon the text rather than the reader. It is that close reading of the text that uses structuralist or post-structuralist applications to reveal the underlying ideological skeleton in the first case or in the second to detect a "spoiler", a contráry[6] other in tension with the dominant ideological voice in the text. This other approach heralds a broader discussion of those features of the feminist critiques that have most influenced my own queer reading of the *marriage metaphor.*

Close literary readings of the *marriage metaphor* are not restricted to structuralists or poststructuralists. Many reception critics, in particular, base their conclusions on a detailed literary exploration. One could point also to Angela Bauer's use of rhetorical criticism in her hunt for traces of female voices in Jeremiah (1999).[7] To find an example of a structuralist third approach, one could turn to an important article by Diamond and O'Connor (1996). It has to be said immediately that this article is not purely "third approach"; for instance, it concludes on a very firm receptionist note with a Dalyesque echo.[8] But the article's most memorable feature is its codification of gender shifts. Diamond and O'Connor note the juxtaposition of male and female addressees in Jer. 2:2–3 and argue that it "functions to identify them with one another and to highlight their symbolic equivalence ... Jer. 2:1–3 therefore introduces the collection of poems in chapters 2–3 by equating male Israel with bride Israel" (Diamond and O'Connor 1996: 293). The authors then map out the complex patterning of such gender shifts, which they say "reveals a literary composition structured as a drama enacting the marriage metaphor" (Diamond and O'Connor 1996: 293); moreover they conclude that the alternation in the gender of the addressees "plays a large part in 'telling' the reader (implied audience) to treat the marital story as a national, religious parable" (Diamond and O'Connor 1996: 300). Their use of the gender of the addressees as a "heuristic device" has been enormously influential in my own approach to Jeremiah; I too have found significance in these shifts, but with the crucial difference that a queer view understands them as not a carefully structured play of polarities but an anti-heteronormative spoiler.

This reference to a difference between structuralist and post-structuralist is a timely reminder of the work of Sherwood. *The Prostitute and the Prophet* (1996), a monograph on the *marriage metaphor* in Hosea, is a most significant work on the *marriage metaphor*. What strikes one most in reading her book is her use of (very) different methodologies. It is true that Dijk-Hemmes used three approaches – gender-specific, narratological and intertextual – in her key article on Hosea (1989: 176), but in her case the three elements are wholly integrated. Sherwood, in contrast, introduces her methodological approaches sequentially: Jamiesononian metacommentary, structuralist semiotics, Derridian deconstruction and feminist literary analysis. She uses each to build up a synthesis, "a feminist deconstructive reading" (Sherwood 1996: 6), but even she seems less interested in her own conclusions than in her ability to demonstrate her virtuosic handling of her methodologies. What her book demonstrates is what I have attempted to spell out in this survey, that is, that contrary to what Greenberg and others appear to believe, a feminist approach to the *marriage metaphor* is not monolithic, is not a *methodology* in itself, but a self-consciously ideological stance that can employ a range of methodological weapons in its anti-patriarchal assault. I have followed Sherwood's lead in using a range of methodologies sequentially.

One other important feature of Sherwood's book is her use of metacommentary on male scholars in chapter 1, and on feminist scholars in chapter 4. The focus of metacommentary is ideology. I have just argued that feminist criticism is an ideological stance; but commonly feminist theology is accused not so much of being an ideological stance but of promoting one – hence the quotation from Greenberg at the beginning of this chapter. Traditional (male) critics contrast feminist criticism unfavourably with their own alleged impartiality.[9] What Sherwood's metacommentary on male critics in chapter 1 especially demonstrates is that their work is as ideologically based in gender terms as any feminist's. They will, no doubt, be surprised to hear and reluctant to recognize this, but there is here, I suggest, a practical example of Butler's theory of naturalization – their scholarly enterprise involves a performance of gender the operation of which remains so concealed that it appears to be "natural". Sherwood appears to be aware of this naturalizing process:

> I find it suspicious that the most obvious interpretation, that the prophet did marry a wife of harlotry, is so studiously avoided, and in the next section I want to ask whether the dominant reading is indeed "natural" or "obvious" as the critical reading suggests, or whether it is necessitated by a particular ideology. (Sherwood 1996: 39)

The commentators she proceeds to describe employ various stratagems to deny Gomer's prostitution, a denial the basis of which is likely to be as much masculine solidarity as it is theological embarrassment.

At its best, then, feminist scholarship on the *marriage metaphor* is an interplay between its own ideology and the uncovered ideologies of its opponents; the feminist scholar emerges as a stripper of her[10] enemy's clothes. She resists through knowingness,[11] and it is an important weapon to pass on to the queer theorist.

2.2.4 Queer Anticipations 2: "Raped Men As Well"[12]

The last insight of feminist biblical scholarship on the *marriage metaphor* that I discuss deserves careful attention, since it forms the starting point of my own queer concerns. This insight could be called the "interrogative shift". The usual and legitimate question that feminist scholars ask can be summed up as "What are the implications for women of the *marriage metaphor*?" But suppose one were to ask instead, "What are the implications for *men*?" The question may seem hardly worth asking, since the obvious answer is based on a simple binary opposition: if the implications for women in the metaphor spring from the imaging of woman as at best the submissive lover/spouse, and at worst the humiliated and battered betrayer, the implications for men are the opposite: man is the righteous and innocent partner. If woman has all the blame associated with fallen Jerusalem (or Samaria, or Judah/Israel), man by contrast basks in the reflection of the metaphorical tenor: he is the equivalent of Yhwh. Wacker was the first feminist critic to spot a complication amidst this simplicity (1987). Taking Hos. 4:14 as her cue, she argued that women were not the object of the metaphorical attack; Israel may be imaged as woman but Israel in fact stands for the male population. The tenor is at odds with the vehicle. Wacker's argument meets with Sherwood's disapproval:

> [I]f women are exempt on the basis of that they are not fully members of society, patriarchy is not being subverted but only varied, and patriarchy in the form of misogyny and the identification of the woman as evil is merely being displaced by patriarchy in the form of social subordination. (Sherwood 1996: 273)

Sherwood's criticism is good as far as it goes, but her failure to appreciate the wider potential of Wacker's insight is disappointing. After all, others *have* appreciated it, among them Bird:

> By appealing to the common stereotypes and interests of a largely male audience, Hosea turns the accusation against them. It is easy for patriarchal society to see the guilt of a "fallen woman"; Hosea says, "You (male Israel) are that woman!" (Bird 1989: 89)

Like Wacker, Bird is using the insight as a recuperative ploy (based on the argument that the metaphor is not anti-woman since it is directed against men),[13] and would be equally open to Sherwood's accusation of replacing one form of misogyny with another. Yet, perhaps without realizing it, Wacker and Bird have identified the complication generated by the Interrogative Shift: the implications for men are two-fold – by ancient audiences as well as modern, by female as well as male, men are identified with Yhwh, but if Bird is right about the implied audience, then men should be identified with the female lover/spouse. A position similar to Wacker's and Bird's is taken by Leith in her article on Hosea (1989); she relates the naming of Israel as a woman ("not a frivolous accusation") to Near Eastern treaty curses, that threatened to turn non-compliant signatories into women (1989: 97–98). But she also points to a more positive side to calling male Israelites women:

> [O]ne motivation for Hosea's portrayal of Israel as a woman was to augment his negation of Israel's identity. Yet at the end of the tale, Israel is still a woman; no sex change has occurred to restore Israel's manhood ... It is now acceptable for Israel, if only metaphorically, to be a woman. (Leith 1989: 104)

I find it significant that other feminist scholars fail to refer to this fleeting glimpse of a positive aspect of the metaphor, one which I shall make much of in this book. Sherwood abstains from considering Leith's article, for reasons the rationale of which I cannot fathom (What does she mean when she says (1996: 266) "since the main focus of her work is the inversion of the nation's mythical self-perception and the creation of a 'looking-glass world'"?); yet she finds time to dwell, if somewhat disapprovingly, on Leith's discussion of the negative side of the metaphor.

In her study of Jeremiah, Angela Bauer trembles on the brink of queer insights (1999). She describes Jer. 30:6 "as another instance of gender bending (compare Jer. 4:19–21; 20:7)", and questions "whether concepts of gender are subverted or reinforced by males taking on female personae" (1999: 125).[14] I should like to focus briefly on her discussion of Jer. 20:7, since it neatly illustrates some differences between much feminist writing and a possible queer interpretation; moreover, I allude to this verse at the end of my chapter on Jeremiah. My own comment there on the verse is very brief, but on further reflection I should argue that there are contrasting perspectives underlying it and Bauer's interpretation. Although she and I agree on a sexual connotation to the language of 20:7, I should categorize Bauer's defining stance as heteronormative: Jeremiah "takes on a female persona" (Bauer 1999: 113), so that he safely remains male and heterosexual and indulges in a species of heterosexual rôle play. I view this verse as a piece of homoeroticism: male Jeremiah imagines himself in a sexual relationship with male Yhwh. But what sort of sex? Bauer has no doubt: rape; my own account is ambiguous (what follows is a form of self-metacommentary!): I acknowledge the "overtones of sexual violence" adduced by some commentators ("if they are right"), but imagine the sex as with one who is "a demanding and ineluctable seducer".[15] If I were asked to expand my thoughts on that verse, I should retain the ambiguity but suggest that we may have here an example of a semi- or faux-reluctant desire on the part of one man to be sexually overwhelmed by a stronger man. If such a suggestion were to be made in a heterosexual context by a male writer, it would quite rightly be dismissed as offensive; but in a homoerotic context, with a male prophet addressing a male god, things can seem very different.[16] I should recall Leo Bersani's description of the passive rôle in gay anal sex as the desire for the dissolution of identity (1988), and suggest, as a parallel in tone, John Donne's well-known Holy Sonnet XIV.[17]

If Bauer hesitates to cross the boundaries imposed by heteronorma-tivity, Patton is a little more adventurous. As has been seen already, rape is a familiar feminist cry; one might add to the chorus Pamela Gordon and Harold C. Washington, who look at the metaphor of rape in terms of the humiliation of defeated warriors (1995). Patton sees Ezekiel's handling of the *marriage metaphor* in terms of its supposed historical setting (2000): Ezekiel and his audience are aware of, or indeed have experienced, the humiliation of invasion and defeat. Patton goes further than Gordon and Washington in suggesting that the defeated are "unmanned" and that this might involve castration and perhaps male rape. She concludes that in the metaphor the writer is identifying the men of Israel as women because they have been made so by defeat, and that this is their own fault – it is punishment by Yhwh for their sins. There is an interesting hint of gender play here, but as in all feminist writing on the *marriage metaphor*, with the exception of that brief single comment by Leith (1989: 104),[18] the concentration on the metaphor of the dysfunctional relationship grants no space for a consideration of what is implied by a metaphor that includes a relationship that is more healthy. One might note incidentally a fascinating observation by Baumann in another context about the use of אהב, the gender implications of which are not pursued. Commenting on the fact that the word is not used to describe the wife of the vehicle of the metaphor, she adds:

> We may note in passing that in any case YHWH in the OT shows preference for grammatically masculine love objects. Of 29 passages in which the grammatical gender of who or what is loved (אהב) by YHWH is perceptible, "his" love is directed only twice to a feminine object: in Jer 31:3 to feminine Israel addressed as "you" (singular), and in Ps. 33:5 to grammatically feminine "righteousness" (צדקה, but parallel to the masculine משפט). In all the other passages the love is directed to real men …, to Israel designated as masculine, or to masculine attributions. (Baumann 2003: 93, n. 32)

A queer critic would want to investigate this interesting observation further. For now one notes the possibilities in talking of Yhwh's "preference for grammatically masculine love objects" and his love "directed to real men". Before I leave Baumann, however, it is worth observing another glimmering of a queer insight. She reads Jeremiah 2–3 (where the wife is accused of playing the whore with other divinities) against later books where either the "queen of heaven" (7.16–20; 44.15–19 and 25) or Asherah (17:2) are mentioned as divinities who receive Israelite attention. She concludes:

[I]t appears that the "wife" will also "play the whore" with goddesses like the queen of heaven; she will begin an "affair" with a "woman". We can only suppose that the later expanders of the book of Jeremiah, working against the background of Israelite prohibition of homosexual relations (Lev. 18:22; 20:13) did not harmonize Jeremiah's marriage imagery from the beginning of the book with the later texts. (Baumann 2003: 112)

How seriously we are supposed to take this speculation is not clear. The outbreak of quotation marks appear to soften its impact, and Baumann herself seems to be dismissing it as mere editorial untidiness; nor does she offer any comment on the fact that the prohibition in Leviticus seems to focus on male same-sex sexual acts.

2.2.5 Dilemmas of Masculinity[19]

It is instructive to note the reaction of male scholars to two decades of feminist criticism of the *marriage metaphor*. Even after due allowance has been made for the stately pace at which theological thinking develops, male excitement stirred up by the debate has been scarcely detectable. *A Feminist Companion to the Latter Prophets* (Brenner 1995a), it is true, includes three exceptions, though it must be said that none of them is of much interest from a queer point of view. Francis Landy's close reading of Hosea 2, for instance, gets off to a promising, if by no means original, start by describing his chosen text "as a fantasy of the transfer of gender, of slippage between male and female personae" (Landy 1995: 146); but in denying any "meaning" to the metaphor, Landy fails to follow through:

[T]he male-dominated Israelite society is characterized as female. God is the supreme patriarch before whom all the men are women ... But the metaphor is meaningless; the shift in gender of the men corresponds to no social or sacred reality. (Landy 1995: 155)

John Goldingay is even less interesting to the queer theorist; his "masculist" approach parallels feminist tactics of "using women's experiences as an aid in gaining illumination on the text's own concerns" (Goldingay 1995: 162). He draws positive conclusions from the *marriage metaphor*:

To connect God with it [viz. sexuality, via his relationship with Israel] is to affirm that God is in touch with this fundamental aspect of male being with that potential for joy and hurt. To disconnect God from it [i.e. because Yhwh has no divine partner] is to deny that God is affected by its negative aspect with the possible implication that its tragedy, failure, pain, and rejection are ultimate realities. (Goldingay 1995: 166)

This is too neat: it ignores feminist arguments that the images in the *marriage metaphor* are so violent that they question "ultimate realities"; Goldingay's God resembles Stanley Baldwin's harlot;[20] moreover his analysis of the metaphor ignores the gender slippage.

Robert P. Carroll, the third male contributor to *A Feminist Companion* (1995), reacts to the feminist reader-response rejection of the *marriage metaphor* by agreeing that the charge of violent pornography is just, and his paper should be read with his contribution to *On Reading Prophetic Texts* (1996). One must applaud his willingness to engage seriously with the debate – the sensitivity with which his criticisms are expressed[21] is in contrast to Greenberg's curt dismissal of the issue (1997: 493–494). Sensitivity apart, however, Carroll evidently sees, just as much as Greenberg, an unbridgeable gap between this feminist position and "serious scholarship":

> Offence and outrage may be appropriate responses for modern readers to reading the Whorusalamin material in Ezekiel, but *serious* scholarship has to move beyond outrage to rational discourse. (Carroll 1996: 78; emphasis added)

I end this chapter with a brief consideration of two writers who can help to move the debate, if not beyond outrage, then at least, perhaps, into areas not envisaged by Carroll. Both serve as a reminder that feminists were only one part of the movement away from traditional biblical scholarship. So David J. Halperin's *Seeking Ezekiel* (1993) uses the tools of psychoanalysis to create a psychobiography of the author of the book Ezekiel, with evidence drawn from four sections (8:7–12; 16; 23; 24:15–27). His conclusion is that Ezekiel failed to resolve his experience of the Oedipus complex: not only did he blame his mother for abandoning him for a rival,[22] but the successful rival added to the offence by sexually abusing him; this childhood trauma resulted in a complex of bitter emotions, loathing and fear of female sexuality and a mixture of hatred of and desire for the male rival. He projects this childhood experience and its emotional aftermath upon the history of Yhwh and Israel, conflating in his mind the abusive rival of his childhood with the Babylonian soldiers who carried him off as prisoner after the fall of Jerusalem. The Temple visions of chapter 8, then, and the outpourings of venom against both men and women in chapters 16 and 23, as well as the connexions between the death of his wife, the fall of Jerusalem and his dumbness are all taken as evidence of the author's mental state.

This summary does little to convey the suppleness of Halperin's psychoanalytical reconstruction. To choose just one example, Ezekiel's contradictory feelings for the dominant male rival who both supplanted and abused him are projected on to a "constellation of male figures", amongst whom are "the lovers of Yahweh's wives, the 'righteous men' (23:45), the 'mob' (... 16:40, 23:46–47), and Yahweh himself" (Halperin 1993: 168). And this heterogeneous collection of males draws out of Ezekiel "a range of emotions that shaded from love, through homosexual desire and heterosexual envy (mingled with awe at the adult male's sexual powers) into fear and hatred" (Halperin 1993: 168).

This is an admirable uncovering of ambiguities in the text,[23] but it is the use to which this close reading is put that makes Halperin's approach unattractive to a post-modernist reader. No queer theorist is likely to object to the use of psychoanalysis *per se*, but it is not easy to accept the use of a highly speculative piece of psychoanalysis to bolster an attempt to establish such an elusive historical situation as the emotional history of the author of Ezekiel. Again and again Halperin convincingly demonstrates ambiguities and contradictions thrown up by the text, yet he himself shows no postmodern uncertainties about the concept of author, nor indeed any lack of confidence that, far from simply drawing from a polyvalent text yet another exegetical possibility, he has provided *the* solution to the problem of Ezekiel – by the end of his book, Ezekiel "is dumb no more". Finally, although he acknowledges Ezekiel's debt to Jeremiah and Hosea, his urge to explain Ezekiel's writings as the outcome of his morbid personality leads to an underplaying of the tradition to which Ezekiel belongs. While I should agree with him that there is some "tenderness" in his two predecessors that is absent in Ezekiel himself (Halperin 1993: 142; I should relate this point to the absence in Ezekiel of the Third Movement of the *marriage metaphor*), some of the vicious hatred of female sexuality, so noticeable in Ezekiel, is present in them. The difference between him and them is that of degree rather than of kind.

Turning to Howard Eilberg-Schwartz (1994), I find myself in a curious position. Here is a work that *ought* to make frequent appearances in the present book; after all, Eilberg-Schwartz's primary point of departure is that the relationship between Yhwh and Israel as expressed in the *marriage metaphor* is based on homoeroticism. His canvas covers more than the prophetic material: he ranges from Genesis to Rabbinic commentary and the New Testament; moreover he sees the *marriage metaphor* as integrated into Israelite religious symbolism well before its treatment in the prophetic texts. But the prophetic treatment permeates the book, and it is clear that he understands its gender ambiguities.[24] He points to what he sees as the central causative feature of this ambiguity:

> [T]he heterosexual metaphor, which works so well when speaking about Israel as a collectivity, ignores a critical fact. The primary relationships in Israelite imagination were between a male God and individual male Israelites, such as Moses, the patriarchs, and the prophets. The images of a female Israel, then, were addressed primarily to men and conceptualized the male relationship to God. (Eilberg-Schwartz 1994: 99)

He enriches this central analysis with discussions of such issues as God's gender and physicality, and the part played in Israelite religion by the father-son relationship and with the male gaze, with such virtuosity that one wonders why his book has been so quietly reviewed and only moderately cited.[25] Yet Eilberg-Schwartz will hardly appear outside this chapter. This is not to say that I have not found some of his insights stimulating. Most commentators, for instance, both traditional and feminist, assume that the male reader of the *marriage metaphor* is meant to identify with Yhwh; for my part I have assumed that all a queer argument can do is point out that the logic of the metaphor runs counter to this "natural" assumption (and by "natural" I mean that it is an outcome of the heteronormative process). But in chapter 7 of *God's Phallus*, Eilberg-Schwartz offers us a metacommentary on Rabbinic literature, which demonstrates that the logical implications *have been* noticed by male readers in an early period, if only those of the Rabbinic times.

Yet, despite this and other insights, I find something in Eilberg-Schwartz's stance that is at odds with my own. He sees the suggestion of homoeroticism in the metaphor as a problem or a dilemma (hence the full title of his book). Now it is true that in Butlerian terms (and *Gender Trouble* appears in his bibliography), homoeroticism *is* a problem, one that the heteronormative process aims to overcome. The queer position, derived from Butler, is that the homoerotic will keep popping up despite the best efforts of heteronormativity. Eilberg-Schwartz's position is less clear. Is the homoeroticism implicit in the *marriage metaphor* simply an unforeseen consequence of the metaphorical logic, or, as I tend to see it, a driving force behind the formulation of the metaphor, a maverick

motivator for choosing a risky image? Eilberg-Schwartz seems to believe
in the first position:

> A homoerotic dilemma was thus generated, inadvertently and to
> some degree unconsciously, by the superimposition of heterosexual
> images on the relationship between human and divine males. (Eilberg-
> Schwartz 1994: 99)

He argues that one solution to the dilemma is the "feminization of
men":

> By imagining men as wives of God, Israelite religion was partially able
> to preserve the heterosexual complementarity that helped to define
> the culture. (Eilberg-Schwartz 1994: 3)

This is a curiously circular argument: the terms of the metaphor (a male/
male relationship imaged as heterosexual marriage) create a homoerotic
dilemma, which is countered by means of the terms of the metaphor
(a male/male relationship imaged as heterosexual marriage). Eilberg-
Schwartz's problem seems to lie in thinking of sexual desire along rigid
binary lines. To imagine a man desiring a male Yhwh means that one
has "feminized" that man, as though one has wielded a mental scalpel
upon him and turned him into a woman, as though a man *qua* man
cannot desire another man. Rigidity is further exemplified by his habit of
describing ancient Israelite sexual relations in terms of heterosexuality;
he does not accept that this necessarily implies "homosexuality", its binary
opposite, against which it is defined, and that to a twentieth/twenty-
first-century reader the terms imply sexual identities; Eilberg-Schwartz
is imposing current Western notions of sexuality upon an ancient Near
Eastern society. He candidly acknowledges the personal circumstances
that influenced his writing of *God's Phallus*, which "was written when I
was struggling with my own masculinity, rediscovering intimacy with
my father" (Eilberg-Schwartz 1994: 10). But the relationship between the
subject matter of the book and his own understanding of homoeroticism
has not been worked through. As for the subject matter, the men of Israel
"love, in ways that are imagined erotically and sensually, a male deity"
(Eilberg-Schwartz 1994: 3). He points out how, in the case of Ezekiel,
this erotic imagining is about as physically-focused as it can possibly be.
But his own understanding of homoeroticism, to judge from his final
apologia, is erotically sanitized:

> Embracing the Father involves a willingness to see male-male eroticism
> as an emotionally whole relationship. It does not mean that all men
> are homosexual[!], but it does mean that we recognize the part within

ourselves that craves intimate bonds with fathers and other men, though those bonds do not take the form of sexual relationships. (Eilberg-Schwartz 1994: 241)

It is time to turn from feminist biblical scholarship and the first uncertain glimpses of queer insights towards a consideration of the encounter between queer theory and the biblical texts.

2.3 Queering the Biblical Texts

What does a queer treatment of biblical texts look like? A glance through the growing number of titles of articles and books on theology and biblical studies where the word queer has made an appearance will bear out Goss's comment that "there are many ways to be queer" (Goss 2002: 257).[26] Queer is sometimes used as an identity label, either as a new identity distinct from both heterosexual *and* homosexual labels,[27] or, more commonly, as a hold-all that is meant to cover all those whose sexual desires and/or practices fall outside the boundaries defined by heterosexuality. In general, the collection of essays *Take Back the Word* (Goss and West 2000) uses queer in the holdall sense.[28] The main focus of the contributors is inward-looking in the sense I used in the Introduction,[29] that is, the view that a "queer reading of the Bible" is one that "allows us to 'define and affirm ourselves' in the midst of a social environment that uses the Bible to justify violence and hate toward us" (Goss and West 2000: 5). I should emphasize again that my inward-looking descriptor is not intended to disparage this use of queer. On the contrary, many of the essays in *Take Back the Word* show that an inward-looking approach can produce hermeneutic profundity that opens up new meanings in the biblical text.

Similarly, *Queer Commentary and the Hebrew Bible* (Stone 2000) contains papers that could be classed as inward-looking, but there are also others that use a more outward-looking approach. *The Queer Bible Commentary* (Guest 2006) offers a successful continuation of this diverse approach to queer;[30] on the other hand, *Queer Theology: Rethinking the Western Body* (Loughlin 2007) is more homogeneous: only Gerard Loughlin's introductory essay (Loughlin 2007: 1–34) and Elizabeth Stuart's paper (Loughlin 2007: 65–75) demonstrate an understanding of queer theory.

I end this section with a closer look at one of the essays in *Queer Commentary and the Hebrew Bible* (Stone 2001b), but first I should like to comment briefly on Robert E. Goss's *Queering Christ* (2002) and Theodore W. Jennings's *Jacob's Wound* (2005). Goss's essays cover a wide range of theological, biblical and ethical issues, but what I find particularly fascinating is the ease with which he combines inward- and outward-looking uses of queer, and, in doing so, fully justifies my warning[31] to distrust the rigidity of the inward/outward binary:

> I use "queer" theologically not only as an identity category but also as a tool of theological deconstruction, for "queer" as a verb means "to spoil or to interfere". (Goss 2002: 228–229)

This quotation comes from chapter 11 (2002: 223–238) which is an illuminating exploration of queer theory as a medley of hermeneutical procedures. His use of queer as a hold-all identity label, on the other hand, is not confined to one chapter but is evident throughout the book.[32] What is fascinating about his view of queer theory is not so much his theoretical understanding but his application of it. He sees it as "a resistance to normativity, including heteronormativity and *gay and lesbian normativity*" (Goss 2002: 228; emphasis added). Questioning the stability of gay and lesbian identities is standard practice for queer theory; even to call their discourses forms of normativity may not raise many eyebrows. But Goss's method of resistance is simply to soften the rigidity of its boundaries:

> Gay identity seems too hardened, too mainstream for adequate queer theological reflection and too inflexible for developing a full queer politics of difference. (Goss 2002: 233)

One might characterize Goss's resistance to gay and lesbian normativity as a horizontal rather than a vertical application of queer theory. A vertical application might question the viability of sexual identity labels over historical time, for example, or within an individual lifetime, or between different cultures and races, or in the context of situationality; more radically it might try to situate gay and lesbian as the necessary other that validates and upholds heterosexual normativity. Goss's horizontal application, on the other hand, is more simply to widen the boundaries of gay and lesbian identities to include other sexual minorities, with the effect, that is, of creating a queer identity label. Thus the two uses of queer – queer as identity label and queer theory – that Goss sets out are for him more interrelated than at first appears. One might illustrate his positioning by his treatment of Genesis 19 (together with Judges 19). He condemns, on the one hand, the "centuries-old Christian tradition that relates Genesis 19 to same-sex practices" (Goss 2002: 194). But he equally attacks McNeill (1993: 42–50) and Boswell (1980: 92–98), who in trying to draw attention away from same-sex practices deny a sexual connotation to יָדַע in verse 5, and thereby bracket out "some vital interpretative elements: phallic violence and patriarchal gender codes of domination/subordination and honor/shame" (Goss 2002: 194). The point of his reading is to question the boundaries of gay: male-on-male rape should not be automatically associated with gay sexuality; moreover he wants to draw attention to the gross gender/power relationship in these verses, which is ignored by many non-feminist readings.[33]

Jacob's Wound is a late entrant into the discussion of the *marriage metaphor*, as far as this book is concerned. It may be thought misplaced to discuss Jennings's work (2005; especially pages 131–176) in the context of queer anticipation. After all, he contrasts his work with both "homophobic readers and those who seek to develop a counterhomophobic or 'gay-affirmative' stance" (Jennings 2005: x), and in his search for "traces of homoeroticism in the narrative" he claims to be carrying out his work "in connection with a queer perspective" (Jennings 2005: xi). But in a note he explains what he means by queer:

> In contemporary parlance the term "queer" serves to designate multiple sexualities, practices, and identities that diverge from the norm of conventional heterosexuality. Thus it includes lesbian, gay, transgendered, and bisexual perspectives and practices. (Jennings 2005: xi, n. 2)

Jennings, then, works with a hold-all understanding of queer. This means that at times he does not quite let go of the notion of fixed identities. Admittedly he offers many useful insights in his chapter on the *marriage metaphor*. For instance, he places it holistically in the context of other glimpses of homoeroticism that he finds in the Hebrew Bible. He contrasts, for instance, his depiction of David's homoerotic relationships (characterized as that between heroes and their companions) and that of Yhwh's relationship with Israel; in the case of David and his friends there is no suggestion that the masculinity of the beloved is in question, whereas he certainly argues that it is so in the case of Yhwh and Israel.[34] In the case of Israel, however, there is a "deliberate transgendering of a standardly male subject" (Jennings 2005: 132); that is, the texts "describe a stereotypically male collective (Jacob, Israel, Ephraim, Judah, and so on) as female" (Jennings 2005: 133). What I find problematic in Jennings's discussion is his understanding of "transgendering". So, for instance, the abrupt changes of gender in Jeremiah, which I interpret as symptomatic of subverted gender identities, are seen by Jennings as "metaphorical drag" (Jennings 2005: 152); and while I agree with him when he says that "the prophets do not shrink from the attribution of almost any kind of eroticism to the relation between YHWH and his people", I find his next sentences too dependent on a fixed view of gender identity:

> Since the relationship is one between subjects that are typically cast as male, the eroticism involved is essentially homoerotic in character. Even where YHWH's beloved is dressed as female, the result is not so much the depiction of a conventional heterosexual relationship but one between a male and his transvestite beloved. (Jennings 2005: 165)

Jennings's Israelite has thus turned from someone of ambiguous sexual identity to a male drag artist. As will be clear from my later arguments, I see a much more nuanced and fluid situation than that.

To help convey a flavour of what an outward-looking queer view of a biblical text can look like,[35] I should like once again to call upon the assistance of Stone, whose "Introduction" to *Queer Commentary and the Hebrew Bible* (2001a) has already been referred to.[36] Stone's other contribution (2001b) to that volume is especially interesting, because in it he discusses the book of Hosea, with a focus on chapters 1–3, which I discuss in chapter 6 below. He takes as his starting point the link between food and sex, a topic of interest to anthropologists.[37] The sparse literature on the topic in terms of biblical scholarship is dominated by feminist interest in the relationship between food preparation/consumption and women. Stone turns the discussion into an examination of the relationship between food provision and masculinity. He begins by noting that "Hosea's references to food and drink frequently appear in or near passages in which Hosea's controversial sexual imagery is also utilized" (2001b: 120). He takes as an example 2:7(5);[38] He could also have cited 2:10–11(8–9), 2:14(12), 2:17(15), 2:24–25(22–23) and 3:1–2, especially if food is considered to include wider agricultural products. His next step is to discuss the significance of this conjunction; for Stone it is not indicative of the theory that "the Israelites of Hosea's day were falling away from a pure devotion to Yhwh into some sort of Canaanite 'fertility religion'" (Stone 2001b: 121). Nor does he understand it, following Keefe (1995), as symbolic of a protest against unjust land policies, with the sexual imagery used "as an index of more widespread family disintegration in the eighth century" (Stone 2001b: 122). Instead he argues that in Northwest Semitic religions "concerns about the production of food through agriculture ... as well as concerns about conception and death ... are more often associated with male than with female deities" (Stone 2001b: 123).[39] He points to Baal and El in this context and argues that Yhwh too is credited with the power to decide success in childbirth and agriculture (he cites Hos. 9:11–12a; 14:16). The relation, then, between food and sex in Hosea is "primarily a conflict between the male gods Yhwh and Baal, characterized respectively as a husband and a male lover [viz. of the woman, one should make it clear], between which Israel (characterized as a woman) must choose" (Stone 2001b: 126).

It may be difficult to see anything queer in the argument so far, but Stone's next tactic is to relate this divine battle over food provision to anthropological discussions about masculinity. Conventionally indicators of men's masculinity are "their ability to father children and to be absolutely vigilant with respect to both the sexual purity of the women of their household and the sexual intentions of other men" (Stone 2001b: 127). But he utilizes cultural anthropology[40] to establish the argument that an important indicator of masculinity was the ability to provide food. He argues that the "display of economic success ... may actually be more important for a man's honor than the widely discussed display of sexual vigilance" (Stone 2001b: 128; he appeals to the authority of Davis, 1977: 77–78, on this point). The conjunction of food and sex in Hosea, then, symbolizes a threat to Yhwh's masculine prestige, and it is in this light that one should read, for example, the woman's denial of his ability to provide for her in 2:7(5) and his indignant riposte in response in 2:10-11(8-9) – they articulate "a profound sense of anxiety about masculinity" (Stone 2001b: 135).

To anticipate the discussion in the next section about the ethics of queer theory, I offer Stone's paper as an example of a serious attempt to highlight "troubling components of Hosea's 'theology' in the strict sense of that term as 'speech about God'" (Stone 2001b: 118). Some commentators[41] accuse queer theorists of a socio-politically disengaged approach to the biblical texts. Koch (2001; in the same collection as Stone's paper), for instance, may leave himself vulnerable to such criticism; he offers brief comments, from a homoerotic point of view, on four short biblical texts, in one of which (2 Kgs 1:2–8) he explores the connotations to a gay man of reading Elijah as "the hairy leather-man" (Koch 2001: 176–177). Spencer (2001), in a critique of Koch's paper, comments that "he would like to see further development of how these encounters can contribute to our common as well as individual lives" (Spencer 2001: 199). Koch might reply that his treatment of the texts was intended to shock, and to displace conventional readings, a strategy that informs my own reading of Ezekiel 23 in chapter 9. In fact, it may be said that his "cruising" methodology is more inward-looking than that. In his introduction he states:

> While I deeply treasure any contributions I might make through my work here and elsewhere to lesbians, bisexuals and transgendered persons – indeed to the human community at large – the remarks that follow primarily regard the experiences of gay men, simply because I cannot and do not presume to speak for anyone else. (Koch 2001: 169)

Whatever the case with Koch, Stone is quite clear about *his* strategic aims. He places his work within the tradition of feminist scholarship and calls to witness "those feminist scholars (e.g. Bach 1993: 192–193; Sherwood 1996: 302) who suggest that one important role for male scholars working in the wake of feminism is to analyze critically the ideologies of masculinity constructed by biblical texts and their readers" (Stone 2001b: 119). And he concludes his paper by invoking Butler's model of performativity and its failures; his paper, he argues, highlights just one of a number of ways in which the stylized reiteration of gender norms breaks down in Hosea.[42] Stone declares himself (2001b: 129) to be one of the "gay male readers of the Bible", but it is interesting that his discussion has nothing to do with same-sex desire *per se*, and it might be felt that for the most part his methodological procedures follow conventional patterns. His concern is to expose the "inability of masculinities", and to give space "for alternative, even queer scenarios that could involve the surrender, rather than the embrace, of the structure of agonistic masculinities" (Stone 2001b: 139).

2.4 Queer Convictions

Is queer theory convincing as an ethical methodological approach in biblical studies? Will it help to subvert normative readings of the texts? Or, to exploit the ambiguity of the title of this section, will queer theory stand convicted of the charges laid against it, of being, that is, at worst complicit in masculinist oppression, at best a mere quietist academic plaything? Annamarie Jagose usefully outlines early "contestations of queer" (Jagose 1996: 101–132). Much of this criticism was levelled at the use of queer as an identity label. I share Guest's unease at this usage:

> Although one does find writers who identify as "queer", the idea of "being queer" is something of a misnomer given that queer theory problematizes identity categories and labels. (Guest 2005: 25)[43]

Here is the key to a much more serious criticism of queer theory: that in undermining identity categories, it undermines resistance to male and heterosexual oppression. The criticism is often coupled with the accusation that it is a gay male erasure of feminist and lesbian concerns. Sheila Jeffreys (1994: 459), in an article succinctly entitled "The Queer Disappearance of Lesbians", argues that the effect of queer on lesbian and gay studies is to make them "feminism-free". This suspicion is not without foundation. Gay men may argue that they are in the same position as women in that they are the victims of male heterosexual oppression and that, therefore, they have ample reason to resist, but they ignore two factors that may compromise their ability to make their resistance effective. The first is that for them the oppressor is also the object of desire. Bersani argues that "gay men run the risk of idealizing and feeling inferior to certain representations of masculinity on the basis of which they are in fact judged and condemned" and that "the logic of homosexual desire includes the potential for a loving identification with the gay man's enemies" (Bersani 1988: 208). It may be countered that many heterosexual women will also be attracted to male power, but the sexual dynamic works differently, and it is the desire to identify with, and to model themselves upon, the oppressor that is so dangerous an instinct for gay men.[44] The second factor that compromises resistance is definitely available only to gay men and that is that as men themselves they participate in the benefits of male oppression and are complicit with it; to some degree they are oppressors too. These strictures serve as a warning that if queer theory is to be an authentic tool of resistance, one necessary discipline for the gay male queer theorist is self-reflection, in order to avoid succumbing to the allure of power.

Lynne Huffer (2001)[45] presents a philosophical underpinning for the accusation of antifeminism in queer theory. She begins with a view of ethics as the site of "the empty inscriptional space of the other who had been X'd out by repetition" (2001: 4), and goes on to argue that queer theory, as a "legitimated discourse" has "become more fixed ... in its claims to self-definition":

> Thus a metanarrative has developed in which the fluid, destabilizing queer performance stakes out its difference from that which came before by setting up a stable, fixed feminist narrative as its nonqueer, identitarian other. (Huffer 2001: 7)

Huffer admits that both sides have failings:

> [F]eminism often masks its own heterosexist underpinnings and, at the same time the queer position often masks an equally entrenched misogyny. (Huffer 2001: 8)[46]

But she is evidently more interested in the theoretical problems of queer theory, which centre around "the question of the subject" (Huffer 2001: 8). The problem lies in queer's insistence that "the subject it speaks in the present moment of the utterance is the only subject there is" (Huffer 2001: 9). In Huffer's view the result of this position is that in the subversion of subjectivity, there is no "intersubjective relation", and queer performativity, "self-referential and asocial" (Huffer 2001: 10) as it is, denies "the subject's ethical enmeshment in its relation to others" (Huffer 2001: 12). Huffer finds an ambiguity (indeed a "ruse") in the queer theoretical position: it both defines itself as "radically inclusive" and implicitly lays claim to a self-legitimizing authority, a universalizing "we", that disavows the "unqueer" as the Other. The political implications of such a process are clear. Huffer calls to her aid Cohen (1997), who argues that there are various groups of heterosexual people outside "the heteronormative center" (examples include American black slaves forbidden to marry) who are overlooked by queer theorists. To call such groups queer "would be presumptuous if not downright imperialist" (Huffer 2001: 18). Huffer calls for the "examination of one's own speaking position [as] ... an ethical obligation of theory; because this is what allows theory to remain open to the possibility of hearing and reading the particularity of the other" (Huffer 2001: 18).

While Huffer's recommendation is commendable, the queer theoretical understanding that she criticizes is not one that resonates with my own. A queer theory that creates a binary of queer and nonqueer and places itself in a position where it can be accused of disavowing certain "heterosexual" groups seems to have fallen into an identitarian trap. Huffer's equation of queer theory's "falsely universalizing claim" with Bersani's "bringing out, celebrating the 'homo' in all of us"[47] does not seem to have much to do with a queer theory that destabilizes rather than homogenizes subjectivity.

If Huffer's criticism is of a queer theory that does not tally with my own understanding, it is still important to recognize that her remarks are a register of genuine unease about the queer agenda. A similar unease is expressed by Guest.[48] She describes her own approach as "lesbian-oriented", but it is clearly one that "can use the insights of queer theory to develop its own agenda without abandoning the term 'lesbian' altogether" (Guest 2005: 55). Her discomfort, then, is not altogether about queer theory itself but with its application by queer theorists. For instance, her first (of five) concerns is that queer theory "may turn out to be a critical tool that is insufficiently cognizant of the feminist criticism that precedes it and enabled its birth" and "will not be gender neutral but will install a new universal masculinity at its heart" (Guest 2005: 46). The wording of this objection resembles that of Huffer (and indeed of other feminists, including Jeffreys, quoted earlier). This may be understood as a warning to practitioners rather than criticism of theory.

Guest's second point offers an argument of superfluity:

> There need not be a wholesale move to queer theory if our definition of "lesbian" can be organized in such a way that resists the rigidity of sexual identity labels. (Guest 2005: 48)

I should stress in response that it is not inevitable that queer as a theoretical position and lesbian and gay as political identitarian rallying points are mutually incompatible. Queer theory questions the stability of any sexual identity, but not its existence. It is worth adding that it is the very insights of post-structural theory in general, and of queer theory in particular, that have enabled the reorganization of definitions along the lines suggested by Guest to be conceivable at all. This argument is relevant to Guest's fourth concern, the negative emotions that would be faced by the abandonment of "lesbian" as an identity label; such abandonment is not inevitable – indeed Section III of this discussion might be offered as an example of an application of queer theory with an identity label still showing.

Concerns three and five, to take them together, are on the theme of disengagement, and seem to me the most thought-provoking in Guest's list. I now use them as an opportunity for offering my own thoughts on the ethics of queer theory in an academic context. Guest fears that queer theory, "with its resistance to identity-reinforcement, will not sufficiently engage with the contemporary grassroots" (Guest 2005: 48). More particularly, and with reference to Stone (2001), "the level of political engagement here is worryingly low" (Guest 2005: 48), and finally that "queer will prove to be an elitist discourse, hardly accessible to the lay person or in touch with the lived realities of grassroots communities" (Guest 2005: 51). These concerns are not Guest's alone, of course; she refers to a number of authors who also voice them, for instance Escoffier (1990) and Malinowitz (1993).

I need to ask, therefore, whether my particular application of queer theory is socio-politically engaged. I have already mentioned the criticism by David Anderson of the proposition that Jesus could be called mother, and have argued that his remarks are evidence of a need for such engagement.[49] A strict, indeed strangulating, binary view of gender and desire persists in the churches. What I set out to do is to demonstrate that views such as his cannot be borne out by the biblical texts (or, for that matter, *any* text). I follow Stone, then, in taking as my purpose "a critical interrogation and active contestation of the many ways in which the Bible is and has been read to support heteronormative and normalizing configurations of sexual practices and sexual identities" (Stone 2001a: 33). The aim of Section III is simply to ensure that no reader will ever again read Ezekiel 23 as a "heteronormative and normalizing" text. The methodology employed is radically non-elitist (but not non-academic). Although the purpose of Section II is no less combative, its methodology exploits linguistic features of biblical Hebrew that would resist easy popularization. But would it not indicate a disturbingly low level of academic self-esteem if one were to refrain from taking the opportunity to use such specialist procedures for fear of seeming elitist? The contribution of Section II to the project of contestation, however modest, is as authentic as that of Section III.

I am writing, then, not *for* or *on behalf of* a particular sexual minority, but am using the insights of queer theory as a contribution to that general effort to wrest the Bible from the grip of heteronormativity. It is in this sense, that I see queer theory as very engaged indeed.

There is a further attack on queer theory, in this case from another angle. The undermining of (gender) identity that has caused Nussbaum's objections to queer theory also worries those who are proponents of (confessional) theology. In a paper in *Queer Theology*, Christopher Hinkle comments:

> Based on the complex interactions between feminist theory and theology and between Marxism and liberation theology, one may expect that as queer theology further develops it will both draw on and seek to challenge queer theory. As of yet, queer theological writings seem with a few exceptions unaware or uncritical of queer theory's antipathy towards the most basic Christian commitments. (Hinkle 2007: 196)

This begs the question, of course, as to what is meant by "queer theology"; challenging the use by traditional Christian theology of biblical texts to entrench heteronormativity seems to me a more urgent task than agonizing about Butler's positivist materialism. As far as this book is concerned, "queer theology" is too loaded a term to describe its purpose; rather, it is better described as an example of biblical studies, using queer theory as a literary and ideological tool to undermine preconceptions of difficult biblical texts.

2.5 A Note on Nomenclature

It is evident from these introductory chapters that I do not attempt to be rigidly consistent in my use of terms to describe (non-)heterosexual desire. "Gay", "same-sex", "homosexual" and their binary equivalents jostle with each other. Sometimes the choice of term is context-specific (for instance, "homosexual" may seem more appropriate when the discussion deals with a historical situation in the nineteenth or early twentieth century). At other times, when I am dealing with a particular writer, I may adopt their terminology for convenience or clarity. I put in a plea for this verbal promiscuity to be regarded as a practical illustration of the reluctance on the part of queer theory to ascribe rigidity to categories of desire.

Notes

1. My original intention was to write a standard literature review on Jeremiah, Hosea and Ezekiel, with particular reference to the *marriage metaphor*. A large part of this work has already been carried out by others. Baumann (2003: 1–22) offers a general survey. Others limit themselves to particular prophetic texts. Rowley (1956/7), for instance, remains useful for a review of the earlier literature on Hosea's marriage, and Sherwood has critically examined the work on both feminist and non-feminist writers, again limiting herself to Hosea (1996, in chapter 1 on male commentators and in chapter 4 on feminist critics).

2. Simply to be a female biblical scholar writing in the 1980s onwards is obviously not a necessary qualification. Odell, for instance, at least to judge from her study of shame and forgiveness in Ezekiel 16 (1992), has made no reference to feminist comment on that chapter or similar ones in Hosea and Jeremiah. Perhaps Fontaine is more typical: in *A Feminist Companion to the Latter Prophets*, her 1989 essay on Hosea, written without any mention of feminist concerns, is juxtaposed with her 1995 "Response", which is replete with them; the misgivings she says she felt in writing the earlier essay have at last found a means of expression (1995a, 1995b). But is Galambush's *Jerusalem in the Book of Ezekiel* feminist? This study of the origins and mechanics of the metaphor has certainly influenced feminist scholars, but I have evaded the question of classification by leaving consideration of her work until a discussion of metaphor theory. Moughtin-Mumby (2008) is a special case: she discusses

a set of texts very similar to those studied here, if somewhat wider in scope, and she shows herself very sensitive to feminist concerns about their harmful content, but her main concerns are focused on other literary aspects of the prophetic metaphor.

3. Sherwood (2004) could be cited as an example of such a methodology.

4. On Hosea: Fontaine (1995b), Connolly (1998); on Jeremiah: O'Connor (1992), Brenner (1995a, b and 1996), Brenner and Dijk-Hemmes (1996); on Ezekiel: Shields (1998), Dempsey (1998).

5. Her account of the metaphor explicitly ignores Hosea 3 (Keefe 2001: 17–18); for further comment on this, see Stone (2001b: 122–123).

6. I ask the reader to pronounce *contrary* with the accent on the second syllable in order to convey that sense of "perversely inclined to do the opposite of what is expected or desired", as *The Concise Oxford Dictionary* (10th ed., 1999) puts it.

7. In fact Bauer's approach is a close relative of my third approach in that it is a literary study that can be slotted into neither the receptionist nor the inceptionist camp.

8. "By making God a husband, it [viz. the *marriage metaphor*] also elevates husbands to the role of God" (Diamond and O'Connor 1996: 309).

9. For instance, Greenberg (1997: 494).

10. I use the feminine gender here, since in the case of the literature on the *marriage metaphor* at least, there is little significant male feminist literature.

11. It is in the light of this comment that I prefer to read Brenner's disturbing stripper sequence in "Pornoprophetics Revisited": "I do not want to join in the game of undressing that woman [viz. Jerusalem in Ezek. 16:39]. I do not want to leer at her uncovered body. I am a heterosexual woman. I would rather view Israel, God's chosen son, being paraded naked in the market place" (Brenner 1996: 83).

12. "In the wake of the invasion, any invasion, the ditches fill up with raped women. To be fair, raped men as well. Raped children, raped dogs and cats. Things can get out of control" (Atwood 2001: 582).

13. This attempt at justifying the metaphor can be criticized not only for the reason that Sherwood offers but also because it ignores the two-way effect that metaphors produce (I discuss this issue in chapter 3).

14. She misleadingly calls this phenomenon "transsexualism" and cites, among others, Tyler on gay drag (1999), and Riviere on masquerade theory (1929).

15. The quotations here are from Section 5.5, below.

16. I *could*, as I do in chapter 9, invoke the aid of contact and other advertising material in *Gay Times* to illustrate my point, but perhaps enough has been said by now to make the point.

17. "Batter my heart, three personn'd God ... for I, Except you enthrall mee, never shall be free, Nor ever chast, except you ravish me" (Donne 1967: 385). One might have ascribed the sentiments to Gerard Manley Hopkins rather than the apparently sexually unambiguous Donne; the nearest Hopkins managed, however, was "Thou mastering me God! ... " (Hopkins 1953: 12).

18. Barbara A. Bozak may be considered another exception. In a study of the feminine imagery of Jeremiah 30–31, she comments: "If the Exile was considered a punishment for the sins of the people, then Jer. 30–31 sets out a

blueprint for a life which, more in harmony with the ideal relationship, points to a new beginning" (Bozak 1991: 164).

19. The phrase is taken from Eilberg-Schwartz (1994: 5).

20. The allusion is to Baldwin's well-known comment at an election rally of 1931 on the irresponsible power of the press barons: "What the proprietorship of these papers is aiming at is power, and power without responsibility – the prerogative of the harlot throughout the ages"; see *The Times* 18 March 1931, p. 18.

21. Carroll is as firmly rejectionist of Ezekiel 16 and 23, for instance, as any feminist critic: "this kind of language is the moral equivalent of garbage and every serious reader of the bible ought to say so" (Carroll 1996: 78).

22. The rival is presumed to be Ezekiel's father or quasi-stepfather.

23. Equally admirable is Halperin's refusal to tinker with the text to suit his exegetical ends – something for which he upbraids Zimmerli, amongst others (see Halperin 1993: 146–147).

24. See Eilberg-Schwartz (1994: 99). In a note to that page he acknowledges the contribution to this point made by feminist writers: "In their essays on Hosea, Bird ... and Leith ... both notice the feminization of Israelite men, but do not notice the homoerotic dilemma that this entails" (Eilberg-Schwartz 1994: 258, n. 35).

25. I have found only three book reviews in mainstream theological journals: Fuchs (1997), Harvey (1995) and Hendel (1995); and one in the journal *The History of Sexuality* (Streete 1996); a search in the database *ISI Web of Science* produced 27 citations of the book since its publication (search carried out June 2005).

26. Goss's remark contains an interesting ambiguity: does "to be queer" refer to an identity label, or does it indicate the act of using queer theory? Goss himself uses "queer" in both senses.

27. This version of the identity label is exemplified by movements such as Queer Nation, for which see Jagose (1996: 107–109).

28. The first sentence of the Introduction begins "When queer people think about their relationship with the Bible ..." (Goss and West 2000: 3), and the reader may understand "queer people" to be "gay men, lesbians, transsexuals, and bisexuals from different ethnicities, socioeconomic standings, and religious communities" (Goss and West 2000: 4).

29. Above, pages 2–3.

30. One or two of its chapters are discussed below in chapter 8.

31. Above, page 2.

32. For example: "Coming from diverse erotophobic traditions within Christianity, many religious people – including many *queers* – have been damaged around the issues of sexuality and gender" (Goss 2002: xiii; emphasis added).

33. If I were to examine Genesis 19 or Judges 19 from a queer theoretical point of view I might start by asking the questions "what (necessary?) failure in performativity has created the irruption of same-sex desire in the male population of Sodom? These men are after all usually heterosexual, are they not? Or is one to suppose that Sodom has (far!) more than its share of predatory homosexuals?" Of course these questions are couched in ridiculously anachronistic identity terms, but these are the terms used or

implied by heterosexist traditionalists, and to ask the questions in this way might be more challenging to their assumptions. My conclusions might well be similar to Goss's, but the language in which the questions are expressed may more readily spoil the assumptions about rigid identity boundaries.

34. Jennings (2005: 135); furthermore he offers a socio-historical context for the contrast: that David and his friends represent a warrior subculture, whereas the *marriage metaphor* occupies a social setting where "sexual relations are incorporated into the male-female structure so prominent in agrarian or household contexts" (Jennings 2005: 135).

35. Although one cannot talk of a *typical* application of queer theory, since its appearance varies considerably.

36. Above, pages 1–2.

37. He uses the work of Levi-Strauss (1963), Pollock (1985) and, in particular, Gilmore (1987) and Davis (1977).

38. In those instances where the verse numbering of the English translations differs from that of the MT, the English verse numbering is given in brackets after that of the MT.

39. He later qualifies this theory as being a "*conventional notion*" rather than dependent upon "empirical evidence about the *actual* division of labor in ancient Israel" (Stone 2001b: 127; emphasis original); moreover he concedes that "there may also have been Israelites who associated food provision primarily with female rather than male deities" (Stone 2001b: 127), and he cites Jer. 44:15–19.

40. See note 37, above.

41. Examples are discussed below.

42. One item in his list is a theme that I too discuss in chapter 6, below: the command to the prophet to marry an אֵשֶׁת זְנוּנִים.

43. In the same paragraph, Guest comments on the pejorative "echoes" that this recuperative signifier recalls; Simon Watney voices concern: "Its use only serves to fuel existing prejudice" (Watney 1992: 18).

44. Bersani makes his remarks while discussing the propensity of gay men to mimic *machismo*.

45. The biblical overtones in the title of her article (2001) deserve some comment, even if only because they represent a radical revisioning of a notoriously "anti-gay" text (Genesis 19). Her allegorization of the process of erasure is the relationship between Sodom and Gomorrah, as mediated by Colette; Sodom is "[i]ntact, enormous, eternal" while Gomorrah is "its puny counterfeit" (Colette 1966: 131–132; translation adapted by Huffer). The result is that Gomorrah, the Other, is effaced. The anomaly that seems to ignore the destruction of *Sodom* as well as Gomorrah is explained by the fact that Colette is reading Genesis 19 through Proust who "renders the two destroyed cities of the Plain as the opposition between men [Sodom] and women [Gomorrah]" (Huffer 2001: 5). With the appearance of both Proust and Colette, the relevance of the allegory to the feminist-queer controversy begins to appear: in blatantly ahistorical imagery, "Colette is the feminist taking [the queer] Proust to task for his blindness to the asymmetries and exclusions of gender, even in a context that is arguably queer" (Huffer 2001: 5).

46. A useful note (2001: 25–26, n. 24), expands on the discussion of gay male misogyny in "the queer movement" and feminist antigay bias.
47. Huffer is quoting Bersani (1995: 10); Bersani's position there is more complex than a simple adherence to queer theory; he is attacking those people "who object to being confined within a gay identity [and] have formed a ghetto of their own, based on the assumed superiority of queer culture to what is stigmatized as compulsory heterosexuality"; he sees "homo-ness" as a "mode of connectedness to the world that it would be absurd to reduce to sexual preference".
48. Guest (2005, chapter 1, and especially 38–53).
49. Above, pages 4–5.

Section II

QUEER AND METAPHOR

Chapter 3

A QUEER THEORY OF METAPHOR

3.1 Introduction

A queer theorist who sets out to examine the *marriage metaphor* is fortunate in having the run of a substantial literature on the theory of metaphor.[1] Since the history of that literature has been more than adequately covered by, amongst others, J. M. Soskice (1985: 1–53), Galambush (1992: 4–10) and Stienstra (1993, ch. 1), I propose not to repeat their work, but to follow their examples in isolating some elements of metaphorical theory that seem most relevant to my own project. Accordingly I shall not dwell on the one major preoccupation of many recent theorists: working in a variety of disciplines – literary criticism, philosophy, linguistics and psychology, for instance – they have explored issues of cognitive processes and content-status of metaphors, and not only those that that may be classed as literary figures of speech, but also the metaphorical element of scientific and everyday language. This debate has a resonance with theology; Sallie McFague (1983; building on Paul Ricoeur's work) and Soskice (1985) have offered important discussions on the significance of metaphorical language about God. But what I want to ask of metaphorical theory is what help it can give in exploring how the *marriage metaphor* relates to the queer view of the gender process.

3.2 Definitions

To begin the discussion, I should clarify my own understanding of metaphor. I am happy to adopt Soskice's definition:

> [M]etaphor is that figure of speech whereby we speak about one thing in terms which are seen to be suggestive of another. (Soskice 1985: 15)

Soskice's reason for using the phrase "figure of speech" was that she wished to emphasize the linguistic element of metaphor – as opposed to "process or a mental act" (Soskice 1985: 16); my reason for adopting it is that it suggests a deliberate literary trope, in contrast to the pervasive content of everyday speech. This fits in well with the *marriage metaphor.*[2] A disadvantage of using it is that it may also be suggestive of the small-scale examples of metaphor that theorists, understandably enough, are prone to offer. This would not matter except that Soskice in particular seems to exclude the longer metaphor from her discussion. In distinguishing between allegory and satire, on the one hand, and metaphor, on the other, she argues that allegory and satire differ from metaphor partly in scope "because in many cases ... [they] extend beyond use in the sentence or discrete utterance; their locus being more properly the text, they are not truly tropic" (Soskice 1985: 55). Whether or not the examples of the *marriage metaphor* I am discussing extend beyond the "discrete utterance", I certainly do consider them metaphorical and not allegorical (since they do not contain the detached hidden code or key of allegory).

Before I leave the question of definition, I should like to add a brief aside which emerges from the distinction made between literary metaphor and everyday speech. My synchronic treatment of the *marriage metaphor* will preclude aetiological considerations, but work done in that area is worth a mention.[3] Galambush reviews the literature on the mythological origins of the metaphor.[4] She applies Lakoff and Johnson's idea of the conceptual metaphor[5] to Fitzgerald's argument for the ancient Near Eastern understanding of capital cities as "goddesses who were married to the patron god of the city" (1972: 405). This understanding, Galambush argues, "is deeply embedded in culture so as to be virtually invisible" (1992: 20). The prophets, then, according to this argument,[6] revivified what had become quiescent tradition akin to the "conventional" metaphors discussed by Lakoff and Johnson. Though only tangential to my own concerns, this debate does raise fascinating speculation about the reception of the *marriage metaphor* in its own time. Was the image of a married Yhwh as startling[7] to its contemporary addressees as it is to some modern readers, if it did indeed recall a long-established tradition? Or is it to be inferred that the effect was created by the terms in which the image was expressed? The *marriage metaphor* must have created *some* effect, since it proved a trope of considerable "staying power" (to use McFague's phrase). Moreover it is equally interesting to speculate on the part played by an ancient mythological tradition upon Christianity's imaging of Christ's relationship with his worshippers. There is another, more fundamental, metaphorical element of the Hebrew Biblical and subsequent traditions without which the *marriage metaphor* was inconceivable. That is the practice of ascribing masculine gender to Yhwh. This element will not be in itself a prime focus in this book, but I acknowledge its pervasive influence; it is explored in depth by, for example, Eilberg-Schwartz (1994). I must acknowledge too its power: it is immensely difficult in Western Christian traditions, at least, to think of Yhwh as it, or even It; and despite decades of feminist critique the imaging of Yhwh/God as She has not won widespread acceptance. The fundamental metaphorical gendering of Yhwh is a triumph of gender performativity, and the apparent reluctance to abandon it is a tribute to its effective use of the naturalization process.

3.3 Metaphorical Attributes: Non-Substitution and Interaction

But, to return to the firmer ground of metaphorical theory, I do not wish to linger among the many discussions, except to mention that I take from Richards' classic account (1936) the familiar terminology of *vehicle* and *tenor*, so that in the example "man is a wolf", "man" is the tenor and "wolf" the vehicle. I also take it as axiomatic that the metaphorical process involves more than a simple comparison between vehicle and tenor, but that, in Richards' words, "the co-presence of the vehicle and tenor results in a meaning (to be clearly distinguished from the tenor) which is not attainable without their interaction" (Richards 1936: 100). The significance of this sentence is twofold: first, it suggests what other writers call non-substitution or irreducibility; as McFague expresses it: "A metaphor is not an ornament or illustration, but says what cannot be said any other way" (1983: 50).

Second, the word "interaction" anticipates what Black worked out at greater length (1962: 38–47). The most significant part of his argument for the treatment of the *marriage metaphor* by feminist scholars lies in a single sentence: "If to call a man a wolf is to put him in a special light, we must not forget that the metaphor makes the wolf seem more human than he otherwise would" (1962: 44).

Black fails to develop his remark. Perhaps it is too suggestive of affect rather than of cognition for it to interest him. Perhaps, too, it implies the triumph of the text over authorial control, something with which he would not have much sympathy. But the idea that the metaphorical process produces a genuinely mutual interaction between vehicle and tenor is consonant with the way in which many feminist critics have read the *marriage metaphor*. For the feminist critic, especially one who argues from the standpoint of reception-theory, there is nothing startling in the argument that to talk of Yhwh's relationship with Judah/Israel in terms of a patriarchal view of marriage divinizes that view; it is a feminist insight at least as old as the Dalyesque man/God dictum.[8] This attitude towards metaphorical interaction is fully articulated by McFague (though she does not use the quotation from Black mentioned above), who talks of "the interactive character of models, that is, the way in which the model and the modelled mutually influence one another" (McFague 1983: 147).[9] She expands this theme and includes the comment: "At the heart of patriarchalism as root-metaphor is a subject-object split in which man [viz. qua male] is envisioned over against God and vice versa" (McFague 1983: 148).

While I endorse this understanding of the metaphorical process when applied to the *marriage metaphor*, there remains a need to guard against a reductionist accusation of mere subjectivism. Sherwood is well aware of the danger:

> Because truth is conventionally associated with the literal, metaphor is taken to be a dilute or distorted form of truth, and the force of words and phrases can be made less innocuous by dismissing them as "only a metaphor". (Sherwood 1996: 62)

Sherwood's remark is in fact directed towards those male critics who refuse to accept the implications of the Hosean description of Gomer as אֵשֶׁת זְנוּנִים. Her words could equally well apply, however, to other male critics such as Greenberg and Carroll whose puzzled dismissal of feminist receptionist criticism has already been noticed; indeed, to a great extent their puzzlement stems from the rationalist prioritization of the literal over the metaphorical. To counter their scepticism the work of recent metaphorical theorists, especially that of Soskice, must be recalled.

Soskice is concerned to demonstrate the way in which meaning can be ascribed to metaphorical language about God. A major part of her discussion is devoted to establishing that the metaphors have "conceptual possibility", to scotch once and for all the belief that they are necessarily inferior to literal language in terms of expressing reality. She makes a powerful case, arguing, for instance, that scientific thinking uses metaphors to describe what would otherwise be indescribable phenomena. But I have already suggested a possible complication here: it is implicit in Soskice's argument that, although the reader has an allotted task of thinking through the implications of the metaphor, it is the writer who sets these tasks; conscious authorial intent is taken for granted. But the receptionist view of the *marriage metaphor* challenges authorial pre-eminence – and I too am happily complicit in this postmodern penchant for author-assassination, although not only from a receptionist point of view.

3.4 Metaphor and Ideology

But is the possibility of meaning killed off along with the author? Is there any metaphorical "truth" left? What I am suggesting is that, as far as the *marriage metaphor* is concerned, one should think less in terms of truth, conceptual possibility or reality content, than of power. To obtain a sharper picture of the *marriage metaphor* through the lens of queer theory, it is necessary to look not at its content but its ambivalent functionality as an ideological weapon, to view the metaphor as (dys) functional dominance.

The association of metaphor and ideology should come as no surprise, especially in view of the supra-literary view to be found in Lakoff and Johnson, according to which metaphorical language orders basic concepts: "The conceptual systems of cultures and religions are metaphorical in nature" (1980: 40). Stigliano sums up the ascendancy of the metaphorical:

> Nelson Goodman and Richard Rorty, along with Paul Ricoeur, Hans-Georg Gadamer, Jurgen Habermas, and many other Marxists, phenomenologists, and hermeneuticians, are busily dissolving the literalist ontology and epistemology taken for granted by social and natural scientists. (Stigliano 1985: 286–287)

Metaphorical language, then, in the later twentieth century has been seen to have a function in the marshalling of human experiences that is similar to that of ideology. But it is also necessary to note that that functioning, in the case of ideology, has come to be seen as somehow sinister. To appreciate this, one could most usefully turn from theoretical to applied studies. I should like to offer just one or two examples from the many available, the first being from a critic who will figure prominently in chapter 8 below. In her *Illness as Metaphor* (1991) Sontag traced the distorted manner in which tuberculosis and cancers were symbolized.[10] She examined the use of metaphors of illness by political philosophers and practitioners for the purposes of political propaganda.[11] So, for instance, she observed an increasing intensity of tone, from the seventeenth century, "political philosophy's great tradition" when "the analogy between disease and civil disorder is proposed to encourage rulers to pursue a more rational policy" (Sontag 1991: 78), to the "less lenient assumptions" of the twentieth century (Sontag 1991: 80) – among her examples is Hitler's first political pamphlet of 1919 in which he "accused the Jews of producing 'a racial tuberculosis among nations'" (Sontag 1991: 83).

It is perhaps in the area of political ideology that the study of metaphorical rhetoric has been most energetic. I should like to single out Jansen and Sabo's analysis of the language used in the first Gulf War; they argued that "sport/war tropes are crucial rhetorical resources for mobilizing the patriarchal values that construct, mediate, maintain, and, when necessary, reform or repair hegemonic forms of masculinity and femininity" (Jansen and Sabo 1994: 1). I could adopt this sentence almost wholesale for my present purposes – simply substitute for "sport/war tropes" the phrase "the three versions of the *marriage metaphor* under consideration", and the result will be a close approximation to my view of how the metaphor functions in the three prophetic texts. I am arguing that it bestows divine sanction not only on the hierarchal gender relationships of patriarchy – which is, of course, exactly what feminist scholars argue – but also on heteronormativity, the compulsory code of cross-sex desire. And because it is *divine* sanction, it strengthens the impression that heteronormativity is the only natural way to be – the *marriage metaphor* presents the reader with apotheosized naturalization.

But does it? The whole process of gender performativity is subject to "necessary failures", as Butler calls them (1990: 185), unintended products from the conveyor belt of performativity, that reveal the artificiality of the whole system. What follows in this section are pointers to the inherent quirks in the *marriage metaphor*, which betray the metaphor's systemic artificiality, and question its claims to divine inspiration. As I have already remarked, a few feminist critics have pointed out an intrinsic oddity of the metaphor: that the male addressees of the metaphor are equated with the spouse/lover of Yhwh. This oddity has escaped the notice of most readers, male and female (including the majority of feminist critics). It is my object to nail down this anomaly, so that it is impossible for it to be ignored. But, to help in this project, I must first establish who the addressees of the *marriage metaphor* really are: "Are the Israelites Male?"

Notes

1. It is a literature that began with Aristotle, and by 1971, Warren Shibles was able to list more than 400 pages of entries in his *Metaphor: An Annotated Bibliography and History* (quoted in McFague 1982: 201, n. 2).
2. In the next paragraph, I allude to the aetiological connexions of the *marriage metaphor* to everyday speech.
3. Moughtin-Mumby, it should be noted, more radically distrusts aetiological approaches to the *marriage metaphor* (a phrase which in itself, as we have seen, she distrusts); so, for instance, in discussing Ezekiel 16 and 23, she argues that "in the period during which the prophetic books were written there was no pre-existing, recognized concept of 'the marriage metaphor' consisting of a number of given features which are deliberately recalled whenever sexual or marital metaphorical language is employed" (2008: 161).
4. She includes, for instance, Fitzgerald (1972 and 1975); Lewy (1944); Wakeman (1982).
5. That is, the everyday use of metaphor in the conceptual system; Lakoff and Johnson 1980: 3–6.
6. More recent research, e.g. Dever (2005) and Hadley (2000), however, has amassed evidence to suggest in the period of the prophets Yhwh was considered to be married to the goddess Asherah.
7. "[G]ood metaphors shock, they bring unlikes together, they upset conventions, they involve tension, they are implicitly revolutionary" (McFague 1983: 17).
8. Earlier I suggested that Ortlund offers a clear illustration of such interaction in the *marriage metaphor* (1996: 173; see above page 4).
9. For McFague, a model is "a sustained and systematic metaphor"(1983: 67).
10. She continued the theme in *Aids and its Metaphors* (1991).
11. Sontag (1991: 73–87).

Chapter 4

ARE THE ISRAELITES MALE?

At times it seems as if women are simply not part of Israel. (Plaskow
1999: 406)

4.1 Introduction

When Hosea declares that "the Lord loves the people of Israel' (Hos.
3:1), whom exactly does the Lord love? Or when Jeremiah is told to make
his proclamation "in the hearing of Jerusalem" (Jer. 2:2), who is to be
his audience? Is it to be supposed that the prophets' audience or the
target of their condemnation or cajolery is the whole population of the
kingdom? The question is important. My interpretation of the *marriage
metaphor* assumes a comparison between the vehicle bridegroom/bride
and the tenor Yhwh/male Israelites – that is, that male Israelites are the
brides of Yhwh. Is this comparison justifiable?

Some feminist critics share this assumption. In her discussion of
women's position in a post-patriarchal Judaism, Judith Plaskow argues
that "the Jewish textual tradition treats men as normative Jews" (1999:
403). Citing the inclusion of circumcision in the statement of the Sinai
covenant, she argues:

> This important passage seems to presuppose a religious community
> composed of males only, an impression reinforced by other texts. The
> covenant at Sinai is spoken in male pronouns, for example, and the
> content assumes male hearers. (Plaskow 1999: 406)

Indeed, she qualifies this statement: women are not excluded entirely
from the Israelite community, but at the same time they are part of it
only "in a submerged and non-normative way" (1999: 407). But the point
about gender assumptions in the text is significant.

As for the addressees of the prophetic texts, Leith makes a similar
point, and links them to the covenant partners:

> It is important here to keep in mind that though he uses imagery derived from female sexuality, Hosea is addressing his prophecies to his fellow citizens and Israel's élite, but not to Israelite women. In patriarchal Israel, women were not full partners in the covenant. So Hosea, on one level, is calling the Israelites "women". (Leith 1989: 97)

Similarly, Galambush, in her study of Ezekiel, argues that it is the "male Israelites" who "constituted the legal community of Israel" (1992: 35).[1] This assumption may derive from the view of Israel as a patriarchal society where his privileged position socially, legally and politically renders the male citizen the default object of address. When in the Hebrew Bible characters talk to or writers talk of the Israelites, or when the Israelites speak for themselves, it is the men to whom the speaker speaks, or it is the men who do the speaking.

But is there evidence in the text itself that this is indeed the case? The emphasis here is on literary evidence of the text, a criterion that seems appropriate, not to say obligatory, in a study of the Hebrew Bible that is dependent on a literary rather than a historical or sociological approach.

The first piece of evidence is that, except where it is represented by a grammatically feminine simile or metaphor, the people of Israel are described in grammatically masculine terms. But although the use of grammatical masculine gender to represent both male and female may say something about the relative positions of men and women in their society, it is not in itself convincing evidence of the assumptions of the individual speaker or narrator. There is a need to examine the texts of the Hebrew Bible more systematically to see whether, when referring to Israelites as a group, characters and writers routinely ignore women and assume that their addressees or subjects are male. If such evidence *can* be found, the assumption made by Leith, Galambush and the present writer is all the more justifiable. The survey focuses on the structure of the text, an appropriate way to support a project which, in this section at least, also looks at the structure of the text in its search for breakdowns in the process of gender performativity.

In examining the use and occurrence of יִשְׂרָאֵל, עַם and related words in the Hebrew texts, over fifty passages in all, both single verses and longer texts, were identified as the providers of useful pointers to the gender of the Israelites. A selection of the more significant ones is presented below.[2]

It will be apparent from this use of the Hebrew Bible as a whole, that the approach to this evidence is synchronic rather than diachronic.

Thus the opening sentence of this section mentions Hosea and Jeremiah together, leaving aside the various socio-religious, literary and historical contexts. The terms Israel/Israelite(s) are used flexibly to refer to the unitary nation or to either of the post-Solomonic kingdoms, or indeed, in one or two cases, to the population of Jerusalem.

The situation that emerges from the evidence is complex. The Israelites are addressed or spoken of far more times than in the 50 examples the survey has pinpointed, and in the vast majority of cases it is impossible to say, from the text itself, whether or not it should be assumed that both men and women are referred to. To take an example, on a very simple level, from the several references in the opening chapters of Exodus to the Israelites enslaved in Egypt, one may be justified in assuming that it is both the men and women for whose liberty Moses and Aaron plead before Pharaoh.[3] But it should be stated clearly that in this and the majority of cases in which the Israelites are addressed or spoken of such an assumption is based merely on common sense; the texts themselves fail to make it plain either way.

4.2 Examples of Gender Inclusivity

First then, what is the textual evidence for inclusivity, that is, explicit indications that, when Israelites are speakers, addressees or subjects, women are included along with men? Only a few examples can be identified, and most of them are ambiguous:

1. Exodus 32:2–3. Aaron responds to a request from the people (הָעָם in verse 1) to make gods for them: "Aaron said to them 'Take off the gold rings that are on the ears of your wives, your sons, and your daughters, and bring them to me.' So the people took off the gold rings." Grammatically the addressees are masculine plural (e.g. וַיִּתְפָּרְקוּ in verse 3), and the wording of verse 2 might lead to the conclusion that the people addressed by Aaron, those who are to take the rings away from the earring-wearers, are those who are not on the list, that is, the adult male fathers. Thus so far the inference is that "the people" by default consists of the adult males. Against this, in verse 3, "the whole people" (כָּל־הָעָם) took their (masculine plural) earrings off. Here "the whole people" seems to include the women, sons and daughters, and indeed might even be interpreted as excluding the apparently non-earring-wearers, the adult males! In the light of verse 3, it may be tempting to interpret verse 2 in

some inclusive way, for instance as "all of you Israelites, that is, all who wear earrings", but it has to be admitted that these verses leave an impression of gender confusion.

2. Exodus 35:4–5 and 20–22. Gold also figures in the second example of apparent inclusivity. Exodus 35 describes the response of the Israelites to Moses' injunction that "whoever is of a generous heart" (כל־עָדֵח לבּוֹ) should make contributions to the Tabernacle. In verse 22 it is stated that "both men and women (הָאֲנָשִׁים עַל־הַנָּשִׁים) came, all who were of a willing heart" (compare verse 29). Although this access of goodwill is not explicitly attributed to "all the congregation of the Israelites" (כָּל־עֲדַת בְּנֵי־יִשְׂרָאֵל, 35.1), yet one might identify here a clear indication that the grammatical masculine may not necessarily exclude women.

Yet do these two passages really demonstrate inclusivity? The context in both cases is a call to sacrifice costly finery for sacred purposes; for finery one might even substitute the word frippery – one recalls the errant lover in Hos. 2:13 decking "herself with her ring and jewellery" when she went after her lover. Far from providing us with examples of inclusivity, women are mentioned in these two passages because they are among those in the community who are perhaps more likely to indulge in such finery. Women are introduced here, then, for a specific purpose, and it is difficult to argue from these passages that such terms as בְּנֵי־יִשְׂרָאֵל or הָעָם by default signify both sexes.

3. Deuteronomy 17:2–17, however, seems to present a very different case: the pronouncement on idolatry, addressed to "you" (second singular masculine, referring back to "Israel" in 10:22), specifically and emphatically includes women (אִישׁ אוֹ־אִשָּׁה in verse 2; and twice in verse 5). This is a striking example of inclusivity without parallel in the Deuteronomic code, except for chapters 21 and 22, where female references are an inevitable part of the pronouncements on sexual relations. But scarcity is suspicious in itself; why is idolatry singled out for inclusive treatment? Perhaps what lies behind the female references here, after all, resembles what I have observed in Exodus 32 and 35: woman is introduced here because she is considered to be especially prone to the sin of idolatry. In Jeremiah 44, for instance, it is the women who "had been making offerings to other gods" (verse 15), and (despite the textual problem) verse 19 depicts female intransigence on the matter. It is worth dwelling on this passage a little longer. Jeremiah's response "to all the people,

men and women" (verse 20), recalls Deut. 17:2 and 5, though there are some minor differences of vocabulary (עַל־הַגְּבָרִים וְעַל־הַנָּשִׁים rather than אִישׁ אוֹ־אִשָּׁה), and there is here, as I have argued for Deuteronomy 17, the special need for inclusivity, a need that seems to be soon forgotten, since by verse 24, Jeremiah is proclaiming to all the *people* and "all the women" (אֶל־כָּל־הָעָם וְאֶל כָּל־הַנָּשִׁים), a telling slippage; and by verse 25, the women are further demoted in terms of address: "you and your wives" (אַתֶּם וּנְשֵׁיכֶם).

4. Deuteronomy 28:54–57. Deuteronomy 27 and 28 list warnings to "the people" (27.1; אֶת־הָעָם) in the event of their disobeying the laws. In 28:54–57, the writer relates the desperate straits to which the enemy's siege will reduce the Israelites: the picture depicted by "the most refined and gentle of men among you will begrudge food to his brother" is carefully balanced by "she who is the most refined and gentle among you ... will begrudge food to the husband". At first sight, the verses seem to offer a genuine instance of inclusivity, but further consideration suggests some uncertainty. It could be felt that the inclusion of woman here reflects a desire to create a neat rhetorical balance; moreover the picture of the breakdown of wifely devotion and basic maternal instincts[4] effectively underlines the horrors that follow on disobedience.

5. Deuteronomy 29:9–10 (English versions 10–11). At the renewal of the covenant in Moab, Moses addresses "all Israel" (כָּל־יִשְׂרָאֵל 29:1): "You stand assembled today, all of you, before the Lord your God – the leaders of your tribes, your elders, and your officials, all the men of Israel, your children, your women, and the aliens who are in your camp". This list, then, constitutes "all of you" (כֻּלְּכֶם), and the women are included. But the wording is significant and prompts the question who is this "you"? In one sense Israel is made up of all the groups listed in these two verses, but, apart from the aliens, who presumably may be ignored, the only group not described as "your", is "every man of Israel" (כֹּל אִישׁ יִשְׂרָאֵל). There is no reason why the speaker could not have said אַנְשֵׁיכֶם; instead he adds the nation's name.[5] Is this because Israel = men and so to say "your men" would not have sounded natural, since "you" is the same as "the men of Israel"? Other possibilities are that the phrase sums up the groups mentioned so far as equivalent to "the men of Israel". Perhaps, the phrase אִישׁ יִשְׂרָאֵל should be seen as referring to the ordinary adult males who are of military age (as opposed to elders and children);[6] but this is something to which I shall return.

6. Jeremiah 18:19–23. Jeremiah asks Yhwh to punish his enemies. If the enemies are taken to be the main body of the people of Judah or Jerusalem (as seems to be the case at, for example, 20:4), then it may prove interesting to look at the wording of the list that follows, since it offers a contrast to Deuteronomy 29 (example 5): "let their wives become childless and widowed; may their men meet death by pestilence".[7] Inclusivity does seem firmer here: the list does seem to refer to the different elements of "they", rather than assume by default that they = the men of Judah/Jerusalem. It is tempting to add 2 Sam. 6:19 (לְכָל־הֲמוֹן יִשְׂרָאֵל לְמֵאִישׁ וְעַד־אִשָּׁה לְאִישׁ); David shares out the food but one feels the inclusivity is one of rhetorical emphasis meant to underline David's kingly dignity (in contrast to Michal's subsequent complaint in verse 20).

These examples indicate that, though not entirely absent from the Hebrew Bible, inclusivity makes only very rare appearances. How strong is the evidence to the contrary?

4.3 Examples of Gender Exclusivity

What clues are there in the text for suspecting that, when the Israelites are addressed or described or speaking, it is the men who are uppermost in the minds of the narrator or speaker? The short answer is that there are far more than the contra-indicators already noted but that there is also some ambiguity in the evidence. I should like first to discuss some of the more straightforward examples.

1. Exodus 19:14–15. Among the set of preparations at Mount Sinai, the writer includes the comment that "Moses went down from the mountain to the people (אֶל־הָעָם). He consecrated the people (אֶת־הָעָם), and they washed their clothes. And he said to the people (אֶל־הָעָם), 'Prepare for the third day; do not go near a woman.' (אַל־תִּגְּשׁוּ אֶל־אִשָּׁה)". The masculine plurals following the singular הָעָם are what one expects, and I shall not draw any conclusion from them, but the veto on sexual relations with a woman or wife establishes that הָעָם (repeated twice) signifies "the men".

2. Exodus 22:22–23 (English versions 22:23–24). The recital of the laws includes the consequences of abusing widows or orphans: "If you do abuse them,[8] when they cry out to me, I will surely heed their cry; my wrath will burn; and I will kill you (אֶתְכֶם) with the sword, and your wives (נְשֵׁיכֶם) will become widows". The "you" here,

which refers back to "Israelites" in 20:19(22) is indisputably not just masculine in gender but also male in sense. The Israelites here are male.

3. Leviticus 18 (and 19:20). The ordinances on sexual relations are pronounced upon the people (or, strictly, children, descendants or sons) of Israel (as at 18:2: אֶל־בְּנֵי יִשְׂרָאֵל). Yet implicitly throughout Leviticus 18 it is exclusively men who are being addressed. Verse 23 may illustrate this: "You shall not have sexual relations with any animal ... nor shall any woman give herself to an animal to have sexual relations with it".[9] The need to ensure that women were included in the ordinance demanded a specific reference in the third person, in contrast to the (tacit) male reference in the second person. This is not just because grammatically the verb is masculine, or even because a different verb is required to express the different physical activity. It is because the ordinances are usually addressed to the men – if it were not so, one might have expected two third person expressions here: "a man shall not have ... nor shall any woman give herself".

4. Numbers 14:2-3. In response to the spies' report about Canaan, the people protested: "And all the Israelites (כֹּל בְּנֵי יִשְׂרָאֵל) complained against Moses and Aaron; the whole congregation (כָּל־הָעֵדָה) said to them, 'Would that we had died ... Why is the Lord bringing us into this land to fall by the sword? Our wives and our little ones will become booty'". Whatever the exact force of בְּנֵי יִשְׂרָאֵל or הָעֵדָה in terms of gender,[10] the text might be expected to imply that the whole population was complaining, women as well as men. But from the words "our wives" (נָשֵׁינוּ) it is clear that "we" are males. It is puzzling that in Yhwh's response, the women drop from view completely (verses 28–35): "I will do to you the very things I heard you say ... all of your number, included in the census, from twenty years and upwards ... not one of you shall come into the land ... But your little ones, who you said would become booty, I bring in". The interesting question of censuses will be dealt with in due course, but the relevant point to note here is that it was a census of male adults only. So the men and the children are dealt with, but what will be the fate of the women? Booty or death?[11]

5. Deuteronomy 13:7 (MT 13:6). This contrasts to no. 3 in the examples of gender inclusivity. Both are injunctions against idolatry, but whereas Deut. 17:2-17 specifically includes women as addressees, the present passage is vaguer. It is, as in the preceding chapters,

addressed to "you" (masculine singular), identifiable as יִשְׂרָאֵל in chapter 10:12; until 13:6, there is no clue as to whether the addressee is meant to include women. Among would-be enticers, however, is אֵשֶׁת חֵיקֶךָ, and the absence of a balancing reference to אִישְׁךָ may lead to the conclusion that the addressee is more than grammatically male. But the evidence is indicative rather than conclusive, since from the absence of a balancing partner to אָחִיךָ (that is, no sister is on the list), one might argue that the list contains merely random examples of would-be enticers. On balance, I feel that the presence of the wife is reasonably strong evidence for exclusivity.

6. Deuteronomy 28:30. One item on the long list of the consequences of disobedience to the Deuteronomic laws indicates the gender of the list's "you" (second singular masculine): "You will become engaged to a woman, but another man will lie with her". Men are clearly meant. It is all the more striking that no other item on the list could refer only to women; the only possible exception is verse 18: "Cursed shall be the fruit of your womb (פְּרִי־בִטְנֶךָ). At first glance, this seems to be clearly addressed to a woman: men do not have wombs. It *could* be argued that בֶּטֶן does not have to mean "womb" (see, e.g., Ezek. 3:3, where it refers to Ezekiel's belly), but it often does and would seem to do so here. But the two words are used as part of a stock phrase in Deuteronomy, which includes not only the children, but the person's crops and animals (e.g. 7:12, 28:11, 28:18, 28:53 and 30:9). The anatomical details fade from view and the phrase can be read as referring to a male. Job 19:17b: "and I am loathsome to the sons of my womb" (וְחַנֹּתִי לִבְנֵי בִטְנִי), where Job himself is talking, may be considered as a parallel (compare also Ps. 132:11; Mic. 6:7).

7. Judges 3:5–6. This statement of Israel's racial integration with its new neighbours in Canaan is expressed in terms of the male subject: "So the Israelites lived among the Canaanites, the Hittites ... ; and they took their daughters as wives for themselves". It is interesting that בְּנֵי יִשְׂרָאֵל. is regularly translated as gender-neutral (NRSV: "Israelites"; AV: "children of Israel"), but here it is definitely male in meaning.[12]

8. 2 Chronicles 20:13. "Meanwhile all Judah (וְכֹל־יְהוּדָה) stood before the Lord, with their little ones, their wives, and their children". Judah is just as prone as Israel to exclusivity. Here וְכֹל־יְהוּדָה refers to the male citizens, with the wives and children described as adjuncts.[13]

9. Ezra 9:1–2. In the denunciation of mixed marriages, the charge is made that "the people of Israel (הָעָם יִשְׂרָאֵל), the priests[14] and the

Levites, have not separated themselves … For they have taken some of their daughters as wives for themselves and their sons". There is no possible ambiguity about "the people" here: it is הָעָם that is used, not בְּנֵי יִשְׂרָאֵל. But these verses may be contrasted with 10:9–12, where the accused have now become כָּל־אַנְשֵׁי־יְהוּדָה וּבִנְיָמִן. It seems clear that people = men.

10. Psalm 128:1. "Happy is everyone who fears (כָּל־יְרֵא) the Lord", as long as he's a man, it seems, since his "wife will be like a fruitful vine in the house" (verse 3). Moreover by verse 4, כָּל־יְרֵא has become גָּבֶר. *HALOT* supports a generic use of גבר (and claims as evidence the LXX use of ἄνθρωπος rather than the stronger ἀνήρ).[15] But *TDOT* argues that גבר "does not mean simply a man … nor does it mean man in general".[16] In this its use is contrasted with that of אדם and אנוש. Its force in the Psalms is seen as an indicator of righteousness, and the present passage is cited amongst others. For righteousness as a manly quality, one might compare the relationship between the Latin words *vir* and *virtus*.

11. Jeremiah 6:11–12. The prophecy of doom against the inhabitants of Jerusalem begins inclusively enough: children, young men, husband and wife and the old will all be affected; but in verse 12 the reality of the male force of "they" breaks out: "Their houses shall be turned over to others, their fields and their wives together (שָׂדוֹת וְנָשִׁים יַחְדָּו)". Leaving aside the socially significant fact of lumping together the wives and the fields, I shall content myself with the obvious point drawn from the text that "they", the householders, are distinguished from the wives; in other words, they, as far as verse 12 is concerned, are male. Jeremiah 6:12–15 is reproduced with variation in 8:10–11, where the same conjunction of wives and fields is made, with the same assumption of a masculine subject.

12. Jeremiah 14:16. "And the people (הָעָם) to whom they [viz. the false prophets] prophesy shall be thrown out into the streets of Jerusalem, victims of famine and sword. There shall be no one at all to bury them – themselves, their wives, their sons, and their daughters" (הֵמָּה נְשֵׁיהֶם וּבְנֵיהֶם וּבְנֹתֵיהֶם). Once more the inhabitants of Jerusalem, or at least those who listened to the false prophets, are seen as males, despite the presence of the seemingly inclusive הָעָם.

13. Jeremiah 15:7–8. "I have winnowed them [the people of Jerusalem] with a winnowing fork in the gates of the land; I have bereaved them, I have destroyed my people (עַמִּי); they did not turn from their ways (מִדַּרְכֵיהֶם). Their widows (אַלְמְנֹתָו) became more numerous than

the sand of the seas." The "their" of "their widows" does not exactly reproduce the MT (אַלְמְנֹתָו); the suffix is third person masculine singular, although some traditions reflect a plural reading. In either case, however, the reference seems to be to "my people" or (their ways), and leads us to understand them as masculine.

14. Jeremiah 29:6. In his letter to the exiles in Babylon (who are described in 29:1 as "the remaining elders ... and ... the priests, the prophets, and כָּל־הָעָם)", Jeremiah tells them to settle in their new city, and then once more construes הָעָם as adult males by advising them to "take wives and have sons and daughters".

15. Ezekiel 33:26. Ezekiel's condemnation of the remaining "inhabitants of the waste places in the land of Israel" (הֶחֳרָבוֹת הָאֵלֶּה עַל־אַדְמַת יִשְׂרָאֵל יֹשְׁבֵי verse 24) includes the accusation that "each of you defiles his neighbour's wife". Like Jeremiah, Ezekiel sees the inhabitants as male.

4.4 Discussion: Soldiers and Censuses

The historical books (particularly their legislative passages) and the prophetic books (particularly Jeremiah, with none at all from Hosea) have provided most of the examples of what I argue are unambiguous examples of exclusivity. This uneven scatter is interesting, but of no great significance: the clues detected in them necessarily involve allusions to men and women, and more such allusions may be expected in that type of text that focuses upon the details of everyday life (historical narrative, for instance, or legal precepts), and fewer in the text that stands at one remove from such lived reality (for instance, hymnals or liturgical works).

Not all examples of exclusivity are as unambiguous as these. There is one type of apparently exclusive reference that presents a difficulty. Exodus 13:18 provides an example: "So God led the people (הָעָם) by the roundabout way of the wilderness toward the Red Sea. The Israelites (בְּנֵי־יִשְׂרָאֵל) went up out of the land of Egypt prepared for battle." At first glance, the semantic gender of neither הָעָם nor בְּנֵי־יִשְׂרָאֵל. is clear from the surrounding text. But is the reader not entitled to assume that הָעָם, at least, refers to the whole nation, whom Moses is leading away from slavery? A similar point was made at the start of this section about the gender of the whole nation in slavery. But what can be said about בְּנֵי־יִשְׂרָאֵל? In a nation unfamiliar with either the ways of the Amazons or the twentieth-century CE controversy about the employment of women in front-line military service, it is safe to assume that, in this case at least, grammatical and semantic masculinities coincide. The masculine phrase, in association with the adjective חֲמֻשִׁים, here indicates male soldiers. Examples of the use of phrases such as בְּנֵי־יִשְׂרָאֵל in a military context abound, and the manner of expressing the idea varies.[17] At Ex. 14:19, for instance, it could be argued that it is spelled out in מַחֲנֵה יִשְׂרָאֵל, which NRSV translates as "Israelite army", whereas in the description of the battle between the Philistines and the Israelites (1 Sam. 4:1–11), the latter are referred to simply as יִשְׂרָאֵל ("Israel went out to battle against the Philistines";[18] verse 1 and compare verses 2 and 10). Perhaps the use of Israel(ites) in these cases should be interpreted as synecdoche, in parallel with such modern English usage as "England beat France two nil", when there is no intention of referring to more than the English and French football teams. This military theme is worth further exploration. In Nehemiah's description of the preparations made to defend the half-rebuilt walls of Jerusalem, there is a stirring pre-battle speech: "I stood up and said to the nobles and the officials and the rest of the people … (וְאֶל־יֶתֶר הָעָם), 'Do not be afraid of them. Remember the Lord, who is great and awesome, and fight for your kin, your sons, your daughters, your wives, and your homes'" (Neh. 4:8 = English versions 4:14). It is tempting to argue that here is yet another example of unambiguous exclusivity, where all the people, הָעָם, are addressed, but only the men are meant (as such it will resemble several earlier examples). Yet though there may have been women, old men and children somewhere in the proximity, presumably within the uncertain protection of the walls, this passage must be an example of "people" signifying "fighting men".

But this may be taken a little further. Is it not understandable, given the background of insecurity against which ancient Israel's history is played out, that adult males, precious as the defence against adversity, should dominate concepts of what constituted "the people"? This is at first sight a simplistic statement, but it does seem a point worth making in the light of another apparent instance of exclusivity.

In Num. 1:2–3 Moses is ordered by Yhwh to "take a census of the whole congregation of Israelites (כָּל־עֲדַת בְּנֵי־יִשְׂרָאֵל) … , every male (כָּל־זָכָר) individually; from twenty years old and upwards, everyone in Israel able to go to war (כָּל־יֹצֵא צָבָא בְּיִשְׂרָאֵל)". This seems a clear case of exclusivity: what appears to be a national census[19] turns out to confine itself to males, and not all males, but just fighting males. But the word עֵדָה demands further attention. According to Budd in his commentary on Numbers, עֵדָה "was evidently an appropriate description of Israel gathered in worship … , and is used by P to depict בְּנֵי־יִשְׂרָאֵל as a worshiping community" (1984: 10). In a comment on Exod. 12:3 "Tell the whole congregation of Israel", Houtman argues עֵדָה indicates that "a group of individuals united by a common bond; the term ... is used in Exodus as designation for the people of Israel as a juridical and cultic community held together by a common bond with Yhwh" (1996: 168). The picture emerging from the use of עֵדָה seems to be that of the whole, rather than a part, of Israel. On the other hand, in his commentary on Leviticus, Wenham argues that the "congregation was a clearly defined group of people in ancient Israel with representative and legal functions" (1979: 98). Similarly *TDOT* argues that the word "entered the political sphere in the use of P and in early history, where it refers specifically to the general assembly of Israelite tribes ... [and] was probably an essentially democratic institution accessible to all male adults". It must be countered that this is speculation; it is uncertain how formal an institution עֵדָה was, if formal at all. *TDOT* accepts that at times "the term ... can refer to the people as a whole", and cites Exod. 12:3, 12:19; Num. 9:19 amongst other texts.[20] Evidence for restricted membership (as in *TDOT*'s assertion that it was accessible to "all male adults") is taken from passages such as Numbers 1, yet it seems odd for the text there to belabour the gender and age of the census sample if כָּל־עֲדַת בְּנֵי־יִשְׂרָאֵל is constituted by exactly those criteria anyway.

There is no particular help to be gained from the second census in Num. 26:2–51. The census implied in Ezra 2:2–67 (= Neh. 7:7–69, with some variation) is called "the number of the men of the people of Israel". The census taken by David (2 Sam. 24:1–9), however, is more significant: in verse 1 there is a clear command to count the people of Israel and Judah (הָעָם) but is evident from verse 9 that the recorded numbers were of "soldiers able to draw the sword" (אִישׁ־חַיִל שֹׁלֵף חֶרֶב).

The importance of military preparedness, then, may have influenced the notion of what it meant to be an Israelite. Be that as it may, the conclusion from this survey is that, despite some ambivalence, there is clear literary evidence for my initial assertion that "when in the Hebrew Bible characters talk to or writers talk of the Israelites, or when the Israelites speak for themselves, it is the men to whom the speaker speaks, or it is the men who do the speaking". To sum up, if in the Decalogue we had been told not to covet our neighbour's wife *or husband* (Exod. 20:14(17)), we might have been justified in thinking otherwise.

Notes

1. One could usefully compare Bird in relation to Hos. 4:13–14: "The pericope as a whole envisions the worshiping community as a body of males, although in the author's mind they represent collective Israel" (Bird 1989: 85); she concludes the same paper: "By appealing to the common stereotypes and interests of a primarily male audience, Hosea turns their accusation against them. It is easy for patriarchal society to see the guilt of a 'fallen women' [sic]; Hosea says, 'You (male Israel) are that woman!'" (Bird 1989: 89).

2. The survey did not aim at comprehensiveness; rather, the intention was to provide illustrations of the main issues.

3. One may well note, however, the curious wording used to describe the Israelites upon their departure from Egypt: in Exod. 12:37 they apparently comprised men and children – כְּשֵׁשׁ־מֵאוֹת אֶלֶף רַגְלִי הַגְּבָרִים לְבַד מִטָּף, without any mention of the women, unless it is assumed that they are part of the mixed crowd (עֵרֶב רַב) of verse 38.

4. The woman is depicted as eating her own children, in sharp contrast to the usual picture of maternal instincts, as expressed for instance in Isa. 49:15 ("Can a woman forget her nursing-child, or show no compassion for the child of her womb?").

5. Perhaps this reflects the writer's focus on national identity.

6. It has been suggested by Donald Murray, in a private communication, that the phrase may mean something like "other ranks" (i.e. as opposed to elders, officers and so on). In the context this interpretation of the phrase looks attractive, and, if correct, would strengthen a view of the use of the verse as an example of inclusivity, but I know of no other clear parallel to such an interpretation of כֹּל אִישׁ יִשְׂרָאֵל. The phrase (in all, 59 occurrences) is not elsewhere contrasted to higher ranks, and may even include them in Josh. 10:24 (קְצִינֵי אַנְשֵׁי הַמִּלְחָמָה הֶהָלְכוּא אִתּוֹ), may even include them though this is by no means a secure interpretation of the Hebrew here.

7. The translation in the NRSV (and AV) of "their wives" and "their men" in verse 21 hides the closer parallelism of the original נְשֵׁיהֶם and אַנְשֵׁיהֶם.

8. 'Them' is the NRSV's translation of the masculine singular אֹתוֹ, which seems to refer back to the masculine singular יְתוֹם of verse 21. Either the abuse of the widows of verse 22 is ignored, or the masculine אֹתוֹ is one of those instances where the females *are* included in the grammatically masculine word. The singular remains curious, a feeling evidently shared by the Targum and the Peshitta.

9. This is the only instance in the list of prohibitions where women are specifically addressed, perhaps because it is the only instance where a woman would not be interacting with a human male (who, as the "natural" instigator, is the obvious recipient of the prohibition). The context of bestiality might be considered a rare example of a situation in which a woman, as a member of the superior species, is the instigating agent, and needs to be addressed.

10. The difficulties in interpreting עֶרְוָה are discussed below.

11. It is worth comparing this passage to Josh. 5:6, where the same events are summarized: "For the Israelites (בְנֵי־יִשְׂרָאֵל) travelled for forty years in the wilderness, until all the nation (כָל־הַגּוֹי), the warriors (אַנְשֵׁי הַמִּלְחָמָה) who came out of Egypt, perished". Here the phrase "the warriors" seems to be either a

definition of כָּל־הַגּוֹי as male warriors, or a *qualification* of it, as though it means "all the nation, or, at least, the warriors, who …". The former seems the more natural interpretation of the Hebrew.

12. Compare a similar situation at Num. 25.1: "While Israel was staying at Shittim, the people [הָעָם] began to have sexual relations with the people of Moab."

13. These observations need not be confined to Israel/Judah. In Isaiah 13, for instance, the horrors that befall "them", include the rape of their wives (verse 16); "they", the Babylonians, like the Israelites, are male.

14. A more literal translation may be more helpful here: "The people of Israel, *and* the priests" (וְהַכֹּהֲנִים).

15. Koehler and Baumgartner (1994, s.v. גֶּבֶר, vol. 1, pp. 175–176).

16. Botterweck and Ringgren (1974/1993, s.v. גָּבַר, vol. 6, pp. 377–382).

17. The use of the phrase "Israelite army" should not be construed as offering an opinion as to the formality or otherwise of this fighting force, which is a matter of relative unimportance to the present argument.

18. I am using here the MT (NRSV includes the LXX variant reading).

19. Perhaps the word "census" itself tends to be misleading, with its modern overtones of statistical orderliness; "head count" may give a better impression (it is certainly nearer the Hebrew expression שְׂאוּ אֶת־רֹאשׁ). The "census" of Numbers 1, though carried out with some care, is no more than an elaboration of the sort of numbering reflected in Gen. 46:8–27.

20. Botterweck and Ringgren (1974/1993, *s.v* עֵדָה, vol. 10, p. 479).

Chapter 5

Queering Jeremiah

5.1 Introduction: Two Questions[1]

If, as argued in the last chapter, the addressees of the *marriage metaphor* are the men of Israel, it has equally to be conceded that this is a feature unrecognized by most readers in the past. It is true that a few of the more thoughtful feminist commentators have come near to asking it themselves:

> Interestingly, the image of apostasy as adultery requires that the Israelite audience (and authors) accept the change in gender implicit in the metaphor. The male Israelites, who constituted the legal community of Israel, were cast in the role of the unfaithful wife. (Galambush 1992: 35)

It is indeed interesting that Galambush hovers on the brink of what looks like a queer insight. Disappointingly, she seems to avoid the plunge, by explaining, in a footnote, that "the gender-reversal implicit in the adultery metaphor was a 'dead' metaphor, and was probably not even consciously perceived by its readers" (Galambush 1992: 35). But is she right? Given the (revived) power of the *marriage metaphor*, can it be assumed, in other words, that there are clear and consistently maintained gender polarities in the text? This is the first question that I shall seek to explore in this chapter.

The second question concerns the working out of the metaphor: with whom is the text asking the reader to identify? In the view of Exum and other feminist commentators the reader is invited to identify with the husband. But how does this square with the gender-reversal noted by Galambush? Exum sees the difficulty: "Male readers are ... thus placed in the subject roles of women" (Exum 1995: 265). And suggests a solution:

> They [male readers] are required to see themselves in the wrong and to repent and change their behaviour, and because a female role is not

"natural" for them and identification with a debased woman is shocking and repulsive, they will be anxious to cast it off. The metaphor offers them another role with which they can more readily identify, that of the faithful husband, whose point of view they are already encouraged to identify with by the prophetic rhetoric. (Exum 1995: 265)

But is this really how the metaphor works?

5.2 Question 1: Gender Polarities

One impression left by a reading of Jeremiah 2–3 is that it is an exercise in staccato. The overall theme is reasonably clear: chapter 2 is taken up with Israel's apostasy from Yhwh, intermittently via a metaphor of a wife's unfaithfulness towards her husband. Chapter 3 continues the theme of apostasy and the metaphor makes further appearances, but includes descriptions of the consequences of apostasy and pleas for repentance. If the theme is clear, however, the way that it is conveyed is far less so. Subsidiary themes are begun, continued and dropped without warning. Transitions are abrupt. It is not always obvious who is speaking to whom.

The Hebrew text itself, moreover, evinces a further and fascinating state of confusion, which is generally concealed in Greek, Latin or English versions. For Hebrew is unlike those languages in that it distinguishes gender in the second person, as well as in the third, of verbal and pronominal forms. In Jeremiah 2 and 3 the main person addressed or talked about is at times masculine, at other times feminine, and sometimes, it should be added, singular and at other times plural. It is not always clear whether these variations indicate different people or not.

To take the first 16 verses of chapter 2 as an example, verse 2 addresses Jerusalem in the second singular feminine, with some emphasis (the second singular feminine suffix makes four appearances). In verse 3, the addressee is not mentioned, but Israel is talked of in the third singular masculine – is Jerusalem still the addressee? Or should it be assumed that the direct address has been dropped and that Jerusalem and Israel refer to the same group of inhabitants (a reference, in that case, to the old unified state of Israel)? Then in verses 4–6 there is a change: "O house of Jacob and all the families of the house of Israel" are addressed in the masculine plural and this continues (with one or two variations – such as the call to the heavens as witnesses in verse 12) to the end of verse 15. As with verse 4, the reader is left to decide whether the addressees are in fact identical to the addressee of the preceding verse(s). Finally verse 16 presents an abrupt change to an unidentified second singular feminine.[2] Is this Jerusalem, as in verse 2?

Such curtness and obscurity may not be unique to these chapters, nor to this prophet, but they do seem to be especially prominent here. As for the variations in gender, one may be tempted to dismiss them as a simple response to grammatical necessity, unnoticed by Hebrew speaker and listener alike. But some commentators have seen them as pointers to a gender distinction that is based on *Jerusalem = woman, Israel = man*. Moreover, it has been suggested that the feminine is used when the *marriage metaphor* is in operation, that is, when the text wants to draw attention to sexual misconduct, and the masculine when the politico-religious problem of apostasy is overt. In their discussion of chapter 2, Diamond and O'Connor exemplify this view:

> Thematically ... the four poems [Jer. 2:4–3:5] accuse male and female Israel of analogous crimes. Male Israel (sing./pl.) abandons Yhwh, goes after worthless things, other gods, empty cisterns. Female Israel abandons her husband, pursues other lovers, and plays the whore. Both betray Yhwh and turn to others, but only female Israel's infidelities are domestic and sexual. (Diamond and O'Connor 1996: 296–297)

Such a differentiation is aided by the use of the trope Jerusalem as the wife of Yhwh,[3] and the fact that Israel is normally masculine, presumably in deference to its eponymous patriarch.[4] Commentators who argue for this differentiation, and indeed others who are keen to systematize the process of the *marriage metaphor*, are usually eager to offer a schema which imposes order on unruly texts. Diamond and O'Connor provide a series of such schemata (1996: 294–295); non-tabulated schemata are offered by Stienstra (1993: 124–125) and John J. Schmitt (1983: 122). Schmitt's article demands some comment. He argues that one should not talk about Israel as "she" (and therefore, presumably, one should not talk about the relationship between Yhwh and Israel in terms of man and wife). This is because, he claims, יִשְׂרָאֵל is always masculine in Hebrew. Quite where that leaves the connexion between Jerusalem, which is unequivocally the wife of Yahweh, and Israel is not made clear. Schmitt's arguments about the gender of יִשְׂרָאֵל will be discussed in due course, but for the moment I shall look at his analysis of chapter 2. He sees there a "careful structuring of masculine and feminine forms" (Schmitt 1983: 122), and detects a "chiastic pattern" as illustrated in Table 5.1.

Table 5.1: Schmitt's Chiastic Structuring in Jeremiah 2

Verse 2	Jerusalem	Fem. Singular	i
Verses 3–4	Israel	Masc. Singular	ii
Verses 5–13	People	Masc. Plural	iii
Verses 14–16	Israel	Masc. Singular	ii
Verses 17–25	Jerusalem	Fem. Singular	i

He concludes that:

> This passage can be analysed for structure in a variety of ways. Here I claim that the editors purposively structured the passage, identifying the figures with their respective gender and number in the beginning and elsewhere as necessary. The effect the editors intended is lost if the care they took with grammar is not observed. (Schmitt 1983: 122)

But is the chiasmus really there and is there really such careful structuring? And if so what does it achieve? How does the alleged chiasmus (i, ii, iii, ii, i) fit in with the text that follows? After all, one could chiasmus-spot endlessly. In Table 5.2 I offer a rival chiasmus, and it seems equally (un) convincing; if Schmitt's chiasmus exists then it is equally reasonable for the one in Table 5.2 to exist, but that they *both* exist, overlapping one another as they do, seems hardly likely.

Table 5.2: Another Alleged Chiastic Structuring in Jeremiah 2

Verses 17–25	Jerusalem	Fem. Singular	A
Verses 26–27	People	Masc. Plural	B
Verses 28–29	Judah	Masc. Singular	C
Verses 30–31	People	Masc. Plural	B
Verses 32–37	Jerusalem	Fem. Singular	A

Schmitt's chiasmus looks rather lop-sided in terms of the relative number of verses in each component unit (1:3:9:3:9); the rival in Table 5.2 is a little better, if rather top-heavy (9:2:2:2:6). Anyway, Schmitt could be criticized for assigning verse 16 to the Israel unit, rather than with verses 17–25; the feminine ך suffix of יְרֵעֵוּך, though inconveniently part of a textual crux, does nevertheless suggest a re-arrangement of the verses, which would create an even more uneven pattern of 1:3:9:2:10 (and incidentally equally upset the rival chiasmus – 10:2:2:2:6). No one would be so foolhardy as to dispute the frequent use of chiastic structures in the prose and poetry of the Hebrew Bible, and evidence for them in Jeremiah 2–3 is presented by Lundbom (1999: 124–125). Yet even if it is conceded that both the chiasmi in question do exist, would it not be wiser to regard them as the product of an unconscious mannerism, deeply embedded in the oral and literary tradition of Israel, rather than evidence of conscious craftsmanship, let alone of overall structural unity?

Even Diamond and O'Connor, in their more sophisticated tabular analysis of Jeremiah 2 (1996: 294–295), are guilty of underplaying the untidiness of the text. In Table 5.3, they detect two themes in 2:1–3: (A) the bride's love for her husband, and (B) her exclusive loyalty. These, they argue, are explicitly reversed in the verses that follow (up to 3:5), which they see as forming four "poems", and the process of reversal creates distinctive patterns. So, for instance, the first "poem" (2:4–16) forms a pattern as follows, where A- and B- are the reversals of (A) and (B) above.

Table 5.3: Diamond and O'Connor's Pattern of Reversed Themes

A-	2.5a
B-	2.5b
A-	2.8ab
B-	2.8c
A-	2.13a
B-	2.13b

But this is a clear over-simplification: the pattern is achieved only by omitting for consideration verses 4, 6, 7, 9–12 and 14. How can the reader detect these thematic oases amongst the arid stretches of the text?

To illustrate the real situation it is necessary to construct my own *Anti-schema*, which appears as Anti-schema 1 in the Schedule of Antischemas. Here, following the examples of both Schmitt and Diamond and O'Connor, I have analysed the gender significance of the two chapters. So Column 2 gives or guesses the name of the addressee or principal personal subject/s. Column 3 indicates the grammatical number of the addressee/subject, and Column 4 their gender. Columns 5 and 6 offer a rudimentary thematic analysis: Column 5 indicates whether the *marriage metaphor* appears in the section concerned, that is, the vehicle of the metaphor, and Column 6 whether the theme of apostasy is present, that is, the tenor of the metaphor.

There are two conclusions to be drawn from this anti-schema. The first is the chaotic nature of the text. The general overarching theme is clear, but that the component parts do not cohere has long been recognized as a problem. To take an outstanding example of disjointedness, to which I have already alluded, verse 16 contains not only semantic and perhaps textual obscurities, but also, what is hidden in translation, an abrupt change of addressee, marked by the second singular feminine suffix ך without any indication of who this new person is. The last second singular feminine addressee appears as far away as verse 2; and one is forced to assume, in company with most commentators, that the reference is indeed to Jerusalem. Similar switches occur in 2:33, 3:13 and 3:19.

Commentators offer a number of explanations for this disjointedness: candidates include the complicated redactional history of the text, and a deliberate stylistic device intended to convey the cuckold's overwrought anger. Many commentators have interpreted the form of the "core" poetic sections as embodying "the accusation speech of a *rîb*, a covenant lawsuit initiated by Yahweh against his people".[5] Carroll provides a helpful list of discussions about this interpretation, although he himself does not subscribe to it.[6] Other suggestions have been made: for instance, Diamond and O'Connor see the two chapters as two narrative acts of a poetic drama.[7]

Whatever the reason, the disjointedness of this text is undeniable. Deliberate rhetorical artifice there may be, and small- and medium-scale chiasmi there certainly are, but the expectation of finding crafted patterns in Jeremiah 2–3 is a pipe dream.

The second conclusion to be drawn from the anti-schema concerns the alleged division of the genders. I have already drawn attention to a tendency amongst commentators to assume that "female" Jerusalem is associated with the *marriage metaphor*, that is, sexual misconduct, and "male" Israel with the politico-religious theme of apostasy, the tenor of the metaphor. If this assumption were valid, it could be translated into tabular form, on the lines of the anti-schema. There ought to be a consistent pattern of inverse relationship between Jerusalem and Israel along the lines shown in Table 5.4.

Table 5.4: Jerusalem versus Israel

	Male or Female?	*Marriage Metaphor* present?	Apostasy theme present?
Jerusalem	Female	Yes	No
Israel	Male	No	Yes

In chapter 2 it is generally the case that there is such a pattern (as long as the masculine plural addressees are taken to be Israel-equivalents). But the boundary walls do show one or two signs of weakness:

(a) In the "male" verses 4–6, where one should expect no sign of the *marriage metaphor*, Holladay sees an allusion to divorce in מַה־מָּצְאוּ אֲבוֹתֵיכֶם בִּי עָוֶל ("what evil have your fathers found in me?"). And the phrase וַיֵּלְכוּ אַחֲרֵי ("they have gone after ..."), though ostensibly referring to apostasy, recalls the key opening sequence of verse 2 and the phrase לֶכְתֵּךְ אַחֲרַי ("how you went after me ..."), which in the context has sexual overtones.

(b) In the "female" verses 16–25, there are clear references to adultery in verse 20, but there are also references to the "male" theme of apostasy in the preceding verses; this explains the *yes yes* answers in Columns 4 and 5 in the anti-schema.

(c) In the "male" verses 29–32, there is an oblique reference to the *marriage metaphor*: Yhwh's people (masculine) are contrasted in a curious way to the bride who does not forget her finery.

But it is in chapter 3 that the sex boundary walls tumble down. In verses 6–11 masculine Israel is referred to as female, accompanied towards the end of the section by his/her "sister" Judah. What is more, the *marriage metaphor* is in full flow, though in verse 9 the apostasy language is overtly woven into it in the phrase וַתִּנְאַף אֶת־הָאֶבֶן וְאֶת־הָעֵץ ("she committed adultery with stones and sticks").[8] Yet by verse 12, Israel is masculine once more. Unfortunately this bald statement cannot be left unqualified, since commentators have diagnosed textual difficulties here, and I have to confess to the perilous enterprise of making a crucial text out of what many have considered a textual crux. I have already alluded to Schmitt's insistence that יִשְׂרָאֵל is always grammatically masculine. As for the present passage, he claims that the unequivocally feminine verbs and pronominal suffixes belong not to יִשְׂרָאֵל but to the word מְשֻׁבָה which he interprets as a species of verbal noun in apposition to יִשְׂרָאֵל, rather than as an adjective dependent upon it. Nothing further needs to be said about Schmitt's blatantly circular argument that the word מְשֻׁבָה cannot be an adjective "because this would offend the proposed universal rule that the noun Israel is masculine and its adjectives are masculine" (1983: 122). But he is on firmer ground when he says that, if מְשֻׁבָה were adjectival, it would follow, rather than precede, its noun, and would take the definite article. The situation is complicated by the text-critical arguments of many commentators who question the status of verses 6–12a; they consider the passage to be, in the words of Holladay, "an early prose midrash ... on several phrases and words from the poetry of chapters 2–3" (Holladay 1986: 116). Holladay argues that one of the words that this inserted section has picked up is מְשֻׁבָה in the poetic phrase שׁוּבָה מְשֻׁבָה יִשְׂרָאֵל in verse 12b. There the verb form שׁוּבָה, and the succeeding grammatical constructions, clearly denote Israel as masculine, and Holladay interprets מְשֻׁבָה there as an internal accusative of the imperative verb ("Turn a turning, Israel"). In his view, then, the writer of the inserted passage verses 6–12a picked up the word מְשֻׁבָה in verse 12b, misinterpreted its grammatical function, treated it in this inserted passage as a feminine adjective belonging to the noun יִשְׂרָאֵל, and on the strength of that made the whole passage feminine.

What is the result of this sorry mess? Even if Schmitt's argument that the feminine references belong to מְשֻׁבָה rather than to יִשְׂרָאֵל were persuasive, I should still maintain that the semantic effect, if not the grammatical construction, is that of a feminized Israel, hemmed in by a female rôle and feminine forms, and accompanied by her equally feminized sister Judah. Again, even if it could be accepted that this section were a prose intruder upon the core poetic text and that its contribution should be ignored, there would still be enough sources for puzzlement in the so-called core text. Verses 19 and 20 could serve as final examples. In verse 19, the addressee is second singular feminine (with another abrupt, unidentified change of direction). At first glance, the content is not obviously part of the *marriage metaphor*. Yet what seems to be contained there is the expression of a desire to give to a woman ownership of property (sociologically an unusual situation): "How I would place you among the sons, and give you a pleasant land", though what exactly is meant by "among the sons" is not clear. In verse 20 there is another change of gender (and number); the masculine plural has returned, but only after a *simile*, based upon the *marriage metaphor*.

What must be concluded from this confusion in both content and gender is that there is no neatly consistent distinction made between female Jerusalem with her sexual sins and male Israel and his socio-political apostasy. Here are the first glimmerings of a queer insight. If queer theory views sexual identity, and indeed gender itself, as not innate but the product of continual re-enactment, and is always on the lookout for evidence of breakdowns in the patterns of these re-enactments, then it will certainly find such evidence here in the failure of the text to ensure a consistent distinction between masculine Israel and feminine

Jerusalem, and a curious tendency to confuse the feminine gender rôle entailed in the vehicle of the metaphor with the masculine counterpart of the tenor. At this point it would be as well to be clear about one point: I am not "outing" Israel. I am not claiming that male Israelites were closet gays. What I *am* saying is that behind the confines of the metaphor, male Israelites are invited to consider themselves as wives of Yhwh, bad wives it is true, but wives nonetheless. Moreover, the confusions embedded in the text and the spillover between male and female rôles has made these confines less safe.

5.3 Question 2: Identifying

The second major question to ask of Jeremiah 2–3 is: with whom is the text asking the reader to identify? It is worth recalling Exum's explanation of what is so offensive about the metaphor to the feminist commentator:

> They [male readers] are required to see themselves in the wrong and to repent and change their behaviour, and because a female role is not "natural" for them and identification with a debased woman is shocking and repulsive, they will be anxious to cast it off. The metaphor offers them another role with which they can more readily identify, that of the faithful husband, whose point of view they are already encouraged to identify with by the prophetic rhetoric. (Exum 1995: 265)

The male reader, then, is let off the hook. He is allowed to identify with the wronged husband, while all the burden of immorality is shuffled off on to the woman. There are two key points to be decided here. Who is the "male reader", and what is to be understood by the verb "to identify with"? Once these points have been answered, it may be possible to explore a new way of drawing something valuable from the *marriage metaphor*.

Diamond and O'Connor's tabulated list of characters (Table 5.5) may help with the first point.

Table 5.5: Textual Levels for Jeremiah 2–3[9]

Outside the Text	Inside the Text
Historical poet/writer/redactor – anonymous	Implied speaker/poet – prophet Jeremiah
	Dramatic speaker – husband Yhwh
Historical audience – late exilic early Post-exilic, Jewish communities	Implied audience – Jerusalem's citizenry/ Israel's progeny

They draw a distinction between characters/audience outside and those inside the text. The outsiders include the historical audience, but identifying them depends on the view taken of the textual history of Jeremiah. If it is believed that "Jeremiah" is the result of an editorial reworking of the original prophecies in the exilic or post-exilic period, then the historical audience can be considered to be, as with Diamond and O'Connor, the "late exilic early post-exilic, Jewish communities". But if a hermeneutical view of the text is wanted, it may be as well to abandon what is after all a position dependent on historical conjecture (however well-considered), in order to test whether the evidence of the text in its present state can offer something more profitable. In other words, it may be more helpful to look for the male reader among the "implied audience" of the text itself. Is he easy to spot? In one sense he does not exist. One might say that the metaphor is addressed to "the house of Jacob and all the families of the house of Israel" (2:4), or as Diamond and O'Connor have it "Jerusalem's citizenry/Israel's progeny" (as in Table 5.5 above), and that the masculine plurals so often found in the text are simply grammatical shorthand for both genders. But in the last chapter I set out to demonstrate that the addressees are, to judge from the evidence of the biblical text alone, the "male Israelites", who, as Galambush says, "constituted the legal community of Israel" (Galambush, 1992: 35).

I can now proceed to consider the second point – with whom do they identify? Exum in the passage quoted above claims that the metaphor offers the male reader a way out of thinking of themselves as bad women by giving them a faithful husband to identify with. This interpretation amounts to accusing the *marriage metaphor* not only of demeaning women but also failing on its own terms. Exum has got the ingredients right but has misread the rest of the recipe. She is right to say that there are two characters in the metaphor who could be said to be rivals for the male reader's loyalty, but she has mangled the metaphorical process. The metaphor builds up a picture of a loyal husband, with whom its male readers will readily sympathize – his sufferings represent, after all, a gross assault upon their own cultural values. But at the same time the metaphor makes the unpalatable fact clear that it is not the faithful husband but the faithless wife, whose characteristics more closely echo the readers' own behaviour.[10] The readers want to identify with the husband; the metaphor forces them to identify with the wife. The readers, of course, may choose to reject the metaphor's message, but in doing so they will make a nonsense of it.

If this were all, the text would still give huge offence. It is still demeaning for a woman to be a model of bad behaviour, even though it is in fact the men who are behaving badly.

5.4 A Suite in Three Movements

But there is more to say. The metaphorical process I have noted so far is a diagnosis of past and/or present misbehaviour on the part of the male citizenry of Israel. But the *marriage metaphor* in Jeremiah also looks to the future. It helps the readers to understand what they should do next: they are to repent and return to the covenantal relationship with Yhwh (3.12b–19). Now in terms of the metaphorical process, this pointer to the future could be represented as a suite in three movements:

First Movement	*Second Movement*	*Third Movement*
Loyal Bride ⇒[11]	Adulterous Wife ⇒	Loyal Wife

In other words, not only does the *marriage metaphor* in Jeremiah require the male citizens of Israel to identify themselves with an adulterous woman, it also urges them to return to being a loyal wife. This Third Movement of the metaphor is overlooked by feminist commentators. Their oversight would be justified if the Movement made no appearance; it could then be said that it was an unused potential element in the metaphor, in the same way, for instance, that the fact that a shepherd may kill and eat his sheep has no part to play in the metaphor "the Lord is my Shepherd". But the Third Movement does make an appearance, tentatively at first, it is true, but in full costume later in Jeremiah.

In 3:12b–13, verse 12b is a call for repentance with a promise of mercy – all in the masculine plural; verse 13 amplifies "repentance" as an acknowledgement of sin, pictured as adultery – all in the feminine singular. Here, then, the *marriage metaphor* is concerned not only with past misbehaviour, but is also associated with the call to repentance.

Verse 3.19 contains obscurities to which I have already alluded. What does seem to be present here, however, is the desire to confer status and possessions upon a beloved female, and by inference from the context, the female is his wife in her hoped-for state of repentance. But the appearance of the Third Movement in its full promise is long delayed:

> I have loved you with an everlasting love;
>> therefore I have continued my faithfulness towards you,

Again I will build you, and you shall be built,
 O virgin Israel!
Again you shall take your tambourines,
 and go forth in the dance of the merrymakers.
Again you shall plant vineyards
 on the mountains of Samaria. (Jer. 31:3b–5a; NRSV)

This sunny passage, all in the feminine singular (referring to בְּתוּלַה יִשְׂרָאֵל, usually translated as virgin Israel) is the Third Movement, the fulfilling counterpart to the First Movement of 2:2. Just as Jerusalem/Israel was the loyal bride in the desert, so after repentance will she be the merry wife in a rich land. The male citizenry are urged to acknowledge their adultery and resume their place as loyal wife to Yhwh. The appearance of the Third Movement acts as a restorative from the corrosive effects of the picture of woman as adulteress that precedes it.

5.5 Conclusions

A queer gaze does not wholly contradict the feminist view of the marriage metaphor as a tool that validates an oppressive patriarchy, but it offers an invitation to consider the implications of the loose boundaries of desire pictured within it. First it blurs the distinction between the male element of the tenor (the male citizenry and faithfulness/apostasy) and the female element of the vehicle (the wife and her loyalty/adultery). Second, it requires the male reader to associate himself with the rôle of a woman: your crime, says Jeremiah, is that you have betrayed your husband; your aim should be to win back your place as his loyal wife.

Many feminist commentators find offence in what they consider to be the insistent emphasis on the female as the model of immorality – a sponge to soak up male guilt. The queer point of view does not deny the offensiveness, but it sees it as not an incidental *effect* of the metaphor but a deliberate *device* intrinsic to the metaphorical process. The *marriage metaphor* requires men to think of themselves and their relationship to the divine in a way that wholly undermines their cultural expectations. This requirement makes unnatural, outrageous, demands on them – are they really the wives of Yhwh? If both the implied and historical male readers have one thing in common with the modern feminist biblical scholar, it is that they all misunderstand and/or reject Jeremiah's message.

And finally, who is it that is conveying this queer message to the people of Israel? Is it not fitting that the metaphor comes from the mouth of someone who himself has a queer relationship with Yhwh? "You shall not take a wife, nor shall you have sons or daughters in this place" (Jer. 16:2). If, as the text says, this veto is issued on the grounds that children and wives (and husbands) are all going to die anyway, why is it not issued to other prophets in equally grave crises? Or indeed to the whole population and not just Jeremiah? No, Jeremiah must give himself wholly to Yhwh. Not that of course he agrees without demur:

> Oh Lord, you have enticed me,
>   and I was enticed;
> you have overpowered me,
>   and you have prevailed. (Jer. 20:7; NRSV)

Some commentators have seen here the language of seduction, with overtones of sexual violence.[12] Their interpretation has not won universal approval, but if they are right then it is an odd twist that the prophet urges his audience to view Yhwh as the husband who, though betrayed, is ready to forgive his repentant bride, yet in his own case sees him as a demanding and ineluctable seducer. Here indeed is a new insight on to Jeremiah's gloom!

Notes

1. A version of this chapter was published elsewhere (Macwilliam 2002).
2. The feminine suffix in verse 16 seems safe, even if the verb to which it is attached (יְדִי) has been questioned. In any case the second singular feminine is unequivocal in verse 17.
3. As already noted, Galambush has argued that "the marriage metaphor depends for its coherence on the culturally accepted notion that the female capital city is married to a male god" (Galambush 1993: 23).
4. But this is a contested point, about which there is further discussion below.
5. Holladay 1986: 73.
6. Carroll 1986: 117.
7. Diamond and O'Connor (1996: 293–299).
8. The metaphor wobbles at this point: the female Israel of the marriage metaphor is accused of literal apostasy: the vehicle and the tenor elide.
9. Taken from Diamond and O'Connor (1996: 291).
10. Compare the simple definition of "identify with" given by the *Concise Oxford Dictionary* (10th edn, Oxford, 1999): "regard oneself as sharing the same characteristics or thinking (as someone)".
11. The arrow could be the equivalent of the handy Hebrew verb שוב, which can be used to mean virtual opposites, both to backslide and to repent.
12. The controversy centres around the verb פָּתָה; I shall not discuss the controversy here, except to comment that a queer understanding would parallel the use of the verb in this verse with that of Hos. 2:16(14), at the beginning of Hosea's version of the Third Movement; see below, Section 6.6.

Chapter 6

QUEERING HOSEA

6.1 Introduction: The Complexities of Hosea

The gender issues in Hosea 1–3 are more involved than those in Jeremiah 2–3. Because this chapter in consequence is necessarily longer and more complicated than the last, it may helpful to the reader to have this brief guide to its overall structure.

It begins with a preliminary discussion of the rôle played by the prophet's marriage to Gomer (6.2: "The Anti-schema and Hosea"). The presence of this human marriage might be expected to strengthen the gender polarity of the *marriage metaphor* and therefore make it more difficult for the anti-schema developed in Chapter 5 to reveal gender breakdowns. In fact the anti-schema does prove inadequate, although not because the human marriage strengthens the gender polarity, but because structurally it is difficult to disentangle it from Yhwh's relationship with Israel.

The gender issues in Hosea are further complicated by claims made by some critics that Yhwh is depicted as having feminine qualities, and 6.3 ("Yhwh's So-Called Feminine Qualities") discusses these claims and their implications.

Much of my queer analysis of the *marriage metaphor* depends on the structural interplay in Hosea 1–3 between the human marriage and the divine/human relationship. In 6.4 ("Linearity in Hosea"), I present an understanding of the structure of this interplay, arguing that it is a loose succession of themes, linked together by a consecutive association of ideas in four stages.

This argument of loose association has the effect of freeing the human marriage from the *marriage metaphor* proper, and allows me in 6.5 ("The Unmanning of Hosea") to develop a queer view of its function.

It also allows me to focus with more clarity on the *marriage metaphor* itself, and in 6.6 ("The Three-Movement Model") I apply to Hosea the developmental view of the metaphor offered in the last chapter, with a particular emphasis on the emphatic presence and queer significance of the Third Movement.

After 6.7 ("Queering Hosea: Conclusions"), in which I draw the various strands of the discussion together, 6.8 ("Postscript: Methodological Reflections") follows the precept of self-reflection which in Chapter 2 I urged as a necessary accompaniment to a queer theoretical investigation.[1]

6.2 The Anti-schema and Hosea

Jeremiah has provided opportunities to search for breakdowns in the binary relationship of vehicle (bride/betrayed marriage) and tenor (male Israelites/broken covenant). When turning to Hosea, one may expect to find a sharper and more consistent gender division; for in Hosea the imagery of the divine/human relationship is closely involved with the description of a human marriage. The most that might be left to point out from a queer point of view would be the paralleling of male partners and female bride in the divine/human relationship, but there would be little prospect of a crop of gender ambiguities as rich as that provided by Jeremiah. Moreover the contrasting of the two axes male=divine=right and female=human=sin, a feature of Jeremiah that is at the heart of many feminist complaints, is heightened in Hosea, by the apparent paralleling of Hosea the wronged husband with the wronged Yhwh, and of the sinful Gomer with the sinful Israelites.

It is thus with no great optimism, from a queer point of view, that I apply to Hosea[2] the anti-schema that was constructed for Jeremiah. There the anti-schema provided the means of uncovering breakdowns in the gender divisions; these were indicated by instances in the anti-schema where the answer *m(ale)* in Column 4 coincides with *y(es)* in column 6 (apostasy theme present) and where conversely *f(emale)* coincides with *y(es)* in column 5 (marriage metaphor present).

It is not too surprising, therefore, to find that the anti-schemas for Hosea do not reveal any clear breakdowns in gender division. But this is not so much because there is any demonstrably consistent pattern of gender division in the text as because there is a more complex metaphorical structure in Hosea than in Jeremiah. As Diamond and O'Connor have pointed out (Diamond and O'Connor 1996: 306), in Hosea there are *two* marriages. There is no simple metaphorical relationship between Yhwh's marriage and Yhwh's relationship with Israel. Instead the text offers a conjunction of Hosea's marriage to Gomer, Yhwh's relationship with *his* bride, and the divine/human relationship. Hosea's marriage to Gomer, that element of the text that could be expected to emphasize gender polarity, in fact becomes the means whereby the sharpness is blurred. Without it, there might be a simple metaphorical schema, as there is in Jeremiah:

vehicle	$\rightarrow$	tenor
(Yhwh's marriage to Israel)		(divine/human relationship)

With it, there is instead:

vehicle 1	$\rightarrow$	tenor 1 = vehicle 2	$\rightarrow$	tenor 2
(Hosea's marriage to Gomer)		(Yhwh's marriage to Israel)		(divine/human relationship)

Now, it may be that Hosea's marriage is not a part of the core metaphorical structure, and I shall be arguing presently that such is the case. But if it can be assumed, for now, that it *is* a full participant in the metaphor, it may be arguable that its presence *per se* is not an inevitable cause of confusion, though the fact that tenor 1 and vehicle 2 are identical may alert the reader to potential problems of clarity. What is indisputable, however, is that there are several places in the text where it is impossible to decide whether it is Hosea's or Yhwh's marriage that is under discussion. This will be the case whether Hosea's marriage is considered part of the core metaphorical structure or not; and it is this confusion that has produced the forest of question marks and square brackets in the anti-schemas. The inevitable conclusion to draw at this point is that the anti-schema employed to look at the *marriage metaphor* in Jeremiah is inadequate as far as Hosea is concerned.

As just one instance of its inadequacy, one could highlight the failure on the part of the anti-schema to point out a simple example of gender slippage in the text. At 3:1 there is a direct correspondence between Hosea/Woman and Yhwh/בְּנֵי יִשְׂרָאֵל, in other words, a pronounced link between the female element of the vehicle and the masculine plural element of the tenor, a correspondence in a simile form that is underlined in an allegorical form in 3:3 and 3:4, where the wife's penitential period of quiet withdrawal is paralleled by the prophesied solitariness of, again, the masculine plural בְּנֵי יִשְׂרָאֵל. The male citizens of Israel are compared directly to the woman – no mediating mother is mentioned.

6.3 Yhwh's So-Called Feminine Qualities

Not only is any expectation of finding sharp gender division in Hosea frustrated by the inadequacies of the anti-schema, but it may also be challenged further by the claim made by some commentators that Hosea sometimes portrays Yhwh as having gentler – and therefore more feminine – qualities. The alleged salient evidence is Hosea 11, where two aspects of Yhwh's character are delineated: his torment and change of heart, and his parental tenderness towards Israel. The torment, expressed in the repeated questions of 11:8, and the alleged change of heart of 11:9 have attracted scholarly interest, in the main as examples of biblical inconsistency. Shimon Bakon, for example, contrasts 1 Sam. 15:29 with Hos. 11:9 (1988). In the former passage, Samuel ascribes Yhwh's fixity of purpose to the fact that he is not mortal; in the latter passage Yhwh's change of heart is attributed to the fact that he is God and no mortal. Bakon concludes that: "[The Hebrew Bible] is a record of the relationship between God and man, together with reversals and seemingly conflicting values" (Bakon 1988: 245).[3]

It is interesting to note the depiction of divine quasi-human vacillation, which ends in the declaration of forbearance. The depiction of torment and vacillation is all the more noticeable because it is set in the context of parental imagery, that other aspect of Yhwh's character portrayed in Hosea 11. Commentators' interest in Yhwh as loving parent varies. J. C. Andersen and J. L. Freedman seem indifferent (1980); H. W. Wolff, though talking of the "metaphor of fatherly love" in verses 1–4 (1974: 195), also describes the chapter as a whole as "structured in analogy to a legal complaint made by a father against his stubborn son" – hardly paternal love (1974: 194). Feminist commentators have pointed to the possibility of a new interpretation, chief among them Helen Schüngel-Straumann (1995) and Marie-Theres Wacker (1987), and their work is worth a digression, since it is a telling example of the way in which some feminist scholars have suggested new interpretative possibilities but have not quite thrown off the habits of thinking along the old lines of binary opposition. I shall confine my attention to Schüngel-Straumann's paper, originally published in 1986, since she has set the pace for later work. She argues for a consistency of maternal imagery in 11:3–8, and centres her case around the vocabulary of verses 3–4 in particular. She relates תִּרְגַּלְתִּי, for instance, in verse 3 to the Arabic *rgl* (meaning suck), as opposed to the usual Hebrew רֶגֶל (usually meaning foot); she argues for the more general meaning of רָפָא ("care for", rather than "heal") in the next colon, arriving at the translation "But it was I who nursed Ephraim, taking him in my arms. Yet they did not understand that it was I who took care of them" (Schüngel-Straumann 1995: 195). Similarly in the second half of verse 4 she emphasizes the difficulty of reconciling the abrupt change of image, from the kindly use of the yoke to feeding and bending down, the first allegedly referring to animals, the other to human children. Certainly such abrupt changes of imagery within the same verse do not seem well represented in Hosea. Perhaps 4:10, where food and whoredom are paired, might be cited, though it could be argued that the imagery of whoredom here is so well-worn as to have become a quasi-literalism. Neither the examples of evanescence in 13:3 nor the animal parade of 13:8 in any way match 11:4. Schüngel-Straumann proposes to read עוּל (nurseling) instead of עֹל (yoke) and translates לְחֵיהֶם as "their breast(s)" rather than "cheeks" (in line, for instance, with Ruth 4:16). Her resulting translation of the second half of verse 4 reads "And I was for them like those who take a nursling to the breast, and I bowed down to him in order to give him suck".

If she is right in her interpretation, then one wonders why, in her words, "the entire literature on Hosea 11 speaks from the outset and without exception of a father, fatherly love, and *nothing else*" (Schüngel-Straumann 1995: 204; emphasis original). Schüngel-Straumann herself provides the answer:

> [W]hen the masculine aspect is in the inferior position, namely as "son" in the role of unfaithful Israel while YHWH takes the female part, the ideas have found practically no reception at all. Apparently, since interpretation has been practiced almost exclusively by men, there has been a conscious or unconscious influence of the interpreters' own self-identification. (Schüngel-Straumann 1995: 227)

Schüngel-Straumann's method here of exposing this "unconscious influence" may be compared to Sherwood's detailed critique[4] of how male commentators have dealt with Gomer, the "missing prostitute"; Sherwood labels this technique of uncovering the part played by ideological preconceptions as "metacommentary", a term first employed by Frederic Jameson (1988). But are the two positions, Schüngel-Straumann's and that of the male commentators whom she criticizes, really mutually exclusive? Schüngel-Straumann offers a more coherent interpretation that of her predecessors,[5] and her argument that some male critics have been blinded by their own expectations is convincing.

Yet the situation is more ambiguous than either Schüngel-Straumann or the male commentators admits. She herself points out that no explicit reference to "mother" or "father" is present in the text. She uses a historico-religious argument for the absence of overtly maternal terminology:

> In his time that [viz. to call YHWH "mother"] would have been too open to misunderstanding, for Hosea was engaged in a bitter struggle with Canaanite fertility gods, and in particular the goddesses who, in practical terms, probably played a more important role than the male gods. (Schüngel-Straumann 1995: 203)

She cites no evidence for this assertion, and the word "probably" gives away its conjectural nature. Graham I. Davies, on the other hand, takes a more cautious line:

> It has been usual to speak of God's fatherly love here, but recently it has been pointed out that the imagery is at least as appropriate to a mother's as a father's. (Davies 1993: 29)

He compares Isa. 49:15. This is an interesting passage, but it is clearly different in literary structure and effect. Its structure is that of rhetorical comparison whose logic runs "I can no more forget you than a woman can forget her nursling"; Yhwh here in no way refers to himself as a mother. In Hosea 11, on the other hand, the imagery is more involved in the referent. While it may convincingly be argued that וָאֶהְיֶה לָהֶם כִּמְרִימֵי in verse 4 is an explicit simile, verse 3 is directly metaphorical, and if Schüngel-Straumann is right about the maternal imagery extending beyond verse 4, it permeates the whole chapter. From a queer perspective, both the God-as-father and God-as-mother lobbyists are persuasive: the present passage represents the dynamic tension of a male god describing himself in female terms. It is even more powerful than that: the tension is increased because one may *expect* to be listening to a male god and the expectation might have been fulfilled if the description of Yhwh had been in the third person. But because Yhwh speaks of him(?)self in the first person, which in Hebrew is of itself indeterminate in gender, it is not until verse 9 (if the difficult verse 7b is left out of the account, since its referent is a matter of dispute among commentators) that unmistakable third-person references to a male god appear. Until then the chapter is remarkably ambiguous: it contains a description that may be paternal or maternal, of a God whose gender-specification is long delayed.

One might have expected that the conclusions to Sections 1 and 2 would be in sharp contradiction to one another: on the one hand, the male interest of the *marriage metaphor* might have been expected to be reinforced by the association of Hosea's human marriage with the metaphor of Yhwh's relationship with Israel; on the other, commentators have argued that Yhwh is at times portrayed in gentler, and therefore more feminine terms, in particular through the parental, or perhaps even maternal, imagery explored in Chapter 11.

These expectations have failed to materialize. It is not clear what rôle Hosea's marriage plays in the *marriage metaphor*; certainly it has made the anti-schemas that I applied to Jeremiah inappropriate for Hosea, and a closer look at the structure of the *marriage metaphor* in Hosea is necessary, in order to see why this is so. As for the alleged portrayal of Yhwh as more gentle and therefore more feminine, it would be naïve thus to reinscribe stereotypes of inherent gender qualities, and just as naïve to say that the alleged masculine cruelty described in Chapter 2 is somehow balanced or even cancelled out by the alleged feminine kindliness of Chapter 11. Yet the queer glimpse of a possible gender tension in Chapter 11 may signal the possibility that gender ambiguities may lurk elsewhere in Hosea. Thus I shall look again at the structure of the *marriage metaphor* in Hosea, and from there go on to question the cohesiveness of its gender structure.

6.4 Linearity in Hosea

The hermeneutical difficulties of Hosea's marriage have long been acknowledged.[6] As an introduction to my own understanding of the structure of chapters 1–3, I shall summarize very briefly the most important problems that commentators have identified.

Some problems originate in the text itself. In this category one could place the difficulty of finding coherence in the relationship between chapters 1, 2 and 3. For instance, is Gomer, the woman of chapter 1, the same as the woman in chapter 3, or do the texts refer to two wives, if wives are what they are, of Hosea? And if it *is* one wife under discussion, how does the narrative set out in chapter 1 relate to that of chapter 3? The text throws up a related problem: although it is clear that a particular section of the text refers to the character Hosea in relation to Gomer (for instance, in chapter 1) and that another relates to Yhwh in relation to Israel[7] (for instance, 2:15–25 (13–23),[8] an attribution on which all scholars can agree), there are other sections where the referents are ambiguous. The first half of chapter 2 is the most prominent instance of this. H. H. Rowley attributes verses 4–9 (2–7) to Hosea and Gomer,[9] and verses 10(8) onwards to Yhwh and Israel.[10] Andersen and Freedman share Rowley's opinion that chapter 2 represents a transition in concern from Hosea/Gomer to Yhwh/Israel but place the point of change at verse 16 (14).[11] Wolff, in contrast, seems to consider Yhwh as the referent of the section from the start of chapter 2.[12] Landy argues against a definite position,[13] but to judge from his subsequent remarks he seems to be in favour of taking all of chapter 2 to refer to Yhwh and Israel (1995: 37). Davies is more firmly in favour of Yhwh and Israel as the referents of the chapter: "Chapter 2 portrays the whole relationship between Yahweh and Israel as a marriage broken and restored" (Davies 1993: 91).

A. A. Macintosh seems to agree:

> The section 2:4–15 suggests a prophetic speech ... of Hosea in which he makes use of the parable of a wayward wife and mother in order to indict the perversity of his nation ... The words are spoken by Yahweh and addressed to the children. (Macintosh 1997: 40)

But later in his commentary his position becomes less clear:

> It [viz. chapter 2] contains material largely concerned with the relationship of Yahweh and Israel, but explained by the ubiquitous parable of a man's love for his unfaithful wife. Here there is no explicit testimony. (Macintosh 1997: 114)

The text cannot always be blamed for interpretative difficulties; sometimes problems are imposed upon it by commentators' own preconceptions. The belief that the texts represent a factual account of the historical Hosea has tied some commentators in knots, as has the concern to establish his ethical probity in marrying an אֵשֶׁת זְנוּנִים (or indeed Yhwh's probity in commanding Hosea to do so). Related to this preoccupation with historicity is the desire of source and redaction criticism to establish the original Hosea and to identify (and, for many critics, to discount) editorial accretions.

Keefe's comment on scholarly attempts to clarify the exact metaphorical roles played by the wife and children in Hosea 1 may be expanded to serve as a general warning about the use of metaphor in Hosea and may usefully point towards a new way of understanding the relationship between the description of Hosea's marriage and that of Yhwh's relationship with Israel:

> The search for a clear set of allegorical correspondents to assign to the parts of the metaphor ends in frustration as it is based upon the faulty premise that the trope is an allegory, rather than a complex metaphor. (Keefe 2001: 22)

Keefe is right to reject the idea that there is in Hosea 1–3 "a clear set of allegorical correspondents" (Keefe 2001: 22). But it is possible to go further: perhaps the relationship between Hosea's and the divine marriage is much looser than that, and the text here should be viewed as a succession of themes, whose relationship with each other is no more than that of a consecutive association of ideas, though with some overlap. I now trace the four main stages of this thematic sequence and their significance for an understanding of the structure of the *marriage metaphor* within chapters 1–3.

6.4.1 Linearity: The Thematic Sequence of Chapters 1–3: Stage 1

The root theme is found in כִּי־זָנֹה תִזְנֶה הָאָרֶץ מֵאַחֲרֵי יהוה, the emphatic[14] words of 1:2, which are given as the reason why Hosea should marry Gomer. But this observation recalls the controversy about the figurative usage of the word זָנָה and its derivatives. The use of the word in its figurative sense of "apostasy" is summarized in *TDOT*.[15] This use is found most often in the prophetic books, but *TDOT* cites more than a dozen examples elsewhere in the Hebrew Bible (1980:99). The controversy centres around the question: does this use of זָנָה relate to, if not emanate from, "participation in the Canaanite fertility cult with its sacral prostitution" (*TDOT* 1980: 100)? The hypothesis of a such a cult along with, for some scholars, "sacral prostitution" won wide acceptance in post-nineteenth-century scholarship.[16] As has been already noted, it influenced the interpretation of both Hosea's marriage to Gomer and the *marriage metaphor* itself, and became firmly established among some "traditional" male scholars; Wolff, for instance, suggests that Gomer was merely carrying out the contemporary Canaanite "fertility rite in which the women had sexual relations with strangers to bring new vitality to the clan" (Wolff 1974: 14). The hypothesis attracted some feminist scholars, who saw in it an opportunity for rediscovering a woman-centred fertility religion in opposition to Yahwistic patriarchy, for example, Dijk-Hemmes (1989), Setel (1985), Balz-Cochois (1982).[17] It has been challenged, however, by other scholars, including Hackett (1989) and, most forcefully, Keefe (2001).[18] Keefe's array of evidence against the hypothesis is impressive, in particular her account of the part played by androcentric scholarship in the history of the debate, although her arguments would be even more impressive if one could only forget that she *has* to discredit the hypothesis in order to make room for her own socioeconomic substitute. It is not only feminist scholars, however, who have discredited the hypothesis. Niels Peter Lemche agrees that "we have very little, if any, knowledge of a sexual religion in ancient Palestine of the kind imagined by all too many biblical scholars" (1992: 253), and in a footnote adds:

> The interest in fertility religion that was extremely conspicuous a generation ago has happily diminished by now, as it turned the ancient inhabitants of Palestine and Western Asia into something more likely to be found in the more dark and remote parts of modern Western cities. (Lemche 1992: 253)

The arguments of Keefe, Hackett and Lemche are persuasive, although it should be added that the controversy in general, centring as it does upon socio-historical issues, is not of crucial significance to my own literary approach. And, to make one last comment on the controversy, the text at this point at least is as indifferent to the exact nature of the apostasy as I am: the emphasis in this, the first accusatory expression against Israel (if that is what the reference to "the land" means), is the fact that she is abandoning Yhwh; no mention is made of another lover to whom she is escaping. The focus is on abandonment not adultery.

I argue, then, that the root idea that sparks the *marriage metaphor* is the observation that Israel has abandoned Yhwh, and that this abandonment is expressed in the figurative use of the word זָנָה. Why זָנָה? F. C. Fensham suggests that the *marriage metaphor* in Hosea is influenced by the covenantal language of divine love and jealousy that can be found in such passages as Exodus 34 (1984: 76), where זָנָה is used possibly in the figurative sense of abandonment in verses 15–16. Keefe finds the suggestion problematic:

> How do we know whether Hosea is indebted to the Pentateuch's language of covenant or whether the Pentateuch is indebted to Hosea? There are no unambiguous lines of dependence in either direction. (Keefe 2001: 107)

The answer is that there is no scholarly consensus as to the relative dates of Hosea and the Pentateuch. Some further points are worth making, however. First, Keefe admits that Hos. 1:9c indicates familiarity with, for instance, Exod. 6:7, although she seems to suggest that Hosea may be the original.[19] Second, her arguments, along with those of Fensham, seem too entangled with the בְּרִית terminology of so-called Mosaic covenantal theology. She argues that there is little evidence of interest in such language in Hosea: of the five instances of בְּרִית, only two resemble the Mosaic covenant (6:7 and 8:1); 2:20 (18), on the other hand, is a covenant between Yhwh and creation as a whole, and the other two instances (10:4 and 12:2) are political rather than theological; and adds that "this covenant theology only gains full expression with the writings of the deuteronomistic school, which postdate Hosea by at least 100 years" (Keefe 2001: 107). But why should there necessarily be a concern in Hosea with בְּרִית theology? And why must זָנָה be seen as a term that relates solely to such theology? Perhaps Fensham is at least partly right: Hosea is expressing deep anger about the abandonment of Yhwh by the people of Israel and is doing so in imagery familiar to him and his audience: apostasy as fornication.

6.4.2 Linearity: The Thematic Sequence of Chapters 1–3: Stage 2

I return to the suggestion that the sequence of themes in the text begins with the observation that the land has utterly abandoned Yhwh. Whether or not the figurative use of זָנָה first appears in the book of Hosea, and whatever the exact nature of the land's abandonment, it is the shocking gravity of the offence that is emphasized here. The next step in the thought sequence is that so grave is the land's sin, her fornication, that it demands an extreme response from the prophet: he is ordered by Yhwh to marry a woman of fornications.

As Sherwood has said of the command to marry an אֵשֶׁת זְנוּנִים "critical consensus finds this statement ethically unviable" (Sherwood 1996: 34; compare Rowley 1956/7: 209–230), and her chapter on the topic exposes the almost desperate measures to which commentators have resorted in order to resolve the dilemma. Sherwood herself compares Yhwh's rôle here to that of the English metaphysical poets in that "he forges bizarre and dangerous relations":

> The image of the metaphysical conceit recaptures the audacity of the marriage metaphor, not only by foregrounding the transgression of categories and the threat of sexuality, but by highlighting the precariousness of the prophet-prostitute, and by analogy divine-human, relationship. (Sherwood 1996: 81)

From a queer point of view, the salient word in this perceptive comment is *precariousness*: the reader's understanding of the marriage command is such that Hosea is unmanned, but I shall return to this point shortly. For the time being I shall examine the meaning of this second stage only in its structural relationship with the *marriage metaphor* as a whole.

I take the expression of Stage 2 to stretch from 1:3–2:3 (1:3–2:1). Stage 2 introduces the symbolic act: an extreme, indeed "unnatural", response demanded from Hosea to the desertion of Yhwh by Israel. If there is some metaphorical process at work here, it is not at first what might be expected: Hosea's marriage is not being described in a way that says something about the relationship between Yhwh and Israel. Rather, it is the breakdown of that latter relationship that demands the otherwise bizarre response of the prophet's marriage with Gomer. It is a reaction of despair at the breakdown of the divine/human order.

The birth and naming of the children continue this symbolic reaction to Israel's misbehaviour, but they do also to some extent introduce a shift in the succession of images. The symbolism of the names says little about Hosea's marriage, bizarre or otherwise. Instead, the names are deployed in order to introduce comments about Yhwh's reaction to the breakdown of the relationship: his rejection of the northern kingdom and its eventual collapse. But it should be stressed, this is hardly metaphor; nothing is being pointed out about the children *in themselves*, that will further enlighten the reader about the relationship between Yhwh and Israel; instead in the arbitrary attribution of names the children act as mere pegs on which are hung pronouncements of judgement upon Israel, the details of which are of no relevance to the present argument.

There follows a further shift of theme, so marked a shift, indeed, that it almost represents a further stage in itself at 2:1–2.3 (1:10–2:1). The abrupt reversal of the condemnatory names, in apparent anticipation of 2:24–25 (2:22–23), has, in Andersen and Freedman's words "startled some commentators, who have either excised the ... passage as a later addition, or else removed it to another place where it harmonizes better with the context" (1980: 199). Wolff is apparently one of the "startled" commentators, for he thinks that the passage originally belonged at the end of chapter 2. His reason for so thinking may not be persuasive about the passage's nomadic history, yet in itself it is a forceful comment on the passage's *effect*, which is "to exhibit immediately the entire range of tension in the prophet's message" (1974: 26). The tension is that between the utter condemnation expressed in the original names, and the complete reconciliation in their reversal. This is indeed an anticipation of the contrasting themes of condemnation and reconciliation that can be found in chapter 2, and what is remarkable about it is not so much that it is there at all, but that it possesses the same quality of puzzling abruptness that is found at 2:16 (2:14).

There is then in Stage 2 a change of image, from the land's fornication to the symbolic act of response, and the use of the children's names to signal Yhwh's condemnation of the nation and his reconciliation. But there is as yet no *marriage metaphor*. The transformation of the children's names makes no difference to their bearers' invisibility. Changes of name are familiar in the Hebrew Bible; they commonly mark some critical change in the life of the character, very often acting as signs of divine favour or blessing. So, for instance, Abram becomes Abraham (Gen. 17:5), Sarai Sarah (Gen. 17:15) and Jacob becomes Israel (Gen. 32:28, 35:10). In the case of Hosea's children, the change of name certainly denotes divine favour, towards not *them*, however, but towards the nation whom they symbolize. If anything, the children recede even further into the shadows as attention is focused the more sharply upon their referents. So far, then, in the text, there is narrative and symbolism, but no metaphor.

6.4.3 Linearity: The Thematic Sequence of Chapters 1–3: Stage 3

The impetus for Stage 3 is the association of Israel's abandonment of Yhwh with Hosea's marriage. What emerges at last is the *marriage metaphor*, that is, the breakdown of the divine/human relationship and the prophecy of its restoration described in terms of a failed marriage and reconciliation. Thus I argue that Hosea's marriage, though a precursor of the *marriage metaphor* proper, is not structurally part of it.

This may appear to contrast with my preliminary remarks to this chapter, in which I supposed that Hosea's marriage was a part of a double metaphor, in which Hosea and Gomer illustrate the idea of dysfunctional husband and wife, which in turn illustrates the dysfunctional relationship between Yhwh and Israel. One objection to such a view of the metaphor, voiced by, amongst others, Robert Gordis (1954) is that the semantic balance of the *marriage metaphor* is severely skewed if אֵשֶׁת זְנוּנִים is understood to refer to someone who is *already* a fornicator; in Davies's words the effect then is that "it creates an inconsistency between the symbol and what it stands for, since when Yahweh 'married' Israel she was still pure and faithful … , unlike Gomer" (Davies 1993: 82).[20] As Sherwood and, to a lesser extent, Keefe have demonstrated (Sherwood 1996: 40–77; Keefe: 2001: 38–42), this apparent inconsistency has led to often tortuous attempts to find other interpretations of אֵשֶׁת זְנוּנִים: that, for instance, the phrase should be interpreted as prolepsis (e.g. Rowley 1956: 210), or that Gomer's sin was no sin at all.[21]

The disassociation of Hosea's marriage from the structure of the *marriage metaphor* removes the suspicion of inconsistency caused by אֵשֶׁת זְנוּנִים. There is no longer any requirement to find exact parallels between Hosea/Gomer and Yhwh/Israel. The two pairs are linked simply by sequential association. But there is a further difficulty: where does the description of Hosea's marriage end and the *marriage metaphor* begin? By implication I am placing that moment, the beginning of Stage 3, at

2:4 (2:2). But where is the evidence for this? I have already pointed out that commentators disagree about the transition point. I am inclined to agree with Wolff that Yhwh, not Hosea, is the speaker from 2:4 (2:2): there is no clear change of speaker or addressee, but the tone of the text does seem to change at this point. Most modern commentators treat the passage as verse rather than prose, and there may indeed be a change of tone: instead of the measured, rather formulaic pace of the previous section, the shorter could produce an effect of heightened tension, as the indignant husband details his complaints and issues his threats. Yet it has to be admitted that there is no incontrovertible indication in the text that the focus has shifted from Hosea's marriage to that of Yhwh until suddenly at the end of verse 15 (13), the formulaic oracular indication נְאֻם־יהוה appears. But to what extent this formula should be considered retroactive is not made clear. Rowley makes a pertinent comment:

> It is undoubted that in chapter ii, the interpretation of the symbolism in terms of Israel's experience in relation to God is intermingled with the prophet's words about Gomer, because Israel appears to be in his mind alongside Gomer; but it is hard to exclude Gomer altogether from this chapter, and most natural to find the references to her dissolving into the references about Israel. (Rowley 1956/7: 222)

Rowley, one may conclude, is right to keep Gomer in the picture, but the characters Hosea and Gomer gradually withdraw and the divine/human *marriage metaphor* wins the reader's exclusive attention.

Well after their parents' departure, however, the children stage an unexpected reappearance, right at the end of the chapter; for, at 2:24–25 (2:22–23), after the grand reconciliation section of the *marriage metaphor*, there is a confirmatory allusion to the reversed names of all three children mentioned at 2:2–3 (1:11–2:1). So in this regard, at least, Rowley is right to insist that the theme of Stage 2 not only prompts, but also lingers in, the *marriage metaphor* of Stage 3.

6.4.4 Linearity: The Thematic Sequence of Chapters 1–3: Stage 4

As if the theme of reconciliation has not been spelled out enough in Stages 2 and 3, it makes a further entry in Stage 4, but with a significant difference. In the previous stages, the theme of reconciliation has been expressed through the children, and applied in Stage 3 to Israel as the wife of Yhwh. In Stage 4 (chapter 3) there is a return to the theme of the human marriage. The logic behind this shift in themes seems to be: just as the theme of Israel's desertion prompted the symbolic act of marrying an אֵשֶׁת זְנוּנִים, so the theme of reconciliation prompts the symbolic act of reconciliation between the prophet and his wife. Whatever the redactional origins of chapter 3, and however it is reconciled with chapter 1 in narrative terms, the part it plays in the structure of Hosea 1–3 is as a confirmatory assertion of reconciliation, not, as in previous stages, by means of the children's symbolic names or through the *marriage metaphor*, but via symbolic interaction between the prophet and Gomer. Whatever the details of the reconciliation, there is no doubt about the point of the symbolism: in verse 1, as already noted, the human marriage between the prophet and Gomer is directly related to the relationship between Yhwh and Israel, and indeed Gomer is identified with the male children of Israel. Finally this link between Gomer and the male children is underscored in verses 4–5.

6.5 *The Unmanning of Hosea*

It is time to return to the second stage of the thematic sequence of chapters 1–3, Yhwh's command to Hosea to marry a woman of fornications. It may be helpful to classify Hosea's marriage as a "symbolic action" as Andersen and Freedman do (1980: 166).[22] Symbolic actions are not unusual in the prophetic books; indeed Jeremiah makes a speciality of them.[23] But Hosea's marriage is more than a symbolic action and it is the book of Jeremiah that is helpful in explaining its significance. I have already observed that the extreme situation in which Jeremiah is described as living elicited from Yhwh the veto on marriage. That there is a parallel here between Hosea's marriage and Jeremiah's lack of one is almost recognized by Andersen and Freedman:

> In ancient Israel it was usual for a man to be married. It required special instructions to Jeremiah to restrain him from taking a wife … Hosea's case was the opposite. He had to be told to get married, as if he were not disposed to do so, or had even made up his mind to be single. (Andersen and Freedman 1980: 163)

The effect of this comment seems to be to make a man out of Jeremiah and to queer Hosea, though a further comment by Anderson and Freedman ascribes Hosea's reluctance to marry not to his own inclination but to "his loyalty to Yahweh" (Anderson and Freedman 1980: 163). All this is fantasy – nothing in either text gives a hint of the prophet's own feelings on the matter, unless, that is, one approaches the texts with a predisposition to the opinion that the prophetic experience is a projection of the prophet's psychological state. Where Andersen and Freedman do make a telling point is in their first sentence: "in ancient Israel it was usual for a man to be married", though this is an understatement. It is more accurate to say that it was unnatural for a man not to be married, and therein lies the shockingness of Yhwh's command to Jeremiah, a command unparalleled in the Hebrew Bible.

Holladay's discussion of Jer. 16:1 is more helpful than that of Andersen and Freedman for an understanding of the prophetic marital situations; he clearly sees the parallel between Jeremiah and Hosea:

> If one believes that Hosea deliberately married a harlot, then one can go further: Hosea married a harlot to demonstrate the corruption of Israel's relation to Yahweh, while Jrm married noone at all to demonstrate the end of Yahweh's relation to Israel. (Holladay 1986: 469)

Holladay then goes on to discuss the marriage veto and remarks that "celibacy was virtually unknown in Israel" (Holladay 198: 469). He quotes Koehler:

> It goes without saying that the Hebrew will marry, for that is the natural course of events ... The Arabs still call the bachelor "azab", "forsaken, lonely". The Old Testament has no word for this at all, so unusual is the idea. (Koehler 1956: 89)

Perhaps the nearest word is uttered by the prophet Jeremiah himself, and it echoes Koehler's Arabic allusion: "I did not sit in the company of the merrymakers, nor did I rejoice; under the weight of your hand I sat alone (בָּדָד)' (Jer. 15:17). Lundbom's comments on the same passage are helpful here. He stresses that marriage was a "natural state in ancient Israel", and cites some of the many Hebrew Bible passages that emphasize its value.[24] He recalls Yhwh's command to "be fruitful and multiply" (Gen. 8:17, 9:1,7, as well as 1:28), and concludes that "celibacy was therefore highly unusual" (Lundbom 1999: 756).

So unusual, indeed, was celibacy that some commentators have been unable to accept that Jeremiah was commanded not to marry: there has been speculation, for instance, about an earlier marriage (complete with children) or some hitherto unrecognized limitation on the marriage veto, for instance, M. D. Goldman (1952). The claim that Jeremiah had children is based upon the flimsy evidence of one variant reading, not of the MT but of the Targum at Jer. 37:12, where one manuscript claims "Jeremiah set out from Jerusalem to go to the land of Benjamin to divide his inheritance there in the midst of the people *with his sons and his brothers* (לבנהי ולאחוהי)" (Sperber 1962: 223; emphasis added). The MT, it should be emphasized, has none of this, nor does LXX.

Yhwh is telling Jeremiah to lead an unnatural life, to fail to ensure the patrilinear succession. The shockingness of Yhwh's command to Hosea is related in kind. A man has a right to the assurance that access to his wife's sexuality and fertility was guaranteed before the marriage and a duty to safeguard his exclusive possession of that access during it. Thus, in a discussion of the place of the prostitute (זֹנָה) in ancient Israelite society, Bird describes the conflicting desires of men for, on the one hand, exclusive control of their wives' sexuality (and hence a guarantee of their children's paternity), and, on the other, sexual access to other women (1989: 79). She notes that Collins "emphasizes male concern for legitimacy of offspring as the primary motive in identifying activity by *znh*" (Bird 1989: 91, n. 20).[25] Underlying these imperatives is the need to ensure a verifiable patrilinear succession. Hosea is commanded to break this basic code, to marry a woman whose sexual access is known to be violated, whose progeny cannot be unquestionably his. In obeying this command, he becomes less than a man, just as Jeremiah is less than a man in not marrying at all. Moreover both these prophecies, which are based on sexuality, are uttered by men whose manliness has been subverted, whose virility is negated.[26]

As if this were not enough, the assault on their manliness is in both cases compounded by the references to children. In Jeremiah's case it might be thought enough to leave it implicit that he may not become a father, but instead the lack of children is spelled out (Jer. 16:3), and the fate that would have overtaken any child that he would have fathered is given in detail (16:4). Unlike Jeremiah, Hosea does have children, but it does him little good, since in a phrase that has puzzled generations of commentators,[27] the children are described as יַלְדֵי זְנוּנִים. Keefe may be right to see this phrase as necessarily dependent on אֵשֶׁת זְנוּנִים, and that both phrases "are bound together in a single metaphoric complex such that one cannot be understood without the other" (2001: 22). Yet the children are a further and significant undermining of Hosea's standing as a man: if the point of marriage is to ensure the continuation of the bloodline and safeguard the patrilinear succession, Hosea will fail in his duty if he cannot guarantee that the children are his, and the phrase זְנוּנִים יַלְדֵי clearly points to such a failure.

I argue, then, that the manhood of both Jeremiah and Hosea is subverted in these texts, but it is interesting how differently the subversion occurs. In the case of Jeremiah, the main exposition of the *marriage metaphor* and the command not to marry are widely separated; indeed the veto comes well into the prophecies. On the other hand, as has already been noted, the marriage ban is not the only text that prompts the reader to question Jeremiah's manhood. His personal agonizing is familiar to us, in particular his attack on Yhwh in 16.4 where he seems to be making the charge of quasi-sexual seduction. Indeed, *whose* masculinity is being subverted here? After all, it is Yhwh who forbids the marriage. Whatever the case, the subversion of masculinity in Jeremiah works through both the marriage veto and the expressions of personal agony. The case of Hosea is different. Indeed the subversion might have escaped attention, had not the more obvious example of Jeremiah given notice of its possibility – one happy consequence of examining the prophets in my unorthodox sequence. Of Hosea's feelings nothing is learned. Instead there is only a description of his marriage from the two points of view of chapters 1 and 2. But if there are no clear textual clues in expressions of angst, yet there is some emphasis in the positioning of this, the oddest of commands: Hosea is introduced at the very beginning of the book as a man whose masculinity has been undermined by Yhwh himself.

Further, although I have argued that the connexion between Hosea's marriage and Yhwh's relationship with Israel is that of a close association of ideas rather than an intertwined metaphor, yet there is some drift between the two images, a drift encouraged by the ambiguities of chapter 2: just as one wonders about a Yhwh who seduces Jeremiah and forbids him to marry, so one wonders about a Yhwh whose rôle as masculine partner has been to some degree paralleled by a human husband whose masculinity is under question.

6.6 The Three-Movement Model

If in this study of Hosea I have jettisoned the anti-schema developed for use in Jeremiah, will the same fate befall the Three Movement Model?[28] I noted in Jeremiah a progression from the golden age of marital harmony (first movement) to unfaithfulness and marital discord (second movement), then on to reconciliation and a new golden age (third movement). While the largest portion of the text of Jeremiah and virtually all the attention of feminist scholars were focused on the acrimonious middle movement, both outer movements were undoubtedly present in the text. The appearance of the first movement at Jer. 2:2, though brief, is emphatic – it introduces the *marriage metaphor* and is reinforced in verse 7 by a non-metaphorical rehearsal of the first movement's referent – Yhwh's safe deliverance of Israel from Egypt "to a plentiful land to eat its fruits and its good things". The third movement, however, is alluded to in 3:12b–14, but the writer waits until chapter 31 before giving an unequivocal account of happy reconciliation. Before I compare this to the situation in Hosea, it is important to be clear about the terms of the reconciliation in Jeremiah. The main exposition of the *marriage metaphor* ends in chapter 3 with an extended plea for repentance: Yhwh's mercy is assured (verse 12b) but only on the condition that faithless Israel repents (verse 13). The rest of the chapter sets out the non-metaphorical mechanics of Yhwh's fulfilment of his promise and ends with Israel's confession of guilt. The full description of reconciliation in chapter 31 is set in a surround of repentance (for instance, 38:19), but the emphasis is more on restoration after punishment. Yhwh not only threatens punishment (for instance, 30:11, 30:24) but also carries out his threat (30:15, 31:18). The sequence of punishment and repentance is summed up in 31:18: "Indeed I heard Ephraim pleading: You disciplined me, and I took the discipline; I was like a calf untrained. Bring me back, let me come back, for you are the Lord my God."

In Hosea there is a very different situation. To begin with, the first movement of the three movement model is missing, except for one brief allusion in 2:17 (15): "There she shall respond as in the days of her youth, as at the time when she came out of the land of Egypt." The problem is that, structurally, this is placed as a retrospective allusion in the *third* movement. It cannot be said to be a structural element in the three-movement suite, which has none of the progressive logic of that in Jeremiah. There is a good reason why a first movement cannot be found in Hosea: its absence is the price paid for the association of the divine and human marriages. I have already argued for a structural disassociation between the human marriage (= Stages 1 and 2 above) and the *marriage metaphor* proper (Stage 3), and have suggested that the latter starts at 2:4 (2) At the same time, I have acknowledged that although the structural disassociation is clear cut, the effect produced by the human marriage not only leads to but also permeates the *marriage metaphor*. Since the human marriage apparently had no golden age of connubial innocence, it would seem rhetorically inappropriate, though logically justifiable, to emphasize the very different start to Yhwh's relationship with Israel. The effect of this omission is interesting. Although one might expect that to pass over recollections of happier times would allow the description of unfaithfulness all the more limelight, it could be argued that just the opposite happens. In Jeremiah the recalling of past happiness emphasizes the contrasting gravity of Israel's unfaithfulness. To forgo this rhetorical crutch leaves Hosea's description of unfaithfulness to stand unaided.

Further, the treatment of the third movement in Hosea could hardly be more different from that in Jeremiah. In Jeremiah there is an allusion to reconciliation in 3:12b–14, then several verses in chapter 31. In Hosea, on the other hand, the promise of reconciliation, heralded as early as 2:1–2 (1:10–11) is proclaimed at some length in 2:16–25 (14–23), and finally re-affirmed in 3:1–4. Hosea's third movement, then, in simple terms of prominence, has a dominating presence, and its presence would seem to be borne out by several modern commentators. Andersen and Freedman, for instance, argue that the formula נְאֻם־יהוה at 2:15 (13) "comes after the climactic statement that concludes the unit 2:14–15. The tone changes from this point on" (1980: 262). Macintosh deals with 2:16–25 (14–23) as a separate section, though he emphasizes the cohesion of the chapter as a whole:

> The soliloquy continues but the mood changes abruptly from punishment and coercion to coercion through love. The transition, abrupt as it is, does not break the underlying unity of thought. (Macintosh 1997: 69)

Andersen and Freedman's reference to the "climactic statement" that concludes 2:4–15 (2–13) deserves some attention. In addition to their comment on the נְאֻם־יהוה formula, they point to the rhetorical force of the chiastic word order of

וַתֵּלֶךְ אַחֲרֵי מְאַהֲבֶיהָ
וְאֹתִי שָׁכְחָה ...

and finally argue that the position of the perfect verb שָׁכְחָה at the end of its clause indicates paragraph closure (Andersen and Freedman 1980: 262).

This would seem convincing, but to leave the argument there would be to overlook the wider debate that the second half of chapter 2 has excited, a debate which might seem to challenge the contention that there is a strong third movement in Hosea. Modern commentators agree that chapter 2 consists of two distinct sections, the first detailing Israel's crimes and Yhwh's threatened punishment, the second, equating to the third movement of the three movement model, promising reconciliation and restoration. Some commentators, however, have questioned the integrity of the second section; an understanding of their arguments can best be gained by focusing on the question of where the second section (or third movement) begins.

6.6.1 Where Does The Third Movement Begin?

As has been already noted, Andersen and Freedman insist that the turning point of chapter 2 is at verse 16(14). Wolff, on the other hand, argues from a form-critical standpoint that the first section stops at verse 17 (15), and that it forms a complex of sayings which "all have their setting in a legal process against an unfaithful wife" (1974: 32). His salient argument is that the three passages introduced by לָכֵן[29] should be considered as a unitary group, three pronouncements of judgement after the statements of accusation. He criticizes the argument that the third לָכֵן acts as the introduction "to a new speech unit" (1974: 32); rather it is one of the three "judicial decrees [which] seek to heal the broken marriage ... They are therefore to be taken as attempts to achieve conciliation" (1974: 32). For him, their unity is not in doubt, since they possess a "structural connection [which] makes it necessary to take vv 16f with the preceding verses" (1974: 41). But it is difficult to avoid the conclusion that the third occurrence of לָכֵן introduces a passage that is in marked contrast to what has gone before. The first two occurrences of לָכֵן herald pronouncements of punishment, but the third marks an abrupt change of subject, an announcement of forgiveness. Wolff acknowledges the contrast, but surmises a redactional cause:

> In 2:4–17 we found a collection of prophetic sayings that have been carefully connected with each other, according to both form and content. In clear contrast to these verses, 2:18–25 consists of a loosely knit series of sayings and fragments of sayings. (Wolff 1974: 47)

For Wolff, then, the third occurrence of לָכֵן introduces a suspect potpourri of texts, which are out of kilter with the thematic thrust of the preceding passage. In his insistence that there is a "structural connection" between the three occurrences of לָכֵן, Wolff may well be assuming that they conform to what Andersen and Freedman call "the classical pattern" (1980: 235), and that here there is what D. Clines calls a "developing movement" (1979: 86). But is such a climactic rhetorical pattern of repeated לָכֵן phrases observable elsewhere in the prophetic writings? Certainly this is the sole example in Hosea, who uses לָכֵן only four times in all. In the 54 examples of לָכֵן in Jeremiah, there seem to be very few groups of three or more: one can point to 6:15, 18, 21, though the effect is somewhat spoiled by the position of the first לָכֵן in the middle rather than the emphatic beginning of its verse. Other examples are even less clear cut: for instance, the לָכֵן rash in Jeremiah 2 (2, 7, 12, 15, 30, 38, 39) is rather a mixture of isolated instances (2, 7 and 30) and two pairs (12 and

15; 38 and 39), unless one can accept that a gap of five or more verses makes no difference to the climactic effect or that there has been some later editorial rearrangement of the verses.[30] The same doubts apply to the series 49:2, 20, 26 and 50:18, 30, 39, 45 and 51:36, 47, 52, where the effect of climax is absent.

Like Jeremiah, Ezekiel has a fondness for לָכֵן (61 instances), and, more than any other prophet, a habit of long series, though there are only three with less than a five-verse gap – 5:7, 8, 10, 11; 25:4, 7, 9, 13, 16; 36:3, 4, 5, 6, 7. These three are indeed examples of rhetorical climaxes, the first and last in particular piling up the horrors of punishment.

But Ezekiel is exceptional; it is doubtful that he provides evidence for a "classical pattern" of לָכֵן groupings that act as a "developing movement", and it is equally doubtful whether it is necessary to see the three examples of לָכֵן in Hosea 2 as inevitably a tight-knit unit. It is just as likely that they are as loose-knit as the trio in Amos 5 (11, 13, 16), where verse 13 does not fit into the characterization of לָכֵן as an announcement of divine judgement or threat. In fact Wolff himself seems, to some extent at least, to share this opinion: pointing out the differences in imagery between 2:5 (3), 8–9 (6–7) and 16–17 (14–15),[31] he argues that:

> Thus, although vv 16f probably do not form an original rhetorical unit with the previous verses, here we certainly have a kerygmatic unit according to the sense of the present literary composition. (Wolff 1974: 41)

In other words, he is arguing that the Hosean editor has taken a previously independent לָכֵן statement and joined it to two others. Wolff may be right, but unless it is obligatory to accept redactional criticism, what he says may be viewed with an open mind. Similarly, because there is no obligation to explain chapter 2 in terms of editorial activity or of form, and although a clear change of mood or theme is perceptible halfway through chapter 2, this does not mean that the chapter must be read as a marriage of two sharply defined kerygmatic units. Rather it would be better to regard the לָכֵן string in chapter 2 as a splendid example of rhetorical undercutting: with the third לָכֵן the reader is primed to expect a third announcement of punishment; instead, totally illogically, there is a description of divine seduction, and the rest of the chapter builds on this change of theme. Verse 16 (14), therefore, both ends the old theme and launches the new.

6.6.2 *The Content of Third Movement*

If, then, it is reasonable to argue that the third movement of Hosea's version of the marriage metaphor begins at verse 16 (14), and is thereby all the more powerful, the next task is to consider its content. I shall not attempt a comprehensive (re-)interpretation, but shall highlight some notable features that are relevant to the overall argument.

One obvious feature is what Andersen and Freedman call "the abrupt shifts ... signalled by changes in the pronouns" (1980: 264), something familiar from the discussion of Jeremiah in the last chapter. Andersen and Freedman comment that "it is easy to see why some scholars can divide the whole passage into several small oracles, each with its own integrity" (1980: 264). Scholars with a bent for redaction criticism have long attempted to unpeel the editorial layers, and in the process turn it into a second-class text. Wolff, for instance, sees the passage as an accretion:

> Since this literary composition is far less logically connected than vv
> 4–17, we should probably not ascribe it to Hosea, but to the redactor
> responsible for 1:2–6, 8f. This is suggested by the expression "on that
> day" ... This formula is evidence of his concern to elucidate the final
> event in 2:4–17 with the help of Hosea's later sayings. (Wolff 1974: 48)

His view of the redaction as northern in origin is challenged by, amongst others, Grace I. Emmerson, who argues that while the individual verses are Hosean, a different theological message has been achieved by a subsequent Judaean rearrangement (1984: 36–48). I must return to the hermeneutical implications shortly. For now, it is enough to observe that, despite their disagreement about the history of the redactional processes, both Emmerson and Wolff leave the impression of a text that is a belated tailpiece to the previous section; as Emmerson expresses it: "The fragmentary sayings of 2:18–25 serve, in their present position, to fill out the expectation of future restoration presented in 2:16–17" (1984: 37). If, however, objections to the authenticity of the text are left aside, one remarkable feature that can be observed is that of the unconditionality of the promises it describes. Andersen and Freedman put the case:

> By contrast [viz. To 2:4–15], the promises in 2:16–25 are not attached to
> conditions of reform ... no indication that the amazing transformation
> between 15 and 16 is brought about by a dramatic alteration in the
> woman's (Israel's) character. (Andersen and Freedman 1980: 263)

This seems to be the inescapable conclusion to be drawn from the passage, but for many scholars it represents an unacceptable offence against justice. Andersen and Freedman themselves share this unease, for they argue that if no conditions were imposed upon the woman, nevertheless the punishments threatened in 2:4–15 (2–13) "correspond to" those carried out in chapters 4 to 14, and that therefore "restoration comes after justice has been satisfied" (1980: 263). They also question the lack of repentance: "While none of the redemptive acts which follow in 2:16–25 necessarily presuppose repentance on the part of the woman, they may be linked to it through verses 8–9" (1980: 263).

Neither of their arguments is convincing. The punishments allegedly meted out in chapters 4 to 14 are no more realized than the threats in 2:4–15 (2–13), and even if they were, it is difficult to find in the text such a correspondence as Andersen and Freedman suggest. As for verses 8–9 (6–7), the repentance depicted there, if such it is, is motivated by self-interest rather than consciousness of sin committed.

Macintosh also argues that a change of heart is recorded in the text, but he takes a different course:

> Logically, then [i.e. because there is an underlying unity of thought in the two halves of chapter 2], as ibn Ezra noted long ago, the threats and punishments are devised solely to bring her to the point where she is amenable to reason. (Macintosh 1997: 69)

Macintosh seems to imply that the third לָכֵן in verse 16(14) should be interpreted as Yhwh's recognition that Israel has succumbed to his threats and is ready to respond positively, an ellipsis that is not obvious. Moreover it is a Yhwh who makes threats that he does not mean to carry out. Could the justice of so duplicitous a deity be believed in?

Macintosh reports, with some approval, another attempt by rabbinic commentators to demonstrate repentance. This time it is the image of the desert in verse 16 (14) that is seized on as the focus of repentance:

> For ibn Ezra, it is the land of Israel reduced by Yahweh to a desert that constitutes the site of her repentance ... For Rashi and Kimchi it is the exile to which Yahweh will lead Israel and there she will learn that it was better for her then than now ... Both views have the merit that they see the unity of punishment and loving exhortation. (Macintosh 1997: 70)

This may be an interpretation that appeals to the generation of the diaspora, but, as far as the text is concerned, the desert symbolizes not repentance but the innocence of the golden age of Israel's relationship with Yhwh, as is made clear in the next verse, and as argued by many scholars.[32] Arguments, then, for the conditionality of Yhwh's promises in 2:16–25 (14–23) are unconvincing. The third movement in Hosea contrasts sharply in this respect with its equivalent in Jeremiah.

Another feature that is worth consideration is the continuing presence of the *marriage metaphor* in 2:16–25 (14–23). Some commentators have argued that the metaphor disappears in this section. According to Sherwood, for example:

> [The] two statements, which enclose the text [viz of chapter 2], step free from the semiotic entanglements of the intervening chapter; the passages are comfortably unambiguous, because the domestic signifier recedes into the background and the emphasis is placed firmly on the universal signifier. (Sherwood 1996: 135–136)

On the contrary, the *marriage metaphor* is the very means whereby what Sherwood calls the "cosmic promise" of the passage (1996: 135) is expressed. But nevertheless her point is interesting, because it highlights the nature of the sexual allusions in two places in the text, and because of this it is worth looking at the language of the vehicle in a little more detail.

It is undisputed that verse 16 (14) speaks the language of seduction. Commentators have raised an eyebrow at the presence of the verb פָּתָה: "The language is daring",[33] "A quite unusual act of Yahweh",[34] "The usage here is striking".[35] It is the very verb that Jeremiah uses at 20:7, and as Andersen and Freedman remark: "It must be admitted ... that, in its typical use, the verb indicates deception for sinister purposes, whether by sexual wiles ... or by other means" (1980: 272). As for וְדִבַּרְתִּי עַל־לִבָּהּ, the phrase, in Wolff's words, "belongs to the language of courtship" (1974: 42).[36]

The third movement, then, is emphatically introduced as part of the *marriage metaphor*, and the metaphor remains perceptible throughout the passage. Verse 18 (16), for instance, contains the prophesied response on the part of the woman, and verses 21–22 (19–20) present the seal of the relationship. What is interesting about these last two verses, however, is not the exact significance of the emphatically repeated אָרַשׂ,[37] but the ambiguous role of the first of two contested issues of vocabulary.

6.6.3 Hos. 2.22(20): יָדַע

There are two interpretations of יָדַע: one insists that, in Wolff's words, it "should be interpreted in view of its other uses in Hosea" (1974: 53), that is, as part of Hosea's theological thought. The other interpretation views it in the context of the *marriage metaphor*, that is, as an expression of sexual intimacy.

Supporters of the first interpretation take pains to ignore the second. Although Wolff, for instance, makes no explicit reference to יָדַע in the sense of sexual intimacy, his choice of words ("should be interpreted") does perhaps hint that there *is* an alternative that is unworthy of consideration. Davies follows Wolff in linking יָדַע here to Hosea's concern for "knowledge of God", a "much rarer expression in the Old Testament but one which is particularly common this book" (1993: 25). He understands by this phrase two things: "a knowledge of and obedience to the divine law" and "a respect for specific traditions about history and law" (Davies 1993: 24),[38] the forgetting of which plays such a part in Hosea's accusations against the Israelites. Although he acknowledges that "knowledge of God" was also "simply a way of expressing the special bond, as between intimate friends, that was believed to exist indissolubly between Israel and their God" (1993: 23),[39] yet to see that same sense in Hosea "is ... an example of the way in which too much concentration on Hosea 1–3 can lead to a distortion of the prophet's real teaching" (1993: 23). As for any thought of *sexual* intimacy, Davies has nothing to say.

Other commentators dither. Emmerson, for instance, relegating her comment on יָדַע to a footnote, leans rather heavily on Mays:

> [יָדַע is p]robably not here to be understood with a sexual connotation, although it is in the context of the marriage metaphor, but as Mays comments ... "in the context of the thematic and crucial use which Hosea makes of 'knowledge of God', the expression is best interpreted in terms of its theological meaning". (Emmerson 1984: 174, n. 67)

Andersen and Freedman also prevaricate. Their rejection of "sexual connotations", however, is based on linguistic criteria: "The idiom does not describe sexual intercourse, although the verb is so used elsewhere in the Bible, since in that usage the subject is male" (1980: 283–284). This is a mistake, as Macintosh makes clear: he gives four examples of a female subject of יָדַע in the sexual sense: Gen. 19:8; Num. 31:17; Judg. 11:39, 21:12 (1997: 85).[40]

Supporters of the second interpretation of יָדַע are not numerous. Macintosh himself is the best example of a recent commentator:

> [I]t is likely that Hosea sails close to the wind by the use of this term, for where the parable of marriage is concerned, the word is likely to have had the nuance of sexual knowledge, and thus of the consummation of the marriage. (Macintosh 1997: 84–85)

Commentators' reluctance to accept sexual overtones, despite Macintosh's reassurance that the sex is wholesome (1997: 85), leads them to miss the possibility of wordplay here. Wordplay is, after all, a familiar device in Hosea (that on the children's names at 1:4–9 is an example). That יָדַע conveys the theological message claimed by commentators is perfectly reasonable. What is unreasonable is that, given the context of the *marriage metaphor*, the author(s) could be so crass as to be unaware that a sexual pun could also be read into יָדַע, particularly since the pun enriches the theological message: the importance of the knowledge of God is underlined by comparing it to sexual knowledge, the *sine qua non* of marriage.

The presence of a variant reading in the MT is of relevance.[41] It replaces אֶת־יהוה with כִּי אֲנִי יהוה. Wolff comments that this has the effect of "interpreting Hosea in terms of Ezekiel" (1974: 46, n.i). It should be noted, however, that the phrase is found elsewhere, particularly in Exodus (e.g. 6:2, 10:2, 12:12. 14:4, 20:2), with which, or at least a version of which, Hosea may have been familiar. It is equally possible to see here an acknowledgement of discomfort at the sexual nuance, and an attempt to get rid of it.

6.6.4 Hos. 2:25 (23): וּזְרַעְתִּיהָ לִי בָּאָרֶץ

As for the second controversial expression of the *marriage metaphor* that I wish to highlight, it might be expected that the second occurrence of the portentous בַּיּוֹם הַהוּא of verse 20 (18) confirms Sherwood's assertion that the cosmic replaces the domestic, that the *marriage metaphor* finally disappears. The female object is replaced by the masculine plural "them", and the terminology is covenantal.[42] But by verse 21 (19), the feminine singular returns for the declaration (and, as I have argued, the consummation) of the marriage. The masculine plurals reappear in verses 23–24 (21–22), but in the last verse they give way to a recall of the children's names. But it is arguable that verse 25 (23) signals the reappearance of not only the children of the marriage, but also the *marriage metaphor* itself. The feminine singular pronominal object of וּזְרַעְתִּיהָ has puzzled commentators. Some have suggested replacing it with the masculine singular in order to link it with Jezreel in the preceding verse. Wolff conjectures a missing protasis, which referred to Jezreel's mother, and interprets the phrase as a prophecy of the re-population of the Jezreel valley following the deportation of 733 BCE (1974: 54).

Macintosh argues forcefully but not very cogently against the interpretation that זָרַע here means "impregnate", pointing out that the verb in the *Qal* is "never used with a woman as the object and with the meaning to make pregnant ... Objects of the verb are either the ground or soil in which seed is planted or else the seed sown (i.e. a cognate accusative)" (1997: 89). It is difficult to apply any of these meanings to this verse; Macintosh seems to take "her" in the last of his three senses: Israel (i.e. the population of Israel) is sown in the land, so that the sentence becomes "an agricultural metaphor of the repopulation of the land by Israel" (1997: 89). Andersen and Freedman make better sense when they comment that "the insemination of a woman is like the sowing of a field" (1980: 288). They therefore claim that זָרַע does convey the meaning of impregnation here, citing Num. 5:28 in support. What seems to be in this passage, then, is the *marriage metaphor* employed to convey the idea of the repopulation of the land, but doing so in *agricultural* terms. It is as though she, Israel, is being thought of as both fertile woman and fertile land, as though the terms of the metaphor (woman = Israel = male Israelites) is being questioned within the metaphor itself. I conclude from this discussion of יָדַע and זָרַע that in this third movement there are daring hints of a sexual intimacy between Yhwh and Israel.

6.6.5 *The Third Movement: Conclusion*

Summing up Hosea's version of the third movement of the *marriage metaphor* could be most effectively done by contrasting it with the version of Jeremiah. A good start could be made by observing a basic similarity: both are prophecies spoken by Yhwh, declarations of love directly addressed to Israel (though in the Hosean version some straying into the third masculine plural). But the dissimilarities are much more significant. I have described the version in Jeremiah (31:4–6) as "sunny", and so it is, but it is also very short; moreover it hardly describes the *relationship* between Yhwh and Israel, except by implication. That it is a happy one can only be judged through Israel's happiness; Yhwh as speaker is invisible, sitting back in the shade, as it were, content to watch his dancing wife. In Hosea, by contrast, there is a genuine development in the relationship, a sudden rush of seduction, response, betrothal, and, if I am right about יָדַע and זָרַע, consummation. Moreover, the dénouement of chapter 2 may be a surprise, but it is also developed in full and in effective proximity to the second movement (features absent in Jeremiah).

There is also a sharp contrast in tone. In Jeremiah it remains domestic, in the sense that, via the restored relationship of Yhwh and Israel, there is a depiction of agricultural prosperity and contentment. Now it may be that, as Emmerson maintains, little more than that is described in Hosea,[43] but the *way* it is described is very different to the version of Jeremiah: prosperity is indeed predicted but apparently the whole of creation is drawn solemnly into the process, in a covenant that bears little resemblance to that announced at Sinai and only partly resembling that proclaimed to Noah.

6.7 Queering Hosea: Conclusions

To set the scene for the conclusions, it would be helpful to recall the charges levelled at Hosea's *marriage metaphor* by feminist critics. Setel offers an overall view:

> In summarizing Hosea's use of female sexual imagery, we may note indications of an objectified view of female experiences as separate from and negative in relationship to male experience. (Setel 1985: 94)

Weems pinpoints the offensiveness of the sexual imagery: "[H]ow are we as biblical theologians to come to grips with the prophet's association of God with physical violence?" (1989: 100).

There has been a trend to view the sexual violence and the *marriage metaphor* in general "as not only abusive but pornographic" (Brenner 1995a: 35) and to label such texts as "pornoprophetic". One interesting allegation of some feminist criticism is that the metaphorical structure has helped to portray an unbalanced view of male/female relationships. Weems presents a thoughtful critique:

> The problem arises when the metaphor "succeeds", meaning that the *dissimilarities* between the two are disregarded. In this case, a risky metaphor gives rise to a risky distortion: here, to the extent that God's covenant with Israel is like a marriage between a man and a woman, then a husband's physical punishment against his wife is as warranted as God's punishment of Israel. (Weems 1989: 100; original emphasis)

Connolly is both more specific and more combative:

> We hear the husband's constant threats and accusations from vv. 4–15 and we are finally greeted with the phrase, "declares Yahweh" (2:15). This appellation was not placed at the beginning of the speech, nor interspersed, but attached to the end. As has been shown, we have been allowed to forget the large scale of the metaphor and have been caught up in the extended, specific picture of a violent and jealous husband. "Declares Yahweh" is not effective in returning us to the metaphorical level, for the passage is over. (Connolly 1998: 59)

There is no doubt about the forcefulness of the language in 2:2–13 (4–15), but is it really the case that, in Connolly's words, this is an "extended, specific picture of a violent and jealous husband" (1998: 59)? Part of the reason why this picture is questionable lies in what I earlier called the "unmanning of Hosea". It was argued that the terms of the marriage command to Hosea subvert his masculinity. It was also argued that, although Hosea's marriage is not part of the *marriage metaphor* proper, nevertheless its influence lingers: I have suggested, for instance, that the nearly total suppression of the first movement is due to its incompatibility with the dubious start of the human marriage; in contemplating Yhwh as husband, moreover, it is difficult to forget completely the unmanned human husband who immediately preceded him.[44] A comment by Connolly is particularly interesting here:

> It is possible that the husband's punishment, taken into his own hands, is a power trip, an attempt to show her who is boss ... But beyond the social assumptions of the day – and the text is being read as sacred outside those assumptions today – the husband's threat sounds impotent and ridiculous. (1998: 61)

Connolly seems to base this judgement on the assumption that the husband "is not the only one who can provide food and clothing: her lovers can, and she can for herself" (1998: 61). But it is not only in the assumptions of today's reader that the husband's threats sound impotent and ridiculous, nor is it because his rivals and/or his wife are able to undermine him. What is more startling is that the husband undermines himself and the text itself allows him to do it.

If Hosea is unmanned, Yhwh is disempowered in 2:4–15 (2–13); not only are his threats not carried out, but they are laconically brushed aside by the third לָכֵן of 2:16 (2:14). Connolly is right to emphasize the late arrival of the stamp of divine authority נְאֻם־יְהוָה, but it can be read as an undermining not so much of the metaphor but of the force of the threats made against the wife – were they after all uttered merely by a bombastic human husband? Connolly says that chapter 2 "speaks of physical action *taken* against the wife" (1998: 58; emphasis added). It does not. It speaks only of *threatened* action, just as the threats in the rest of the book are never depicted as carried out.

But there is a problem here. If the threats of the husband cannot be trusted, why should his declarations of love carry any more weight? Is the reader expected to accept what the second half of chapter 2 says any more than the first half?

Connolly's remarks about the delay of נְאֻם־יהוה again helps to produce an answer. If the subject of the first half of chapter 2 is ambiguous until its very end, there is no such problem with the second half; for enjoying the assurance of that נְאֻם־יהוה, verse 16 (14) speaks with a new authority; the next verse gives a clear indication that it is Israel's past and future that are under discussion (that is, not Gomer's); the next underlines the divine authority of the prophecy, once with the portentous בַּיּוֹם הַהוּא, and again with the repetition of נְאֻם־יהוה; verse 19 (17) sees the defeat of Yhwh's rivals; verse 20 (18) contains a second appearance of the בַּיּוֹם הַהוּא formula. The shifting of the gear to the "cosmic" features of the prophecy lasts until the end of the chapter, and includes the divine name in verse 22 (20), the third occurrence of בַּיּוֹם הַהוּא and the final emphatic ending on God (אֱלֹהָי). I argue, then, that the language of 2:16–25 (14–23), despite the allusion to the human children in the last two verses, is unambiguously part of the *marriage metaphor*, and takes every trouble to assure the reader that this is the reliable and authentic word of Yhwh.

I conclude that, as in Jeremiah, the male Israelites are asked to identify with a sinful woman. In Jeremiah this is underlined by gender ambiguities in the handling of the vehicle and tenor of the metaphor. This feature is not as evident in Hosea, though it is relevant to recall the striking passage immediately after the end of chapter 2, where at 3:1 a clear parallel is drawn, not between the woman Israel and the male Israelites, but, between Hosea's fallen wife and the sons of Israel, in a simile that, as has already been noted, cuts out the divine/human *marriage metaphor* and reverts to its human precursor.

But, with this one exception, queer attention has concentrated on other aspects of Hosea's version of the *marriage metaphor*. It has been argued that Hosea is unmanned by the command to marry an אֵשֶׁת זְנוּנִים. This subversion affects the view of the divine bridegroom: the threats of 2:4–15 (2–13) can no longer be taken seriously. This may not make them palatable – the rages may be those of a martinet but they are still rages. Yet because they *are* those of a martinet, this suggests that the male (threatened) violence against women does not win the divine authority asserted by some feminist critics.

The final point in this conclusion is to comment on the queer significance of the Third Movement: a considerable proportion of this chapter has been devoted to demonstrating that there is an even stronger expression of the Third Movement in Hosea than that in Jeremiah. At first sight the connexion between this discussion and a queer theoretical approach to gender construction may seem obscure. Showing how the prophet Hosea is unmanned is more obviously queer than arguing that there is a positive side to the *marriage metaphor*, where the reader is invited to view the future relationship between Yhwh and Israel as a happy and fulfilled marriage. Indeed it might be argued that such a discussion is an example of the criticism expressed by Guest that "when it comes to destabilizing the male dominance inherent in heterosexism, the keen edge is sometimes found wanting" in queer theory (2005: 46); perhaps this discussion is a masculinist and reactionary attempt to rehabilitate the text. To address this possible objection, it would be helpful to recall and underline the remarks about Jeremiah's handling of the Third Movement made in the last chapter. There it was argued that the presence of the Third Movement in Jeremiah was overlooked by feminist commentators. In the case of Hosea, it is not only that the Third Movement is overlooked but that when it *is* noticed, it is interpreted in wholly negative terms. Those commentators who read the Hosean handling of the *marriage metaphor* in terms of spousal abuse view the change of heart at 2:16 (14) as a mere stage in the abusive process. Commenting, for instance, on the "sudden gentleness" of that verse, Connolly makes the point concisely:

> It sounds like the cycle of abuse in which, when the abuser apologises and shows love, the abused is made to forget the violence and act as though it never happened, rather than facing and solving the problem. The reconciliation at the end of ch. 2 is sinister rather than loving or hopeful. (Connolly 1998: 62)

This would be persuasive if the text did then describe a return to violence, in which case it would be reasonable to view the *marriage metaphor* as a *cycle*; but the structure of the text is not cyclical but *linear*, a progression in which the Third Movement is the culminating act.

Sherwood attacks the Third Movement as "a patriarchal fantasy ... a dream of submission" (1996: 309). But the emphasis of the text is on not female submission but male declaration of passion, a declaration which, as has been argued, whilst grounded in sex, is at the same time elevated to a cosmic level. This is not to say that a positive view of the Third Movement dispels the ugliness of the Second; rather it is to argue that the two movements are in uneasy juxtaposition, and that one has to accommodate this ambiguity. Queer theory may help in this attempt by insisting that a positive view of the Third Movement, far from being a defence of patriarchy, is as effective a means of undermining heteronormativity as is the unmanning of Hosea. I have argued that the female partner of the metaphor's vehicle is the male citizenry of Israel in the tenor: the male Israelites are the brides of Yhwh. In pre-queer anticipations of this observation, described above in Section I, the emphasis was placed on the negative implications of envisaging male Israelites in a female rôle: for Gordon and Washington (1995) the point was to underline the humiliation of the defeated; for Patton (2000) it was castration and male rape. This feature in the text is well observed, but if it were all that there was to say about male Israelites in female rôles, then it would have to be conceded that it contained no challenge to heteronormativity; on the contrary, the *negative* implications of men in female rôles underscores the "naturalness" of clearly segregated genders. But the inexorable logic of the *marriage metaphor* also demands in the Third Movement that male Israelites are foretold a bond with Yhwh that is expressed *positively* in explicitly sexual terms: male Israelites will be Yhwh's happy brides. Here is a very odd situation in the Hebrew Bible, that exemplar of patriarchal values, where men envisioned as women do not symbolize only shame and humiliation, but also sexual fulfilment expressed in cosmic terms. This for me is the most significant queer aspect of the *marriage metaphor* in Jeremiah and Hosea. To emphasize the positive qualities of the Third Movement is neither an attempt to rehabilitate the texts nor a masculinist reaction to feminist criticism of them; rather, it shows how the terms of the *marriage metaphor* subvert notions of normality in gender rôles.

6.8 Postscript: Methodological Reflections

It is time to review the effects of my methodological procedures. I do this in the spirit of my remarks about the need for self-reflection in order to maintain queer theory's credibility as a tool of resistance.[45] I chose to examine Jeremiah's version of the *marriage metaphor* first, without reference to the parallel texts of Hosea and Ezekiel, and explained the reasons for this choice. The study of Hosea has been carried out intertextually with Jeremiah, or rather, intertextually with both Jeremiah *and* my own reading of the version of the *marriage metaphor* there.

The results show clearly not only the differences between the two biblical texts, but also between the two readings, one of which reads intertextually and the other which does not. The Hosean reading clearly feeds off the reading of Jeremiah: I have shown how the anti-schema model that successfully exposed the gender ambiguities in Jeremiah is less appropriate when applied to Hosea, and have suggested that this is accounted for by the very different structural handling of the *marriage metaphor* in the two texts. On the other hand two other arguments put forward for Jeremiah, that is, first, that the character Jeremiah queers himself and, second, that the *marriage metaphor* can be read as a suite in three movements, can be applied to Hosea even more effectively. But there has been a further result: not only has it been possible to develop in this Hosean reading ideas discovered first in Jeremiah, but it has also been possible to take these ideas back to the original reading of Jeremiah and develop that further.

So, for instance, my original brief remarks about the veto on Jeremiah's marriage and his complaints of enticement by Yhwh prompted a parallel with Hosea's marriage command; the development of this parallel led back to a more detailed look at Jeremiah. Again, the comparison of the three movement structure in Hosea and Jeremiah brought about a better understanding of the limitations of Jeremiah's third movement – it is possible to see more sharply not only its dislocation from the other two movements, but also its emphatic conditionality. I could provide a further example of this intertextual reflexivity, so far unreported: I have argued that the third movement in Hosea is more sophisticated than its counterpart in Jeremiah, that in Hosea it was both more extensive and unconditional. In the course of demonstrating the continuance of the *marriage metaphor* in Hos. 2:16–25 (14–23), I argued for the presence of a sexual nuance in the use of the verbs יָדַע in verse 24 (22) and זָרַע in verse 25 (23). Commentators often compare the covenant language of Hosea 2 with that of Jer. 31:31–34. A further look at this passage (Jeremiah's third movement has already been identified in verses 4–6), reveals two features. The first and obvious one, already noted, is that Jeremiah's covenant language is conditional on, or more accurately, consequent upon, Yhwh's punishment of Israel (verse 28 can be taken as one pointer to this from within the passage under consideration, and I have discussed other pointers outside it). The second feature is the similarity of some of the language used in both versions and, by contrast, a dissimilarity of tone. For example, both the verbs discussed above in Hosea appear also in Jeremiah 31 (זָרַע appears in verse 27 and יָדַע in verse 34). But the sexual nuances are not present in the Jeremiah version. In verse 27, the verb יָדַע uses the agricultural motif to express populating rather than inseminating; the house of Israel and the house of Judah are imaged as soil rather than as women. Similarly in verse 34, without the marriage language that appears in Hosea, knowledge of Yhwh, if universal, is markedly asexual. There may be faint echoes of the *marriage metaphor* in the word בְּעֻלְתִּי (which both the AV, NEB and the NRSV translate as "husband"), and in the memory of the third movement of verses 4–6, but these are not strong or consistent enough to prevent the conclusion that Jeremiah not only has a different view of the nature of the covenant but also to a large extent expresses the *marriage metaphor* in less sexualized terms.

My view of the handling of the *marriage metaphor* in Jeremiah has developed by a comparison with Hosea, and I have decided to expose the process of development by leaving the original reading of Jeremiah unaltered, and retaining the developments within my reading of Hosea, from which they originated

Notes

1. See above, Section 2.4.
2. Schedule of Anti-Schemas, Anti-schemas 2 and 3.
3. Indeed it might be considered that there are "conflicting values" in 1 Samuel 15 itself, regardless of Hos. 11.9: in contrast to the firmness of purpose reported at verse 29, in verse 11 Yhwh *regrets* (נִחַמְתִּי) that he made Saul king (a position re-affirmed in verse 35). But "contrast" is overstating the case, since Yhwh's regret is a matter of justice: Saul has disobeyed the divine command. Verse 29 simply asserts that Saul's repentance cannot reverse the inexorable logic of sin and punishment.
4. As discussed above, Section 2.2.3.
5. It is significant that in their attempt to make sense of the "yoke" image in verse 4, Andersen and Freedman pepper their comments with expressions of puzzlement. Admittedly they are trying hard to preserve the MT, an effort with which I strongly sympathize. Schüngel-Straumann's interpretation does involve a change to the MT, if only minor (e.g. עַל to עוּל in verse 4).
6. Rowley, for instance, reports the lamentations of a number of his predecessors, and quotes the well known words of Jerome: "Si in explicationibus omnium prophetarum Sancti Spiritus indigemus adventu … quanto magis in explicatione Osee prophetae orandus est Dominus, et cum Petro dicendum Edissere nobis parabolam istam" (Jerome in *Patrologiae Latinae* 25: 815, quoted in Rowley 1956/7: 200–201).
7. I shall refer to the errant wife of Yhwh thus, *pace* Schmitt (1989, 1991, 1995), whose arguments I discuss in due course.
8. In those instances where the verse numbering of the English translations differs from that of the MT, the English verse numbering is given in brackets after that of the MT.
9. "Here it would seem the prophet's wife and children are referred to" (Rowley 1956/7: 204).
10. "But in the following verses it is clear that he has not Gomer in mind … but the people of Israel" (Rowley 1956/7: 204–205).

11. According to them verses 4–15 (2–13) "make sense on a personal level ... ; in verses 16–25, the focus is mainly on the nation" (Andersen and Freedman 1980: 218).

12. So one must gather from his comment on verse 4 (2): "The God of Israel appears first as plaintiff against his unfaithful wife" (Wolff 1974: 33).

13. He remarks that the "reference of the metaphor in Hosea is quite opaque" (Landy 1995a: 37), and it is equally unclear whether he uses "quite" here to mean "completely" or "somewhat"; and on the same page he comments that the "metaphor may ... be interpreted in a number of ways, none of which is decisive."

14. The emphasis is conveyed in the intensive absolute infinitive זָנֹה.

15. *TDOT* s.v זָנָה (4:102). My use of the word "apostasy" does not imply that זָנָה necessarily entails the abandonment of a *covenant* with Yhwh; at this stage it should be taken in the sense of an abandonment of a less specified relationship. It ought to be added that apostasy is not the only figurative meaning as both *TDOT* and Keefe point out: זָנָה is also used in connexion with commercial trade, e.g. Mic. 1:7 and Isa. 23:17.

16. The theory of cultic prostitution is contested in recent scholarship, for instance, by Hackett (1989) and Keefe (2001), discussed below; but champions of the theory still occasionally make an appearance, of whom Day (2004) is one example.

17. Cf. Hornsby (1999), whose interpretation envisages Gomer not as a promiscuous wife, but an independent prostitute who is pursued by her client and eventually controlled by him.

18. Moughtin-Mumby describes the use of this hypothesis as an example of an "'etymological' approach to metaphor" (2008: 10), the consequence of which has been to treat the metaphor as though it were a metonym, by "insisting that the metaphorical prostitution of the prophetic books must pronounce unacceptable *cultic* practice because such metaphors are based on '*cultic prostitution*'" (2008: 11, emphases original).

19. Her counter-suggestion is not convincing: the Hosea passage gains much more weight if it can be seen as a daring subversion of a familiar predecessor.

20. It is relevant to observe here that the golden honeymoon period pictured, for instance, by Jeremiah (for instance, 2:2) is almost entirely absent in Hosea. Davies offers Hos. 9:10 and 11:1, but these brief and distant allusions do not form part of the *marriage metaphor*. An application to Hosea of the three-movement structure of the *marriage metaphor* which was noted in Jeremiah will receive attention in due course.

21. Sherwood (1996: 40–77) traces this rehabilitative view of Gomer in Rabbinic literature, the Christian Fathers, Calvin and Luther and in modern commentaries.

22. Although one may note that Andersen and Freedman also argue for the historical reality of the marriage.

23. Two examples are the broken jug in chapter 19, and the yoke in chapter 27.

24. Instances are. Gen. 1:28; 2:18–20; the "great blessing" bestowed by children (Gen. 22:17; Ps. 127:35; 128:3–4).

25. Collins, A. E. *The Stem ZNH and Prostitution in the Hebrew Bible* (unpublished doctoral thesis, Bradeis University, 1977). Frymer-Kensky, on the other

hand, disputes "the standard explanation ... that men want their wives to be virgins so that they can be sure that any babies are theirs" (1998: 81); her own account, which seems to be that virginity was prized as evidence that a woman was *controllable*, if correct, does not materially affect my argument. Stone argues that the control of female sexuality was "a way of insuring their [i.e. the husbands'] own reputation and status, the paternity of their children, and above all their ability to be ... 'good at being a man'" (Stone 2001b: 127–128). Of course, as I have already noted, Stone argues that food provision was another important concern to a husband (2001b: 127–129).

26. Stone recalls Deut. 22:13–21, and considers that the incident "may also undermine the divine manhood" (2001b: 138).
27. For a brief summary of opinions, see Keefe (2001: 21–24).
28. See above Section 5.4.
29. 2:8, 11 and 16 (2:6, 9 and 14).
30. A gap of five or more verses may maintain a sonorous impetus, but it requires closer repetition to create a crescendo of intensity.
31. That is, in the first image, the woman has to flee the land because of its desolation, whereas in the second she is brought back from the desert into the fertile land.
32. For example, Mays (1969: 44): "Wilderness is more than a place: it is a time, a situation in which the pristine relation between God and people was untarnished"; as in Jer. 2:2–3; compare Ps. 105:39–43. But it should be noted that this is not the case in the accounts of the wilderness experience in Exodus and Numbers or in Ps. 78:87–93 or 106:3–33. (I am grateful to Donald Murray for these observations.)
33. Mays (1969: 44).
34. Wolff (1974: 41).
35. Macintosh (1997: 69).
36. The phrase is sometimes used simply to express encouragement (in 2 Chron. 30:22 and 32:6, for instance); at other times to persuade someone of one's good (or better) intentions (for instance 2 Sam. 19:7). But commentators also point to its use in male/female courtship (especially Gen. 34:3; compare the interesting examples of Ruth 2:13, where Ruth seems to be (unconsciously?) referring to a potential relationship between her and Boaz; and Judg. 19:2, where the Levite is trying to persuade his concubine to return to her relationship with him.
37. For a discussion of this point, see, for example, Wolff (1974: 52), or Mays (1969: 50–1).
38. Other, lengthier, views of the "knowledge of God" theme in Hosea are listed by Emmerson 1984: 174, n. 65.
39. An expression that "appears to have been ... used in the public prayers of Hosea's day" (Davies 1993: 23), as exemplified at 8:2.
40. Ullendorf also points out this wider application of the verb, emphasizing that the sexual sense is well-established – "one of the most obvious and well-attested euphemisms in the language of the OT", and commenting that there are parallels in "Akkadian, Syriac, Greek and no doubt elsewhere" (Ullendorf 1979: 445).
41. For further details see Wolff (1974: 46, n.i).

42. It is not relevant to the present argument to discuss the nature of the covenantal language used at this point.
43. "The sayings fall into two groups: verses 18, 22–22 and 25 tell of the restoration of Israel's relationship to Yahweh. Verses 20, 23 and 24, on the other hand, speak of future hope in terms of peace and prosperity in the land" (Emmerson 1984: 25).
44. It is important to recall here the confusion about the identity of the husband and wife in 2:2–13 (4–15).
45. See above, Section 2.4.

Chapter 7

QUEERING EZEKIEL, PART 1

7.1 Introduction

In Ezekiel chapters 16 and 23 I continue the search for breakdowns in the separation of the vehicle of the *marriage metaphor* (male/female "marriage") and the tenor (apostasy of the male Israelites). I shall apply to Ezekiel, as I did to Hosea in the last chapter, the anti-schema originally designed for Jeremiah; it may help to spotlight similarities and differences in Ezekiel's handling of the *marriage metaphor*.

In chapter 16, Ezekiel presents few surprises. Column 4 of the anti-schema[1] remains consistently feminine (and singular), and for the most part the *marriage metaphor* stays in the forefront. The only possible exceptions are one or two places where the apostasy tenor seems to oust the vehicle of the *marriage metaphor*. One example may be verse 2 where אֶת־תּוֹעֲבֹתֶיהָ may refer to cultic misdemeanours.[2] But this is insignificant, since the passage is only a preamble to the *marriage metaphor* proper. Once the metaphor does begin, the anti-schema reveals no further oddity until the end of the chapter, at verses 59–63, where, although the addressee remains feminine singular, the *marriage metaphor* seems to give way to the tenor. That is to say, the בְּרִית language (the word appears three times) belongs more to the world of the tenor than to that of the vehicle. But the conjunction of feminine singular and the apostasy theme is not of real significance here. Rather one could say that the intense expression of the *marriage metaphor* has now faded, and that the use of the feminine Jerusalem is now nothing more than simple synecdoche.

Chapter 23 presents a very different situation. For the first 38 verses the anti-schema shows no irregularity. In verse 39, however, the two sisters suddenly become masculine; in the list of charges against them verse 38 presents that of profanation of the sanctuary. The gender of the subjects of verse 38 is left undefined, but there is no reason to think that it is not the feminines of the preceding verses. But verse 39 clearly breaks out into the masculine; in particular in the phrase וּבְשַׁחֲטָם אֶת־בְּנֵיהֶם לְגִלּוּלֵיהֶם the anti-schema points to the masculine gender of the pronominal form. It is the significance of this sporadic outbreak of masculine gender of the pronominal suffixes from verses 39–47 that forms the major subject of this chapter.

7.2 The Case of Masculine for Feminine Forms[3]

Comment on these verses is mixed. Walther Zimmerli views the problem as one of textual corruption; he contrasts the gender mixture of chapter 23 with 16:45–55, "where the feminine form of the suffixes is preserved throughout", a useful comparison, since that section of chapter 16, as the present passage, deals with the relation of Jerusalem and her sister(s) (1979: 102). Daniel I. Block (1997: 760) makes little comment, except that "the bewildering inconsistency of gender and number reflects the prophet's ambivalence"; his footnote concentrates exclusively on inconsistency of number. Greenberg, on the other hand, in commenting on v.39, offers a choice of two solutions:

> The suffixes and pronouns of this verse, though referring to the women, are all masculine plural, either as a feature of later Biblical Hebrew … or as an intrusion of the real referents of the allegorical women – the Israelites. (Greenberg 1997: 485)

From a queer point of view, Greenberg's statement is highly significant. If his second alternative is valid, then there is here as clear an example as could be wished for of an identification of the vehicle of the *marriage metaphor*, the female lovers/wives of Yhwh, with the tenor, the male citizens. It may be wise to qualify this statement, by noting that the subject matter of verse 39 may be more the world of the referent than that of the vehicle; this becomes more evident when in verse 40, with the renewed sexual focus and a dramatic switch to the second person plural, the gender reverts to the feminine. But in verses 45–49 the gender seems less secure; masculine and feminine suffixes coexist; there is an apparently random change from masculine to feminine and back again, and a similar change from into and out of the metaphor, until in verse 49, the focus finally reverts from feminine lewdness to masculine idolatry.

This apparent confusion of genders may lure the reader into accepting Greenberg's first alternative, that the *m for f forms* are simply examples of a late Hebrew linguistic trait. Greenberg cites as evidence the work of Mark F. Rooker, who argues that "the beginnings of this tendency … is [*sic*] heralded by the book of Ezekiel" (1990: 78–79), and that there are

80 examples in the book, compared to only 64 examples of the "regular" feminine plural suffix with a feminine plural antecedent. But what is significant about the phenomenon, according to Rooker, is not so much its frequency but its apparent arbitrariness:

> This practice is ... by no means uniform, however, as different preferences are reflected in different sections of the book ... What is perhaps more indicative of the state of confusion in the use of these suffixes in the book of Ezekiel is the occurrence of the feminine plural suffix for a masculine plural suffix! (Rooker 1990: 79)

Such evidence suggests a challenge to Greenberg's second explanation and prompts the question: is the use of *m for f forms* a mere linguistic trait entirely without semantic significance, or are there any indications that the choice of such forms creates at times effects that one should be unwise to ascribe to mere chance? If mere chance is always the only likelihood, then the initial excitement caused by the gender reversals will be short-lived.[4] To answer the question I must examine some of the 47 examples listed by Rooker.[5]

7.3 Chance or Design? Rooker and the M for F forms in Ezekiel

The first observation to make is that for the most part the *m for f forms* presented by Rooker appear in groups, and this is even more the case when one looks at the apparently isolated examples cited by him, 3:13, 13:20 and 18:26. In 3:13 the context is the prophet's vision of chapter 1 (compare especially 1:24) and the verse should be considered in conjunction with that section. The case of 18:26 is different: for it is not clear that this is a genuine example of an *m for f form*, since there is no obvious feminine plural antecedent for עֲלֵיהֶם. The only possible candidates are the feminine singular צִדְקָתוֹ and the masculine singular עָוֶל, and there seems to be no reason why together they should be thought of as feminine. Greenberg, indeed, seems to dismiss the idea of a particular verbal antecedent: he compares this verse to 33:18–19, and adds the comment:

> [I]n Hebrew the plural pronoun may be used to refer to a single act/ thing that is expressed in two terms ... Here the two terms are the two clauses describing the single act of reversal. (Greenberg 1997: 674–675)

The case of 13:20 presents peculiar problems. It is true to say that here is a real example of an isolated *m for f form* (אֶתְכֶם with antecedent אֶל־כִּסְּתוֹתֵיכֶנָה). One may hazard the conjecture that the use of the masculine helps to distinguish the object from the intervening feminine plural לִפְרָחוֹת הַנְּפָשׁוֹת, a not altogether convincing example of a phenomenon to which I shall return in due course. But the perhaps unavoidable conclusion is that there is no obvious reason for the form here, and that in addition there seems to be an apparent arbitrariness in the sequence of *m for f forms* of which verse 20 forms a part, where the suffixes that refer to women (in verse 17) are for the most part feminine.

These examples indicate that isolated cases of *m for f forms* do exist, though the tendency is for the forms to appear in groups. Moreover, an element of arbitrariness cannot be ruled out; arbitrariness is evident also in the groups of *m for f forms* that Rooker lists. The best example of this is the group found in 42:4 and 11, where there are two masculine plural suffixes that refer back to the feminine plural הַלְּשָׁכוֹת. If it seems odd to label these two examples a group, it is worth noting that the noun in question makes sporadic appearances in the Temple prophecy of chapters 40–42, and that within this section there is one other example of *m for f forms* that refers to that noun: וּפְנֵיהֶם in 40:44. Arbitrariness is indeed the impression of this passage, and it is possible to chart some characteristics of arbitrariness in the use there of *m for f forms*. First, generally only the plural form of the noun and its related suffixes is involved. So, at 40:38 the singular לִשְׁכָּה is followed by the "regular" feminine suffix of וּפִתְחָהּ. Second, other parts of speech relating to the noun remain in the "regular" feminine form. So, at 42:5 in the sequence וְהַלְּשָׁכוֹת הָעֶלְיוֹנֹת קְצֻרוֹת, there are no masculine forms at all. Third, *m for f forms* are juxtaposed with "regular" feminine suffixes relating to the same noun. So at 42:11 the masculine suffix of לִפְנֵיהֶם is quickly followed by a string of feminine plural suffixes. If any rationale is to be found here at all in the use of *m for f forms*, it must be concluded that this is an example of the phenomenon noted by Zimmerli, that is that in Ezekiel certain feminine nouns commonly attract masculine suffixes (1979: 102; he cites, for example, חֻקָּה at 5:6, 18:19, 20:16 and 37), but this is not a very helpful conclusion.

Of the other five groups of *m for f forms* listed by Rooker, one group, 46:19, 22 and 23, can be passed over quickly, since it adds little to what has already been said. Indeed verse 19 is not obviously a valid example of an *m for f form*, since the masculine suffix is an uncertain reading. In verses 22 and 23 there are three cases of masculine suffixes depending on the feminine noun חֲצֵרוֹת, for no obvious reason. Four other groups, then, are left for consideration. Two small ones are the Two Women passage of chapter 23 (verses 37, 39 and 45) and the vision of the dry bones (37:2, 4 and 8). The other two groups are much larger: they are the vision of the living creatures in chapter 1 (16 examples), and the metaphor of the sheep and shepherds in chapter 34 (again, 16 examples). What these four groups have in common is that not only do they occur in passages that employ figurative language – two are visions and two are extended metaphors[6] – but also the use of the *m for f forms* creates effects that are distinct enough to appear deliberately crafted. I must now attempt to justify this claim by examining the Living Creatures (1:5–26), the Sheep and the Shepherds (34:1–31) and the Dry Bones (37:1–14) and read them against the Two Women (23:36–49).

7.4 Chance or Design? Case Study 1: The Living Creatures (1:5–26)

The sequence of gender formations in 1:5–26 is fascinating and complex. A reversal of grammatical gender begins with לָהֶם at the end of verse 6. The referent of the pronominal suffix must be חַיּוֹת of verse 5, a word in the feminine plural that forms part of the noun complex דְּמוּת אַרְבַּע חַיּוֹת; and this masculine form of the pronoun follows two other references to the same noun that are in the "regular" feminine (מַרְאֵיהֶן and לָהֵנָּה, not to mention the repetition of the feminine singular in לְאַחַת, leading up to the appearance of לָהֶם). Why the sudden appearance of this masculine form? Is it merely the arbitrary use of a new linguistic habit?

Two answers, possibly interrelated, come to mind: one is that the writer is aware of the presence of another feminine plural noun כְּנָפַיִם (actually dual rather than plural, but the potential confusion is still present) much nearer than the earlier noun phrase, and that the masculine suffix is chosen deliberately to make it clear that the referent is not that nearer noun.[7]

A second answer may be that of conceptual rather than grammatical gender: in chapter 4 above I maintained that for the biblical writer the Israelites were conceptually masculine. This argument could be extended to assert that, when thinking generically of humankind, the biblical writer would do so in terms of the masculine, and that similarly when referring back to the "four living creatures" of verse 5, particularly under the influence of the descriptive term דְּמוּת אָדָם, would tend to think of them as הֵם rather than הֵן. Indeed commentators point to chapter 10, obviously similar to chapter 1, where the masculine plural noun כְּרֻבִים (verse 2) takes a parallel place to חַיּוֹת.[8]

This conceptual tendency is continued strikingly into verses 7–9; in verse 8, for instance, it occurs five times in a string of masculine suffixes. Another mention of אָדָם may be noted, in verse 8, which may have further underscored the masculine feel of the referent.

Verse 9 presents particular problems. Recent commentators seem to understand כַּנְפֵיהֶם as the subject not only of חֹבְרֹת, but also of the main verbs יִסַּבּוּ and יֵלְכוּ; and they then understand the creatures of verse 5 (חַיּוֹת) to be the subject of בְלֶכְתָּן, thus restoring the expected grammatical gender of the noun. But this would make a feminine noun (כַּנְפֵיהֶם) the subject of verbs in masculine form (יִסַּבּוּ and יֵלְכוּ), a situation barely acceptable even if it were to be argued that the subject was not just the noun in question, but the combination of it and the masculine פְּנֵיהֶם. Such a joint subject might be conceivable if verse 8b were read as referring forward to verse 9, translating as, for example Greenberg does, "As for the faces and the wings of the four of them, their wings were joined one to another". The repetition of כַּנְפֵיהֶם by itself makes the idea of a joint subject less attractive, and there seems no reason not to take verse 8b as a normal verbless clause, just like verse 8a. Is there not a more plausible masculine plural subject for יִסַּבּוּ and יֵלְכוּ? Masculine plurals have been persistently appearing as pronominal suffixes; do they not imply that the subject of the main verbs is חַיּוֹת, whose notional masculinity has been repeatedly emphasized? This would make better sense: it is the creatures, not the wings, that "do not turn but move forward". This leaves the subject of בְלֶכְתָּן to be understood as כַּנְפֵיהֶם, not an ideal solution, since wings may flap but they do not walk – but then to suppose that כַּנְפֵיהֶם is the subject of יֵלְכוּ is open to the same objection. Extending the notional gender of the creatures so that it affects not only pronominal suffixes but also the verbs has the advantage of distinguishing here between nouns of the same grammatical gender.

In verse 10, my argument meets with another difficulty: there are two occurrences of the masculine plural suffix near the beginning of the sentence (פְּנֵיהֶם and לְאַרְבַּעְתָּם), but toward the end, there is a slide into the feminine (לְאַרְבַּעְתָּן, twice). This is all the odder in that three of the four suffixes follow the same word (אַרְבַּע). Perhaps the conclusion must be that the conceptually masculine gender of the creatures gradually weakens once their human appearance gives way to the non-human; the lion, coming next to the man, leaves the creatures masculine, but the ox and the eagle are no match for the creatures' grammatical gender, which belatedly reasserts itself. Moreover the absence of feminine plural nouns obviates the necessity for distinctions to be made between them and the grammatically feminine creatures.

Whatever the case, the masculine plural suffixes reappear emphatically in the first two words of verse 11 (perhaps, once more, influenced by the presence of the feminine plural of כָּנָף); verse 12 is very like verse 9 in form (and problems); thus, it is my contention that the conceptual masculinity of the creatures is maintained in the masculine forms of the main verbs and that the feminine בְּלֶכְתָּן refers back to the feminine noun וְכַנְפֵיהֶם of the previous verse.

The explicit reappearance of הַחַיּוֹת in verse 13 is followed at once by a masculine suffix (מַרְאֵיהֶם), which I understand as a reassertion of the notional masculine gender of the subject, but in verse 16 there is a very different situation. The occurrence of a *feminine for masculine* form here (לְאַרְבַּעְתָּן, referring to הָאוֹפַנִּים) is unrelated to my study of the main sequence of *m for f forms* in this chapter; but it has already been cited as an example of arbitrariness, and it deserves a brief mention. The oddity of the form is underlined by its juxtaposition to the more regular וּמַרְאֵיהֶם, which has the same referent. The likeliest explanation for its presence is that it is an unconscious reminiscence on the part of the writer(s) (or, if it is not objectionable to question the integrity of the text in a minor way, on the part of a copyist) of the regular use of the word in verse 10. In verse 17 the gender confusion seems complete: there is no indication that the subject of the masculine plural verbs is not that of the preceding verse, that is, the wheels; but what is the referent of the three plural suffixes, only one of which is masculine? I suggest that the writer is conscious here of the grammatical gender of the living creatures and uses it to distinguish the referents from the wheels. The verse would then mean: "When the wheels moved, they did so towards the living creatures' four sides, but they did not turn when the living creatures moved". There seems to be here, then, a conscious manipulation of gender as an aid to semantic clarity, such as in verse 9, except that there it is the notional rather than the grammatical gender of the noun that the author uses as a device of clarification.

If this interpretation of the feminine is valid, it will affect the reading of verse 18, where the two instances of feminine plural suffixes can now be taken to refer to the living creatures; this leaves the curious וְגַבֹּתָם: here the notional gender of the living creatures briefly reasserts itself – there is no semantic need for the feminine, since the only other masculine word available is the very word to which it is attached, whereas at the last word of the verse, the author does need to distinguish the referent, and, in any case, will be influenced by previous appearances of לְאַרְבַּעְתָּן.

For the rest of the passage, verses 19–26, the notional masculine gender of the living creatures predominates, and not only in the suffixes: in verse 19, it is the creatures who are the most likely subjects of the masculine verb יֵלֵכוּ. The only exception to all this masculinity is the juxtaposition of masculine and feminine in the repeated phrase of verses 24 and 25, בְּעָמְדָם תְּרַפֶּינָה. The masculine is useful here to distinguish the referent from the feminine wings. The effect created is a reminder, as the reader draws near the end of the passage, of the real grammatical gender of the living creatures.

7.5 Chance or Design? Case Study 2: The Sheep and the Shepherds (34:1–31)

As already noted, Rooker cites 16 examples of *m for f forms* in chapter 34, from verses 11–31 (1990: 79); for the verses concerned see footnote 5. In fact almost the whole chapter requires examination. The key word is the collective noun הַצֹּאן, sheep or flock, which makes its first appearance at verse 2. The word is usually feminine, and, initially at least, is so treated here, to judge from the string of related feminine words in verse 4.[9] But אֹתָם, near the end of verse 4, puts an end to this consistency of gender. One might be tempted at first to dismiss its presence as merely an isolated and arbitrary example of an *m for f form*, especially as it is not only preceded, but also followed, by feminine forms. This is how Zimmerli appears to view it; for him its significance is evidence of a late intrusion into the text (1983: 205). Block points to the various attempts by LXX and other versions to cope with what he calls "the difficulties of the text" (1998: 78). Greenberg agrees that אֹתָם may indicate textual corruption (especially in view of a "notable variant" in LXX). Nevertheless he also offers an alternative explanation of אֹתָם as an "intrusion of the referent" which he claims "is a common feature of Ezekiel's extended metaphors", a comment which echoes his remarks on chapter 23, quoted earlier. He cites as evidence for such intrusion the vocabulary of the verse, especially in the choice of the verb רָדָה, which with the notable exception of Gen. 1:26 and 28, "otherwise has a human object":

> Hence while its figurative meaning as used here is to bring animals harshly to heel … , it evokes the referential meaning – the rulers' harsh oppression of their subjects. (Greenberg 1997: 697)

I have implied that one weakness in my case is that אֹתָם is an isolated example of masculine forms. But this is not so. I have noted that it is followed by a number of words in the feminine, but in verse 6 there is the masculine plural יִשְׁגּוּ. The word is odd in that it is a plain imperfect without the vav, but for Zimmerli its inauthenticity is demonstrated "above all by its lack of agreement with the feminine plural subject" (1983: 205). Another item on his charge sheet is that "elsewhere it always describes human behavior" (1983: 205). Greenberg also sees the word as an interpolation, but he sees points in its favour, chief among them being that its meaning, unlike that of the surrounding verbs, has moral overtones, and that therefore it "expresses perfectly the figurative as well as the referential meaning of verse 6a: 'for lack of a leader to constrain them the flock strayed/the people practiced an erroneous worship on the mountains'" (1997: 698). Greenberg is as convinced of the "incorrect" gender of the verb as Zimmerli, but bearing in mind my observations concerning 1:9 and 1:19 above, I am more inclined to accept its authenticity.

For the rest of verse 6 and continuing to verse 10, the feminine gender and the metaphorical language reassert themselves. From verse 11 to the end of the chapter, however, there are the 16 examples of *m for f forms* listed by Rooker. The passage is a prophecy of future restoration, in contrast to the previous condemnation of past error. Ostensibly it retains the sheep metaphor, but the tendency for the referent to intrude that has been argued for in verses 4 and 6 is even more marked in this later passage. Indeed at times it is as though the writer has forgotten that he is engaged on composing a metaphor at all, so much so that in verse 12 he sees no strangeness in illustrating a sheep/shepherd metaphor by means of a sheep/shepherd simile. The original dynamic metaphor has declined into a system of soubriquets: shepherd is merely another name for Yhwh, suggestive of the relationship between him and his people. The *m for f forms* are predominant, and in some verses the feminine forms have disappeared; this is particularly the case in verse 13, where the metaphor has more or less broken down – why, for instance, should sheep be brought "from the peoples" (מִן־הָעַמִּים)? One may contrast this feminine effacement with verse 16, where masculine forms are entirely excluded – even the feminine suffix maintains its position (אֶרְעֶנָּה). But because this verse is a close parallel to, and contradiction of, verse 4, its feminine format should not be a surprise.

The situation becomes more complex from verse 17, which begins with an emphatic feminine. Here the sheep remain in the feminine to distinguish them, the flock *en masse*, from their corrupt leaders, the rams and he-goats of verse 17, both masculine; the *m for f forms* that Rooker identifies in verses 18, 19 and 21 are in fact masculine forms referring to the male rams and he-goats, in contrast to the general flock (and the same is probably true of verse 20). There is here a careful distinction between genders for the sake of semantic clarity, a phenomenon already encountered in the Living Creatures passage of chapter 1.

It is not surprising that, after such painstaking gender delimitations, the author decides to relax enough to play with the reader's expectations in verse 23, where there is an alternating a-b-a-b pattern of masculine and feminine forms: the same verb רָעָה (with the same subject, David) governs first a masculine then a feminine object. Block sees only inconsistency here, "attributable to the lack of a clear distinction between the figure (the sheep) and the reality (the people)" (1998: 294). Greenberg, however, sees purpose in the gender patterning:

> The alternation in gender of the pronominal suffixes in this verse ... anticipates the transition from metaphor (flock, feminine) to plain speech (humans, masculine) from vs 24 on. (Greenberg 1997: 702)

Greenberg may well be right, though three points are worth emphasizing. First, the "human" passage of verses 24–31 retains echoes of the sheep passage (the mention of security from wild creatures in verses 25 and 28 and of freedom from hunger in verse 29 although applicable to a human context, and indeed typical of this type of prophecy, both pick up references repeatedly made during the sheep metaphor). The sheep, then, are not entirely forgotten, and this is of relevance to the second point, which is that if the sheep metaphor is still remembered, the sheep themselves have become entirely masculine, even as far as the verbs are concerned (e.g וְיָשְׁבוּ in verses 25 and 28). Third, the passage ends with a splendid piece of gender patterning in verse 31. Greenberg disapproves: "Its inelegant MT form specifically (and to our taste needlessly) identifies the flock with the humans who have taken over the scene since v.24" (Greenberg 1997: 704)

Block casts some doubts about the textual integrity of the verse, observing that LXX omits וְאַתֵּן, "which is difficult in any case, because masc. forms have predominated since v.23" (1998: 295).[10] I prefer to characterize the phrase וְאַתֵּן צֹאנִי צֹאן מַרְעִיתִי אָדָם אַתֶּם (feminine suffix, feminine noun, masculine noun, masculine suffix) as a simple but effective chiastic resolution of the gender puzzles that the author has set in the chapter.

7.6 Chance or Design? Case Study 3: The Dry Bones (37:1–14)

This, the third of the groups of *m for f forms*, was earlier described as small. Rooker lists only four examples of such forms, viz. in verses 2, 4, 8, and 10. This is correct if the definition of *m for f forms* is restricted to '"a tendency ... to use ... the third masculine plural suffix to refer to both masculine and feminine antecedents" (Rooker 1990: 78). As will be seen, however, the definition can be broadened to include other parts of speech. Moreover, the effect produced by *m for f forms* in this passage provides even clearer evidence than that given by the longer examples of a deliberate manipulation of grammatical gender.

Not that Greenberg would agree. In fact, he and Zimmerli have exchanged their usual positions with regard to the significance of *m for f forms*. Greenberg's speculations elsewhere that they may signify an intrusion of the referent into the metaphor are entirely absent in his remarks on chapter 37. Instead he maintains a strict view of them here as an arbitrary linguistic trait:

> Most pronominal elements referring to bone(s) throughout the passage are masculine, such a preference for masculine forms being present throughout the book, and characteristic of late Biblical Hebrew. (Greenberg 1997: 742, n. 2)

Zimmerli, on the other hand, sees much more significance in the gender variations (1983: 254, n. 3). He carefully lists both the feminine and the masculine forms that relate to the word עֲצָמוֹת. The feminine forms are רַבּוֹת and יְבֵשׁוֹת in verse 2; הֲתִחְיֶינָה (singular) in verse 3; and הֵיְבֵשׁוֹת in verse 4. The masculine forms are A) עֲלֵיהֶם – verse 2; B) אֲלֵיהֶם – verse 4; C) שִׁמְעוּ – verse 4; D) בָּכֶם – verse 5; E) וִחְיִיתֶם – verse 5; F) עֲלֵיכֶם – verse 6 (3 times); G) בָּכֶם – verse 6; H) וִחְיִיתֶם – verse 6; I) וִידַעְתֶּם – verse 6; J) אֶל־עַצְמוֹ – verse 7; K) עֲלֵיהֶם – verse 8 (twice); L) בָּהֶם – verse 8. The referent is the feminine plural noun עֲצָמוֹת, which first appears at verse 1. Examples A, B, K and L are the third person plural masculine suffixes that Rooker cites. I leave aside his example from verse 10, בָּהֶם, since its referent is more likely to be the masculine בַּהֲרוּגִים in verse 9. But the other examples are different. A number of them are *second* person plural suffixes and thus fall outside Rooker's strict definition of *m for f forms* (examples D, E, F and G). Examples C, H and I are more interesting still, since all are verbs in the masculine clearly referring to the feminine noun עֲצָמוֹת.

In observing how "in the treatment of the gender of עצמות a remarkable variation pervades the whole section", Zimmerli concludes: "The personal conception which then clearly comes through in the בהרוגים of v 9 already lies behind what has been said about the עצמות" (1983: 254, n. 3). This remark has some similarity to Greenberg's comment about the *m for f forms* of chapter 23. There they could be an intrusion of the referents of the metaphor, the vehicle taking on the gender of the tenor. Here the dry bones take on the gender of the living men.

But before looking at that process, it must be acknowledged that the situation is complicated by the gender of עצם. Zimmerli points out that it is of common gender and that, for instance, in the Mishna, it is treated only as masculine (1983: 255, n. 7). Indeed example J of Zimmerli's masculine forms is the masculine singular version of the noun (אֶל־עַצְמוֹ, verse 7 – closely following a feminine singular version). So it is as well to say that the writer here plays with the established genders of the noun in a way that is not paralleled by חַיּוֹת of chapter 1 or the two sisters of chapter 23. One may note, however, that there is *some* ambiguity about the gender of צֹאן in chapter 34, so it may be concluded that there too some play with established genders is apparent.

However this may be, it is clear that the bones when introduced are feminine in form, and that this fact is emphasized by all the attendant nouns and adjectives; surrounded by these, the first example of the masculine אֲלֵיהֶם in verse 2 has the appearance of an arbitrary linguistic trait. But this trailblazer is soon followed by his fellows, and as the prophecy of their visionary transformation into living men is first proclaimed and then enacted, masculine forms pervade the language, so that by verse 7 the word bone itself becomes masculine (example J, verse 7), is replaced by the masculine בַּהֲרוּגִים in verse 9, and is then triumphantly declared to be כָּל־בֵּית יִשְׂרָאֵל in verse 11. There is only one other appearance of bones, again in verse 11 (עַצְמוֹתֵינוּ), employed as a mere device (and in the feminine form) to convey the feelings of its living possessors, as part of the preparation for the resurrection motif that follows. *M for f forms*, then, in this chapter, far from being a mere linguistic trait, play a significant role in the development of the imagery.

7.7 Chance or Design in Ezekiel's Marriage Metaphor: The Two Women (23:36–49)

Having put the case that, in these three passages, the presence of *m for f forms* cannot be dismissed as a mere linguistic trait, I now return to the *m for f forms* in the *marriage metaphor* of chapter 23 and claim all the more confidently that they too are not mere linguistic traits – they are not just feminine suffixes masquerading as masculine, but are a crafted literary device. And because they are fully masculine, they count as clear examples of breakdowns in the gender separation of tenor and vehicle in the *marriage metaphor.*

The *m for f forms* in chapter 23 are contained in what most commentators have seen as a distinct section: after the judgement on Oholah alone, the prophet is called upon to recount the sins of both sisters and to foretell Yhwh's punishment upon them. The passage is often considered a late addition to the book. Zimmerli, for instance, comments on "a new level of independence from the original text", which is indicated "both in the language and the extent of the dependence on Ezek. 16 (and 23)" (1979: 490). He goes on to claim that "[in] detail the style has strikingly run wild" (1979: 491). His evidence for this is the frequent and abrupt change of person. It has already been noted that elsewhere he views *m for f forms* as textual intrusion alarms. His remarks are worth quoting in full:

> In 16:45–55, where altogether about fifteen plural suffixes refer to the godless mother and daughter, the feminine form of the suffix is preserved throughout. Clearly in 23:3f, 13 in the original text of Ezekiel the pure feminine form is preserved, while in the undoubtedly secondary conclusion of vv 39ff masculine suffixes begin to be mixed. (Zimmerli 1979: 102)

There are two preliminary comments to make. Change of person is indeed a marked feature of the passage, and its effect is disconcerting at times. Verse 40 presents the first surprise with a sudden switch to the second person from the third person of the previous verses, and within the same verse there is a further abrupt change from the opening plural to the singular, the latter extending into the next verse. Verse 42, as far as it is intelligible, seems to switch to the third person plural with a masculine verb in וַיִּתְּנוּ (referring to the women?), and feminine plural suffixes thereafter. In verses 43–47, the third person is maintained with switches back and forth between singular and plural. The passage ends, in verses 48–49, with a last change to the second person plural. It is understandable that some commentators suspect editorial cutting and pasting here. My own position is the same as it was when faced with a similarly staccato passage in Jeremiah. Abrupt changes of person are a fact of the text as it stands and I am content to assess the effect of the text holistically.

One effect is certainly an increase in intensity when Yhwh, the reported speaker, breaks off his more measured instructions to the prophet, and in his anger addresses the miscreants directly at verses 40 and 48–49. Another effect to be observed is related to the tendency to adopt *m for f forms*. It is possible to trace in the third person passages a drift away from the vehicle of the metaphor (female sexual sin) into the tenor (male Israelites' abandonment of Yhwh), and in the second person passages an emphasis on female sexual sin. As already noted, Zimmerli contrasts the presence of *m for f forms* in chapter 23 with their absence in chapter 16, referring specifically to 16:45–55, where the numerous third person feminine plural forms might lead one to expect them (1979: 102). This leads to an interesting question. If *m for f forms* are not merely an arbitrary linguistic trait, why do they not occur in chapter 16? The answer lies not so much in a hypothesis of textual accretion, but in the very fact that, unlike most of chapter 16, the majority of chapter 23 is in the plural, and that the intrusion of the tenor of the metaphor, that is the male Israelites, indeed the (male) (implied) readers, is more likely to occur when the vehicle is expressed in the plural, a tendency certainly encouraged by, but not necessarily entirely attributable to, the availability of *m for f forms*, whose presence may be said to aid the process. But what, then, is to be made of Zimmerli's specific example from chapter 16, verses 45–55, where there are also plural subjects to tempt intrusive forms? The answer may lie in the contrast between the feminine subjects of the respective chapters. In chapter 23 the writer takes pains to make it clear that Oholah and Oholibah are Samaria and Jerusalem, a pairing easily translated in the reader's mind as the (male) Israelites. Such a translation, on the other hand, is not as obvious in the case of the female subjects of chapter 16: they appear first as Jerusalem and her mother, who, as the reader has already been told, is the Hittite, and this mocking allusion to Jerusalem's Canaanite ancestry does not make it so easy to identify the pair with the (male) Israelites. The female subjects of verses 46–55 are Jerusalem's sisters Samaria and Sodom and their daughters. They are not treated as one unit as are Oholah and Oholibah in chapter 23; rather they are used to compare and contrast Jerusalem's sins with those of her sisters.

Masculine forms appear in chapter 23, then, because the subject matter lends itself to such intrusion. It will be instructive to see how they work in detail. They start at verse 39,[11] which expands on the horror of the double crime on the same day. Verse 39 is the first climax in the catalogue of the two women's abominations. Although Zimmerli may be right to dismiss it as an interpolation, it may be equally plausible to interpret it in terms of a particular effect that the verse creates in the catalogue of sins. The sexual sins of verse 36 gradually give way to cultic.

At verse 39, the author uses the opportunity to underscore the horror of the crimes by partially stepping out of the metaphor and attaching the crimes to males. A parallel to this is the handling of *m for f forms* in chapter 1, where I made a distinction between the grammatical and conceptual gender of the living creatures. In the case of chapter 23, the "grammatical" gender of the metaphor – in other words its vehicle – is feminine, but underlying it is the "conceptual" gender of the referent – its tenor – which is male. Because the sexual theme is less evident by verse 39, the author feels free to make the comments here more vivid by alluding to the sinners of the tenor of the metaphor. It is worth adding that this is achieved by means not only of two masculine suffixes (אֶת־בְּנֵיהֶם and לְגִלּוּלֵיהֶם) but also the masculine verb וַיָּבֹאוּ, on which neither Zimmerli nor Greenberg make comment. This clear example of a masculine verb, when grammatically a feminine form is expected, makes the case for masculine verbal forms at 1:9, 1:19 and 34:6 all the stronger.

Having created one climax, the author now has the problem of maintaining rhetorical effectiveness. This is carried out in verse 40 not just by a return to a detailed picture of sexual sin (and thus also to the feminine), but also by that abrupt change of person already noted: emphasis is achieved by direct address in the second person singular.

Queer interest will be very much stimulated by the intrusion of the male referent here. There is ample evidence of a conflation of the errant female wives/lovers of Yhwh and the (male) Israelites. But there is also a problem: if in the verses so far examined there is a careful distinction between the female sexual sinners and the male cultic sinners, the conflation is incomplete; the author has not quite gone so far as to refer to the female sexual sinners as masculine. But this is to ignore the second crop of *m for f forms* in chapter 23. From verse 45, the writer sets out the final judgement against the two women, and in verses 45–47 there is a striking mixture of masculine and feminine plural suffixes, all with the same referent. Having noted that there is "regular alternation" of these forms, Greenberg adds:

> The author of this confusion seems not to have distinguished the two forms in pronunciation. In all these cases some mss. and versions replace with regular feminine forms ... It is as though the copyist preserved maximal variants in a text tradition. (Greenberg 1997: 487)

To talk of "confusion" and "regular alternation" seems as unjustifiable as to make guesses about the author's habits of pronunciation. For it is clear that there is a degree of regular patterning here of masculine and feminine forms:

a (אוֹתְהֶם)
b (בִּידֵיהֶן)
a (עֲלֵיהֶם)
b (אֶתְהֶן)

One may well recall the a-b-a-b patterning in 34:23 (masculine, feminine, masculine feminine, as here in chapter 23). The patterning of verse 47 is also striking:

b (עֲלֵיהֶן)
b (אוֹתְהֶן)
a (בְּחַרְבוֹתָם)
a (בְּנֵיהֶם)
a (וּבְנוֹתֵיהֶם)
b (וּבָתֵּיהֶן)

In a passage, then, in which gender-based sins are in the foreground, the writer is consciously playing gender games by means of a linguistic phenomenon.

Finally, verses 48–49 sum up the ambivalence. The author switches back to a dramatic direct address in the second person plural, and to begin with this is firmly in the feminine: you women are being punished as an example to other women. This feminine theme is carried on at first in verse 49, but suddenly the last second person plural verb is in the *masculine* (וִידַעְתֶּם): the female sexual sinners are none other than the male Israelites.

7.8 Re-reading Jeremiah and Hosea

Continuing the methodological practice introduced at the end of the last chapter, I now discuss whether this reading so far of Ezekiel changes in any way the previous readings of Jeremiah and Hosea.

7.8.1 Jeremiah
M for f forms, in the narrower sense of masculine pronominal suffixes where feminine would be expected are not found in Jeremiah. Does this mean that their function of expressing referential intrusion cannot be matched in Jeremiah? In fact, referential intrusion *is* present, but is managed by juxtaposing differently-gendered addressees/subjects who have the same (sometimes notional) referent.

A simple example occurs at the beginning of chapter 2, where the *marriage metaphor* is introduced via an address to Jerusalem (feminine singular). It is immediately followed in verse 3 by an intrusion of the referent – the (male) Israelites' abandonment of their relationship with Yhwh – by means of a mention of Israel (masculine singular). Considerable time was spent in my discussion of Jeremiah in a search for instances where there was a breakdown in the correspondence between feminine/*marriage metaphor* and masculine/apostasy theme. What I did not lay any emphasis on was the destabilizing effect of continually *juxtaposing* the *marriage metaphor* and the referential vehicle, so that the reader never encounters the metaphor for very long before the apostasy theme, couched in male terms, suddenly appears, only in its turn to be replaced by the metaphor. In the present example, the text is firmly outside the metaphor until in verse 16 it slides, without an explicit mention of the addressee, into the feminine singular, an event which prepares the reader for a re-introduction of the *marriage metaphor* in verse 20. If the force of the metaphor is dissipated by the long gap between its introduction and reappearance, the author makes amends by the way the metaphor is handled; for at verse 20 it is conceived in terms of a further metaphor: Israel's abandonment of Yhwh, is expressed by the vehicle of the treacherous wife, which in its turn is expressed in terms of the lustful camel and she-ass. The process reinforces the *marriage metaphor*, by treating it as though it is a historical fact which can be described in metaphorical terms.

So singular an underlining of the metaphor does not put an end to the gender see-saw; for at verse 26 there is a return to the masculine, which lasts until the end of verse 31, though not without some changes of subject and number (Israel, Judah, the unnamed masculine plurals of verses 29–30 and the masculine singular of the collective nouns הֲדוֹר and עַמִּי of verse 31), not to mention the sudden lone feminine singular לָךְ in verse 28a, which, surrounded as it is by masculine singular suffixes is reminiscent of the reverse *m for f form* in Ezek. 1:16. But then, although the main subject of verse 33 remains masculine, the rhetorical question involving the maiden and the bride prepares the way for a return of the *marriage metaphor* and the feminine singular, which continues for the rest of the chapter.

Does the reading of Ezekiel in this chapter shed any more light on Jeremiah chapter 2? In my original search for breakdowns in the correspondence between feminine/*marriage metaphor* and masculine/ apostasy theme, I came to the conclusion that overall there were only hints of such breakdowns; my main observation was the chaotic nature of the text. I can now take this further and say that the effect of referential intrusion created by *m for f forms* in Ezekiel is created in Jeremiah by this very chaos. The *marriage metaphor* in Ezekiel (and in Hosea) appears in long chunks of text, whole chapters. In Jeremiah it is ragged and intermittent. The effect is that the reader never becomes so involved in the metaphor that the referent is forgotten. The (male) Israelites are always at hand as reminders that they are the spouse of Yhwh. The effect is heightened in the "female" verses at least, and in some of the "male" verses too, by the suppression of the subject. Who, for instance, is the female singular addressee of verse 33? Grammatical case may point to the distant Jerusalem of verse 1, but the literary effect is to equate her with the male subjects of the preceding verses.

Chapter 3 offers different lessons. In Ezekiel 23, I noted that up to verse 44 "the author has not gone so far as to refer to the female sexual sinners as masculine" but that the "second crop of *m for f forms*" in verses 45–49 does take such a further step by mixing "masculine and feminine plural suffixes, all with the same referent". The conclusion of the discussion of Jeremiah 3 emphasized the clear evidence for a breakdown between feminine/*marriage metaphor* and masculine/apostasy theme. The example of Ezek. 23:45–49 may be a spur to look for more in Jeremiah 3, a chapter, after all, whose mention of the two sisters seems to have been particularly inspirational to the author of Ezekiel. What can be now seen in Jeremiah is not just the gender breakdown sought in the original discussion, but also a playing with gender assignment. After the introductory six verses (in the feminine singular), the author launches into a detailed attack upon Israel and her sister Judah (verses 6–11), in terms of the *marriage metaphor* and in the feminine (this is the passage that so excited my attention in the original discussion). Verse 12 is an appeal to Israel to repent, and the terms are outside the metaphor and the gender is masculine (both singular and plural). Verse 13 appeals for confession, couched in terms of the *marriage metaphor* and in the feminine singular. But, at the end of the verse, there is a transitional masculine plural that leads to a lengthy passage of direct address to the children; it lasts until the end of the chapter. This passage is mildly disconcerting: there is a passing reference to Jerusalem in the "regular" feminine, but it is verse 19 that returns briefly to the feminine singular. But the lessening of the impact of the *marriage metaphor* is indicated by the introduction of a *simile* of wifely betrayal in verse 20, where the main subject of the sentence remains firmly in the second person masculine plural.

There is an alternation of genders, then, in chapter 3, as in chapter 2. But just as there is a regular pattern in Ezek. 23:45–49, so there is regularity in the gender alternation here:

A 1–11   (11 verses of feminine)
b 12   (1 verse of masculine)
a 13   (1 verse of feminine)
B 14–25 (11 verses of – mostly – masculine)

A rigid pattern cannot be claimed in these verses: the momentary return to the feminine in verse 19, even if followed by the distancing mechanism in the feminine, spoils the exactitude of the pattern. Nevertheless, there is an overall game of alternating gender assignment in chapter 3, which contributes to the undermining of rigid gender roles in the working out of the *marriage metaphor*.

7.8.2 Hosea

Hosea presents peculiar difficulties. On the one hand, like Jeremiah, it lacks Ezekiel's *m for f forms*. On the other, the handling of the *marriage metaphor* in Hosea has none of Jeremiah's raggedness and intermittency: there is no series of referential intrusions to serve as a reminder of the association between the errant wife and the (male) Israelites. Yet a closer examination will reveal a situation that is less clear-cut.

In the original discussion, I argued that the *marriage metaphor* started at chapter 2:4 (2:2 in the English versions), and that chapter 3 represented a further stage in the thought, picking up and underscoring themes in chapters 1 and 2. If that view of the boundaries of the *marriage metaphor* proper is retained, I must concede that with one exception the feminine gender pattern proceeds uninterruptedly. The exception I claim is not the initial masculine plurals of verse 4 (2). They clearly refer to the children of verses 6–7 (4–5). It might be argued that the mention of the masculine plural children may put the reader in mind of the male referent, but this is dubious. The exact referential relationship between mother, children and the (male) tenor is never made clear in Hosea. I argued that they were shadowy figures introduced for the sake of the naming/reverse naming trope, and that still seems a reasonable position. But what of לָהֶם in verse 20 (18)? Andersen and Freedman argue that it refers to the children (1980: 280). That would be credible if the children were the last masculine plural mentioned, but the lovers and the Baalim have since appeared. A more likely interpretation is that the author has stepped outside the metaphor at this point, and that the mention of בְּרִית

leads to an allusion to the referent, the (male) Israelites (and probably the same should be said of וְהִשְׁכַּבְתִּים in the same verse). Instead of the ך endings of the surrounding verses, then, there is an intrusion of the referent in the masculine third plural – a quasi *m for f form*. It is the ambiguity of this verse that has tempted commentators to take the view that in the reconciliation scene which starts at verse 16 (14), the *marriage metaphor* plays little or no part.[12] A view more consonant with the text would be that verse 20 (18) interrupts an account of seduction and (as I argued in the original discussion) consummation, all expressed in feminine terms.

It has to be conceded, however, that verse 20 (18) is not part of a *series* of referential intrusions on the scale observed in Jeremiah. The bulk of the *marriage metaphor* in Hosea 2 does proceed in uninterruptedly feminine terms. Nevertheless from the perspective of the context in which it is set, this monolithic structure appears less securely founded. In the original discussion I viewed the relationship between *Hosea/ Gomer* and Yhwh/errant wife as part of a linear thematic sequence. But looking back on the three opening chapters of Hosea, the reader may discern a different, and equally valid, pattern.

The *marriage metaphor*, as set out in the bulk of chapter 2, is sandwiched between passages that make explicit the referential meaning of the marriage symbolism. Chapter 1 introduces the idea that marriage can say something about the relationship between Yhwh and his people. This is achieved by the device of Hosea's marriage. Israel's behaviour is immediately identified as the referential meaning (1:2), and is constantly underscored. In the same way, after the high prophetic ending of the *marriage metaphor* proper, chapter 3 brings the reader back to earth with its equally explicit allusion to the referential meaning of the marriage symbolism. Verse 2 of chapter 1 has its counterpart in 3:1, but with the difference that the focus of the referential meaning has swung from Israel's misbehaviour to Yhwh's constant love; and it goes on to spell out the result: restoration at a price. The link between the marriage symbolism is given explicit expression. In Hosea, then, the *marriage metaphor* is not *interrupted* by explicit referential reminders, but *enveloped* or topped and tailed by them.

7.9 Conclusions

I have maintained that the phenomenon of *m for f forms* in Ezekiel 23 is an intrusion of the masculine referent in such a way that the rigidity of gender boundaries is undermined. This is a challenge to many previous assumptions; some feminist critics, for instance, have argued that the maintenance of gender boundaries in the *marriage metaphor* has underscored the male self-exculpating stereotype of the sinful woman. What I argue, on the contrary, is that certain properties of the imagery force male readers not only to identify themselves as sinners but also as the wife of Yhwh.

Two questions remain to be answered. First, is this interest in queer theory not exaggerating the significance of the referential intrusions? After all, if my argument is valid, should not a similar one be made in the case of, say, Ezek. 34:1–31 or 37:1–14? That is to say, if the masculine referent keeps interrupting the metaphors of the sheep and the dry bones, ought it not to be concluded that the Israelites are being identified with, rather than merely compared to, bones and sheep? One answer relates to the effect or purpose of referential intrusion. In the case of chapter 34, the effect is to intensify the metaphor; it is as though the writer is saying, "Look at the cruelty being visited upon the sheep; that would be bad enough if they were merely sheep, but actually we are talking of wronged human beings". The intrusions emphasize both the pathos of the sufferers and the offence of the perpetrators. In the case of chapter 37, the effect is also rhetorical: the masculine interruptions express the gradually awakening living potential of the dry bones. In the case of chapter 23 the effect is not one of rhetoric. Rather the masculine intrusions highlight a tension that is already present in the logic of the metaphor: identifying (male) Israelites with a (sinning) woman. It would be merely ridiculous to insist that Israelites are dry bones or sheep, but to say that they are female sinners challenges the profound beliefs that they as men have learned about their core identities. If the *marriage metaphor* were presented in a smooth narrative, the tension of identifying (male) Israelites with a (sinning) woman might pass unnoticed. But as it is, Jeremiah, Hosea and Ezekiel, in their different ways, present texts that do not allow this gender anomaly to go unremarked.

This leads to my second question. I have spoken of "the effect or purpose of referential intrusion". To what extent can such intrusion be said to be deliberate? Are the effects I have pointed to mere accidents? As far as *m for f forms* are concerned, I have already argued that there is no reason for the presence of some, especially the more isolated examples. But in other cases, I have noted particular artistic effects, which accident seems unlikely to have produced, e.g. the chiastic patterning of 34:31, the a-b-a-b patterns of 34:23 and 23:45–49. This patterning is so marked that I have talked about it in terms of deliberate craftsmanship. But in fact it is impossible to say whether the artistry is conscious or instinctive, and the same conclusion must be made about Jeremiah's intermittency and Hosea's envelope.

Notes

1. See Schedule of Anti-Schemas, Anti-Schema 4.
2. Elsewhere in Ezekiel, the term covers both idolatry (as, for instance at 18:12) and illicit sexual intercourse (as, for instance, at 22:11).
3. This phrase signifies the use of the masculine pronominal suffix (usually הֶם-) instead of the feminine (usually הֶן-), and will be designated in the chapter by the shorthand *m for f form(s)*.
4. Slonim argued (1939, 1941, 1944) that *m for f forms* are a result of deliberate scribal changes to the biblical texts, the aim of which was "to give a special significance to a person, an animal, an inanimate object, or an event" (1939: 400). He pointed to women as one group to whom the use of *m for f forms* drew the reader's attention; he offers a range of purposes for such a strategy: either to underline their "tragic woe", "abominable indignities" suffered by them, their "over-feminine worldliness", or their "impertinence", or to signal "the high standing of certain women" (1941: 139–140).
5. The examples are: 1:6, 7, 8, 9, 10, 11, 13, 19, 20, 21, 22, 23, 24, 25, 26; 3:13; 13:20; 18:26; 23:37, 39, 45, 47; 34:11, 12, 13, 14, 15, 18, 19, 21, 23, 25, 26, 27, 27, 28, 30, 31; 37:2, 4, 8, 10; 42:4, 11; 46.19, 22, 23 (Rooker 1990: 79.)
6. Two other groups, chapters 42 and 46, were also in vision passages.
7. Another answer is to excise the word, as Zimmerli (1979: 81). Block notes that the word is unrepresented in LXX or Vulg., which may be an argument for its inauthenticity (one of a number of discrepancies between LXX and MT in this chapter), but as he comments "it is also possible that LXX is based on a different, less problematic, Hebrew *Vorlage*'" (1997: 93).
8. See, for example, Zimmerli (1979: 102).
9. אֶת־הַנַּחֲלוֹת, וְלֹנִשְׁבֶּרֶת וְאֶת־הַחוֹלָה amongst others.
10. He does however qualify his objection: "nonetheless, these two lines may reflect the ambivalence of the entire paragraph, line 1 speaking more to the flock, hence the fem. form, and line 2 moving from the image to the reality, hence the masc. 'attem'" (Block 1998: 298).
11. Not, as Zimmerli thinks, at verse 37; one should not, in his words, "expect לָהֶן for לָהֶם" (1979: 478), לָהֶם refers back to the (masculine) idols; compare the similar 16:21.
12. Compare Andersen and Freedman (1980: 279–280): "the beneficiaries of the covenant are not identified. We are no longer in the context of marriage, for the discussion has moved from 'her' to 'them'."

Entr'acte

An Orgy of the Ego: Reflections on the Methodology of Section III

> I am aware of the problems of self-disclosure, the possibility that biblical studies could collapse into "what the text means to me," an orgy of the ego. (O'Brien 1995:119)

In Section III, I set off in a new methodological direction, and this Entr'acte is a reflection on my critical strategy. Section II concentrated on the text, with less emphasis on the socio-historical situation of either the biblical writers or the intended audience; by means of a strategy derived from (post)-structuralism and deconstruction, its aim was to demonstrate that there were elements embedded in the text that subverted the writers' gender assumptions. The writer of Section II, however, is almost invisible. His gender can be assumed from the title page, as can be some association with academic life in South West England; the choice of subject matter might suggest some interest in homosexuality, but not necessarily so – anyone can write queer theory without necessarily being gay or lesbian. And, after all, what does it matter? Does the reader need (let alone want) to know anything personal about the author? Is not the latter right to conceal himself behind a mask of academic impartiality? Whatever the case, by Section III the mask has disappeared. In its place a keynote vignette shows the writer in conversation with a friend, two gay men smirking over their camp performance of Ezekiel 23. This personal note plays a crucial rôle in contextualizing what follows: Section III reports a reading of a biblical text that takes its cues from camp. An awareness, indeed an appreciation, of camp is no longer confined to a secretive minority,[1] yet I cannot imagine that anyone but a gay man would notice the camp in Ezekiel 23, let alone consider that such an appreciation was worth a wider audience. One ingredient of camp, in particular, may seem out of place in biblical studies, and that ingredient is evident in the vignette: it seems that the two gay enthusiasts of camp are not consumed by either reverence for the text, disgust at its offensiveness or even academic seriousness; instead, they – but let me dispense with this distancing technique – *we* in our gay smirking seem to revel in, to be complicit with, the text's least commendable features. There is a further aspect of this camp view of Ezekiel that may seem equally inappropriate: much of chapter 9 is "indecent"[2] in style and content. But my indecency is there to set against the indecency of the biblical text, both to underscore and to subvert it. I should call it σπουδογέλοιος, a term usually translated as "satirical", but "laughing in earnest" gives a better sense of its intention, laughter with an edge, something very well conveyed by certain strands of camp.

The methodological stance of Section III is not entirely unfamiliar to biblical criticism. Its move away from the text-focused concerns of Section II owes something to reader-response criticism (RRC). This acknowledgement of indebtedness is expressed with some caution: Moore (1986, 1989 and 1989a) and the Bible and Culture Collective (1995: especially chapter 2, pp. 20–69) have expressed reservations about the use of RRC in biblical studies. According to Moore, for instance, the theoretical position in RRC, particularly in Fish's notion of the interpretive community (1980), which collapses any distinction between text and reader, itself collapses in critical praxis.[3] This tendency is especially noticeable in some biblical scholars, who, Moore observes, have not accepted RRC's central tenet: the text can no longer be thought of as "as a fixed and stable repository of meaning, in principle independent of human subjectivity"; they persist in their attempts to discover "the real meaning of the text" (Moore 1986: 715).

The Bible and Culture Collective has mapped this reluctance of biblical scholars to realize the full potential of RRC. One of a number of changes is that, influenced by the work of Iser,[4] scholars have chosen to define the "reader" as the one implied in the text, and in so doing, they validate the text as the repository of meaning. RRC, then, "has functioned as a safehouse for biblical critics who prefer to stay within the secure confines of traditional biblical scholarship and not plunge into the defamiliarized world of the postmodern" (Bible and Culture Collective 1995: 3).

How then do you prise the biblical scholars' fingertips from the cliff tops of historical criticism? One way, perhaps, is to persuade them of the illusory "naturalness" of the reading habit. Fish's insistence that we read in the traditions of our interpretive community suggests to me a certain Butlerian performativity. Moore in a discussion of Fish's interpretation of the reading act comments: "Fish's principles as a 'reader-response critic' directed him to see *readers performing acts*" (Moore 1986: 709; emphasis added) and

> These things [viz. the complications of the reading process] may be hard to see, Fish confesses, when interpretive strategies have become *so habitual* that the forms which they yield *"seem part of the world"*. (Moore 1986:709; emphasis added)

Reading (and the critical process?)[5] is a repeated act whereby we apply to a text the critical criteria dictated by our interpretive community; we assume that the meaning that emerges is a "natural" constituent of the text itself. This reading process echoes, in its creation of naturalness by repetition, Butler's account of gender performativity.[6] We *perform* reading just as much as we perform gender. The important question here is, as in the case of gender performativity: is there an escape from this apparently inexorable process?

It is feminist critics who have come to the rescue, and the key to the escape that they have offered is ideological analysis. They insist that the reader in RRC is not the one implied *in* the text, but the real flesh-and-blood reader *in front of* the text today. Further, when the reader's own social and political situation is a subordinate one and when the text s/he is reading reinscribes the system whereby such subordination comes about, then the reader can respond by refusing complicity with the text. In feminist hands, then, RRC becomes an effective (anti-)ideological weapon: "[R]eader-response criticism has commonly revealed its sharpest political, ethical, and ideological edge when wielded by feminist critics" (Bible and Culture Collective 1995: 37).

It is true that, while citing Fetterley (1978) as a pioneering work in ideological RRC, the Bible and Culture Collective also worries that Fetterley's advocacy of the resisting reader reinscribes the traditional view of the text's ontological stability:

> Paradoxically Fetterley's comparatively radical social/structural version of reader-response criticism depends upon a comparatively conservative belief in a stable and determinant text. (Bible and Culture Collective 1995: 38)

But if reading is a performative act, so is writing, and both are a product of the dominant ideology. To resist is to uncover the determinant ideology, and this has certainly been an effective strategy employed by feminist scholars when tackling the *marriage metaphor*; and if, in Section II, I have offered an alternative strategy to theirs not derived from RRC (though, of course, no less driven by ideology), I now turn to a reading of Ezekiel 23 based on a personal positionality, the point of view of one gay male reader. But who is this "gay male reader"? Is there not a danger of *a* "gay male reader" surreptitiously attempting to become *the* "gay male reader", an unwarranted ploy to represent a "sexual minority" as a whole, and, in so doing, to reinscribe in a very non-queer way gay/straight as a binary of sexual identity?

To prevent this eventuality I link the positionality of RRC to another critical strategy. Fowler may help both to demonstrate the link between the two and to hasten the transition from the one to the other:

> Granted, in my early practice of reader-response criticism I tried to remain cool and dispassionate, seeking the reader implied in the text ... , but as time passed it became increasingly clear that the reader I was talking about was really myself, and that the meaning I was finding was the meaning I manufactured in the here and now. (Fowler 1995: 231)

It is an easy step from Fowler's realizations to autobiographical criticism, from a self-reflexive methodology to an explicitly self-revealing strategy.

Autobiographical criticism (AC) has appeared under various names,[7] with a number of alleged derivations. According to Veeser, two important sources are *écriture feminine*, and pedagogical theories of expression writing (1996: xiv). Freedman adds Latin-American *testimonio* and African slave writing (1996: 7). Moore chooses geographical precision; he names the English Department at Duke University, "that sizeable stable of expensive thoroughbreds assembled by Stanley Fish in the 1980s" (Moore 1995: 32), as the originators of AC. The mention of Fish here is another link between RRC and AC. And a glance through the list reveals another important factor – that of feminist criticism (Kaplan, Tompkins and Sedgwick are among the named thoroughbreds). The link with feminism is very significant: it gives a clue to the fundamental epistemological and methodological issues raised by AC.

Incidence of AC is now a commonplace. It began to emerge in the 1980s, the most quoted example being Tompkins' *Me and My Shadow* (1993; originally published in 1989). Since then there have been several important collections of essays that both reflect on, and are themselves examples of, AC.[8] The autobiographical habit has spread well beyond North American English Departments, to such an extent that by 1996, according to Brownstein, it had lost its freshness, become formulaic and was merely a feature "of a period of excessive, obsessive concern everywhere with persons and personalities".[9] Its appearance in biblical theological studies is marked by a collection of essays in *Semeia* (Anderson and Staley 1995); a recent example is a brief introductory self-portrayal in her study of lesbian biblical hermeneutics by Guest.[10]

There are many comments upon the value of AC as well as the risks involved. Anderson and Staley, for example, give as good a summary as any of what moves a critic to self-revelation:

> To write about how our personal lives, economic situations and prejudices affect our interpretation of the Bible is to reveal the tenuousness and interested nature of our exegetical moves. (Anderson and Staley 1995: 12)

But they also worry that the authors whose essays they are editing have "made themselves too open, too vulnerable" (Anderson and Staley 1995: 12), and in the interests of "critical self-reflection" have risked accusations of narcissistic self-indulgence ("self-critique as self-display"). The writer of AC is always vulnerable to the reader's suspicion that the personal is there for the sake of the writer's self-promotion or self-defence. But, in successful instances of AC, the overt presence of the personal underscores the contention that the personal is present in *all* (academic) writing, usually concealed under the masquerade of impartiality.[11] But here there is yet another Butlerian echo – that of "necessary failure": the writer of AC is always under suspicion, the suspicion not only of self-indulgence but also of choosing the soft option, the easy substitute for "real", "hard" research, and the writer of AC will always have to run the gauntlet of suspicion in order find some means of challenging the normative process of reading.

This mention of softness points to a further, underlying reason for unease about AC, and that is its association with the feminine; Moore follows Miller's lead in characterizing the move to the personal as a reaction to "decades of forced immersion in malestream critical language" (Moore 1995: 19); he (rather confusingly) continues the aquatic imagery by quoting Miller's suggestion that women are good at AC "because they've been awash in the personal so long" (Moore 1995: 19; quoting Miller 1991: 19). This takes us to the heart of AC: it exposes a double binary: theory and personal, male and female, something I must discuss in some more detail.

I found it particularly illuminating to explore this debate in a different discipline with the help of *The Sage Handbook of Qualitative Research*, in its third edition.[12] In the very name of their discipline, social scientists underline their struggle to be accepted as academically respectable, on an equal footing with the "physical" sciences. They have a history of reliance upon methodological analyses that are (statistically) measurable and indubitable (quantitative methods), where a clear distinction is made between the impassive researcher and the subject of research. With the appearance of qualitative research in the 1970s, however, "many scholars began to judge the days of value-free inquiry based upon a God's-eye view of reality to be over" (Denzin and Lincoln 2005: x). *The Sage Handbook* reviews a range of "multiple methodological practices" that constitute qualitative research, including AC, directly addressed by Jones (2005: 763–791) and referred to by others.[13] This social sciences debate expresses more forcefully[14] than that in literary or biblical criticism the relationship between the researcher and the object of research, perhaps because the social scientific model of research is typically – at least in those areas of concern to contributors to *The Sage Handbook* – the field study, a survey by an anthropologist, sociologist or psychologist of a group of (living) people, a human-to-human situation. In such cases, issues such as the relationship between observer and observed, the dynamics of gender, ethnicity and class, are that much more sharply highlighted.

It is particularly easy to spot the double binary of theory/personal: male/female in the social science setting.[15] Traditional positivistic theory is conceived of as *hard* science, the product of *rigorous* evaluative methodology; qualitative research, including AC, is *soft science*(?), a process involving fuzzy procedures. Hard science requires cool heads, qualitative research and AC warm hearts. The picture that emerges will come as no surprise to anyone familiar with the arguments of second-wave feminism. The contrast between quantitative and qualitative research, or traditional scholarship and AC is coded as theory/emotion = male/female. It is small wonder, then, that Moore can speak of only a "few men" that have practised AC (he himself is one of them). Johnson expresses it in another way:

> Not only has personal experience tended to be excluded from the discourse of knowledge, but the realm of the personal itself has been coded as female and devalued for that reason. (Johnson 1987: 44)

But are AC and "traditional" scholarship necessarily mutually exclusive? Miller is helpful here:

> If one of the original premises of seventies feminism (emerging out of sixties slogans) was the "the personal is the political", eighties feminism has made it possible to see that the personal is also the theoretical; the personal is part of theory's material. (Miller 1991: 21)

AC is another way of using theorizing, and as such it does not replace traditional scholarship; it simply demands that self-reflexivity is built into whatever methodologies are chosen. And I use that last plural deliberately: by choosing to work with both species of methodology I aim at least to go some way to fulfilling Denzin and Lincoln's prediction:

> The combination of multiple methodological practices, empirical materials, perspectives, and observers in a single study is best understood ... as a strategy that adds vigor, breadth, complexity, richness, and depth to any inquiry. (Denzin and Lincoln 2005: 5)

It is worth adding a word about writing. I did not expect to find the following remarks in a work about academic methodologies, let alone one that deals with the social sciences:

> I have been taught ... not to write until I knew what I wanted to say, that is, until my points were organized and outlined ... When I thought about these writing instructions, I realized that they cohered with mechanistic scientism and quantitative research.

And again: "Writing *is* thinking, writing *is* analysis, writing *is* indeed a seductive and tangled *method* of discovery." And finally: "Thought happened in the writing."

At last I had discovered someone daring to articulate what I recognized as my own preferred method of academic thinking. Thinking through writing would seem a reasonable slogan for the creative writer, the belletrist. But Richardson and Adams St Pierre (2005: 968–969; emphasis original) have contributed a chapter in *The Sage Handbook* defending this very procedure in the social sciences. In this book it is chapter 9 that most closely resembles this procedure, while chapter 7 resembles it the least.

Chapter 7 was challenging to write (proposing a new interpretation of a key Hebrew construction, amassing evidence, planning and adhering to a careful structure) and challenging to read (at least for me, and, I suspect, for others too). There *was* a pleasure, even an excitement, but it resided not in the writing but in the quasi-laboratory situation: conceiving an idea, testing it in the evidence drawn from the text, and discovering that it was persuasive. Chapter 9, however, was a pleasure to write – thought did indeed happen in the writing, and the ideas fell over themselves to be presented to the reader; yet the chapter is no less authentic an essay in biblical criticism. Both chapters are confronting the problem of the *marriage metaphor* in Ezekiel from a queer theory perspective, the first from within, the second from outside the text. My aim is that after reading both chapters, you will never be able to read Ezekiel 16 and 23 in the same way again.

Notes

1. Ross (1989) provides a good account of commercial or "crossover" camp.
2. It is difficult to find the right word here: obscene? immoral? Ullendorff (1979) favours the word "bawdy" for his biblical examples, a term I find too redolent of the innocent bumptiousness of a naughty seaside postcard. My indecency is much more nuanced.
3. "But what would be the consequences of such a theory [viz. that of interpretive communities] for practical criticism? Fish's reply is a paradoxical 'none whatever', the reason being that the position he presents is not one that anyone could live by ... Thus, as soon as we descend from our theoretical assumptions, we once again inhabit them, and criticism goes upon its merry way" (Moore 1986: 711).
4. Especially Iser (1974 and 1978).
5. There has been an ambivalence in RRC about not only who the reader is, but also – a related question – is RRC a theory about reading or about critical theory/praxis?
6. I have described this process in Section I, chapter 2 above.
7. Freedman (1996: 3–4), Moore (1995: 19).
8. Miller (1991); Freedman *et al.* (1993); Veeser (1996) – this collection is enlivened by a number of essays that are critical of AC.
9. Brownstein (1996: 31–32), an essay, which with (deliberate?) irony is itself an example of the genre it criticizes.
10. Guest (2005, especially pp. 3–7).
11. This self-concealment is another echo of Butlerian gender performativity, where the mechanics of the gender process are hidden in order to promote the appearance of naturalness.
12. Denzin and Lincoln (2005).
13. For example, by Chase (2005) in her discussion of "narrative inquiry".
14. As well as more freshly and urgently, in contrast to the *ennui* apparently common in literary critical writing, as reported by Brownstein (1996: 31–32).
15. To be fair, this is something that has not gone unnoticed in biblical criticism; Moore, for instance, in a remark already partially quoted, argues that "[r]eacting sharply to decades of forced immersion in malestream critical language, many female critics, followed by a few male critics, have begun to contest that abstruse idiom's (spurious) separation of theory and biography, reflection and emotion, public and private, political and personal" (Moore 1995: 19).

Section III

QUEER AND CAMP

Chapter 8

The Methodological Potential of Camp

8.1 Introduction: A Telephone Conversation

The origins of this new treatment of Ezekiel 23 lie in a telephone conversation with a friend, which took place shortly after the completion of Section II; I was discussing the difficulties encountered in this problematic text. At one point in the conversation, one of us declaimed verses 11–21 in a faux-dramatic style. The other's response "Oh isn't that camp!" struck us both as significant. The exaggerated manner of reading caused us to find the text outrageous, but it was an outrage different to that described by many feminist theologians. While sharing with them a recognition of the grossness with which female sexuality was portrayed, our outrage was much more complicit with the text than theirs, for it involved a certain frisson, an enjoyable shock at the text's offensiveness.

This unlooked-for reaction was so striking that it was decided that this encounter between camp and Ezekiel 23 deserved further exploration. This exploration marks a different strategic move. Until this point I have argued that the features discerned in the text are intrinsic to it, unnoticed before and only uncovered by means of a particular reading, but there nonetheless. I now offer a reading from the point of view of a particular reader of today. I have moved from the inside to the outside of the text. Moreover, I am viewing the text not just from the point of view of a particular reader, but also through the lens of camp; this more or less novel point of view requires some justification.[1]

An obvious first step towards the successful negotiation of these hazards is to ask what camp is. It is as well to be wary of attempting a direct answer, for the same reason that one may hesitate to explain the meaning of a joke: the joke's effect disappears in the explanation. "It's embarrassing to be solemn and treatise-like about Camp", Susan Sontag famously remarked, "One runs the risk of having, oneself, produced a very inferior piece of Camp" (Sontag 1964: 106).[2] Yet somehow I must run that risk. It is fortunate that the subject has attracted a corpus of critical comment, which has the merit of being contemporary with its subject, for the most part, and of having developed along parallel lines. Indeed the corpus has become sufficiently extensive as to have led to a collection of its highlights: with the appearance of *Camp: Queer Aesthetics and the Performing Subject* (Cleto 1999), camp seems to have sidled successfully on to the academic stage, with a star billing that includes such names as Butler, Sedgwick and Dollimore.[3] Chuck Kleinhans even claims that one particular essay on camp substantially changed the nature of its subject. He talks of crossover camp[4] in terms of "the broadening of concepts of Camp based on the appropriation that took place *due to* the publication of Sontag's 1964 essay" (1994: 187; emphasis added). It may seem fanciful to attribute even in part the increasing visibility of camp in the mass media to a brief essay in a high-brow, low-circulation literary journal,[5] yet Kleinhan's claim is supported by Fabio Cleto:

> "Notes on 'Camp'" certainly captured the ultimate sensation of the 1960s, projecting its subject-matter and author to intellectual and public stardom ... It's hard to underestimate the currency value the term gained during the rest of the decade ... Isherwood's disconcertion at its absence from public discourse had been fully satisfied. (Cleto 1999: 302)

In one case at least, then, the literature on camp helped to change its subject; and it should be said that Sontag's essay (1983) remains the most significant account of camp and makes several appearances in this chapter. Moreover, there is a significant reflexive relationship between camp and the literature about it. *Because* she is writing on camp, Sontag is self-conscious about the way she writes: the subject she chooses is reflected in her elliptical and epigrammatic style. So, if she influenced camp, camp influenced her in its turn, and one may observe in her a process whereby the power of the subject affects its commentator. Other writers may have had much less influence on camp than Sontag, but its influence on them is just as noticeable: Mark Booth (1983) and Philip Core (1984), for example, produced serious contributions but in showy packaging, with as much photography as text, and a fondness for pithy quotation and their own versions of camp wit.

In the next section I set out to exploit this corpus of critical comment in order to demonstrate some of the qualities of camp, not least the way that it presents concurrent opposites, how, that is, beneath camp's glittering surface the observer can catch glimpses of a disturbing undertow.

8.2 Resolute Frivolity:[6] Some Features of Camp

Camp: ... Used chiefly by persons of exceptional want of character. (Ware 1909: 61)

If Sontag's claim that camp is "third among the great sensibilities"[7] exhibits a *blasé* exaggeration that echoes her subject, the emergence of camp, nevertheless, as a significant phenomenon in the twentieth century merits closer attention from cultural historians than it has so far received.[8] This is not the place to attempt such a project, yet it is important that I illustrate some features of camp that I feel may help to shed new light on Ezekiel 23.

8.2.1 Camp, Gays and Effeminacy: Who Owns Camp?

My remark in the last chapter that no one "but a gay man would notice the camp in Ezekiel chapter 23"[9] may imply that gay men have a special claim on camp. This is not to say that camp is unfamiliar to anyone else; after all, the foremost writer on the subject is female (Sontag 1983), and a number of writers, perhaps most usefully Andrew Ross (1989), have described the adoption of camp by popular culture for a general audience during the later twentieth century.[10] The historical complexity of the relationship between camp and same-sex desire is something that is worth a more detailed exploration. It will clarify my claim that gay men in particular will recognize the camp potential of Ezekiel 23, without excluding the probability that this potential can be appreciated by any early-twenty-first century reader who has come across camp performances in films or television. Moreover some understanding of camp's origins will explain why I shall suggest in due course that you imagine Ezekiel chapter 23 read by a popular (comic) actor "whose rather nasal actorly hauteur and cultural pretensions overlie petit-bourgeois London speech sounds".[11]

I begin with J. Redding Ware's definition of camp in his 1909 dictionary *Passing English of the Victorian Era*:[12]

> Actions and gestures of an exaggerated emphasis. Probably from the French. Used chiefly by persons of exceptional want of character, e.g., "How very camp he is". (Ware 1909: 61)

Who are these "persons of exceptional want of character"? Since Ware published his work 14 years after Oscar Wilde's trials, it is tempting to see here a reference if not to Wilde himself then at least to those whom his downfall made painfully prominent: homosexuality[13] is being coded here. But is it? Perhaps it is not homosexuality but some such other factor as effeminacy[14] that is in Ware's mind.

This ambiguity in Ware's definition foreshadows two debates. The first is about the relationship between camp and same-sex desire. Sontag was the first to articulate indecision. She argues that "homosexuals, by and large, constitute the vanguard – and the most articulate audience – of Camp" (1983: 117), but that "even though homosexuals have been its vanguard, Camp taste is much more than homosexual taste" (Sontag 1983: 118). Sontag's partial disassociation of camp and homosexuality should be viewed in the context of the cultural history of the mid-1960s when her essay was first published. On the one hand, crossover camp was beginning to appear,[15] and, on the other, gay liberationist campaigns gathered momentum.[16] Some gay writers made claims for a gay monopoly of camp. Richard Dyer, for instance, is clear about where camp resides: "It's just about the only style, language and culture that is distinctively and unambiguously gay male" (1992: 137).[17] Jack Babuscio similarly sees a gay element[18] as essential to camp:

> People who have camp, e.g. screen "personalities" ..., or who are in some way responsible for camp ... need not be gay. The link with gayness is established when the camp as aspect of an individual or thing is identified as such by a gay sensibility. (Babuscio 1977: 41)

But, increasingly, gay writers had to acknowledge the existence of crossover camp with its considerable non-gay input. Dyer characterizes this phenomenon as an adoption or take-over by straights, and argues that "it loses its cutting edge, its identification with the gay experience, its distance from the straight sexual world-view" (1992: 145). Such a formulation foreshadows the later attempt by some queer theorists to re-appropriate camp. Moe Meyer, for example, sees the very purpose of camp as resistance to heteronormativity: "I define Camp as the total body of performative practices and strategies used to enact a queer identity, with enactment defined as the production of social visibility" (1994: 5). Camp, then, requires a performer who is not heterosexual: "Camp is solely a queer (and/or sometimes gay and lesbian) discourse" (1994: 1).

Since the existence of crossover camp cannot be ignored, Meyer's solution is to regard camp in terms of authenticity. His attempt to (?re)claim camp as a queer-only political weapon was challenged by Cleto in his introduction to his 1999 reader. Like Meyer, Cleto sees a close link between queer and camp: he claims that they "share the contemporary critical stage, the latter being a central issue for 'queer theory', one of its partially definitional objects of analysis" (1999: 12). But queer and camp also share a lack of definition. Cleto argues that to impose a definition upon camp is to universalize it – an inappropriately essentialist thing to do. He notes how often camp is talked of in terms of dichotomies, binary opposites (high/low, genuine/fake, and my own public/private).[19] Perhaps this is the result of imposing definitions, since to say what something is also to say what it is not. Since the whole *raison d'être* of both camp and queer is to undermine dichotomies, to describe them in terms of dichotomies makes little sense.[20] Cleto concludes that we should be content to think of camp as culturally determined performances and effects, which will vary in time and context.

If camp and same-sex desire are thus not inevitably linked, perhaps the conclusion ought to be that Ware's definition after all codes effeminacy rather than same-sex desire? It is not my intention to engage with this historically complex debate in any detail, except insofar as it accounts for that element of faux-aristocratic affectation often found in camp, an element very much present in my reading of Ezekiel 23. Sontag was the first to link camp with the survival of dandyism, arguing that "the history of Camp taste is part of the history of snob taste" (1983: 117). Ross expands her remarks to trace the artificiality of camp's aristocratic pretensions. He argues that far from being the echoes of a superseded elite, both the old and the new dandyisms are the tactics of the marginalized: "camp belongs to the 'self-presentation' of arriviste groups", who parody their own lack of power and status (1989: 146). This was the position of the nineteenth century camp poseur, himself often the product of the middle classes (Wilde is the most famous example), whose show of aristocratic world-weary foppish affectation set him apart both from bourgeois morality and "the threatening embryonic power of the popular classes" (1989: 147). The same pose was performed by the camp intellectual of the twentieth century, who found a niche in commercial entertainment "as the representative or stand-in for a class that is no longer in a position to exercise its power to define official culture" (1989: 147). Ross, then, interprets what others may see as the effeminate or homosexual element of camp as a contrived aristocratic mode. Moreover he reconciles its aristocratic and democratizing elements by viewing the first as a cultural weapon wielded by the second. Ross's account has been reinforced by Alan Sinfield, who demonstrates that effeminacy in early modern Britain coded a deviant heterosociality rather than homosexuality.[21] The difference between the manly and the effeminate man is that both liked to *go with* women, but the latter also liked to *be with* them, and in so doing he took on some of their "softer" characteristics.[22] But by the end of the nineteenth century, Sinfield argues, after a period of gradual if uneven evolution effeminacy had become firmly associated with both dandyism and same-sex desire.[23] This abbreviated account may further an appreciation of the nuances and tensions that I invoke when asking the reader to imagine Ezekiel 23 read in the pseudo-aristocratic voice of a camp actor of working-class origins.

8.2.2 Camp Stylistics

How can anyone call Ezekiel chapter 23 camp? I have already argued that a gay man might find it easier to do so, but is camp, therefore, a matter of agency, or can one say that something or someone is *intrinsically* camp, exclaiming with Ware "How very camp he is"? Sontag's essay may leave the reader confused about the question of camp agency versus camp object.[24] But Dyer is clearer on the issue: "[C]amp is far more a question of how you respond to things rather than qualities actually inherent in those things" (1992: 136). In Dyer's formulation, how camp works corresponds closely to reader-response criticism's view of reading: camp/meaning does not reside intrinsically in the object viewed/text, but in the viewer/reader. Camp, then, can be a way of seeing, a process rather than a product, and it is with this understanding of how camp works that I approach Ezekiel 23.

Camp, then, is in the eye of the beholder, but what is its mode of expression? I have mentioned faux-aristocratic affectation and alluded to the long and complex history of that phenomenon. I have also quoted Ware's "exaggerated emphasis". This is a *sine qua non* in the catalogue of camp attributes. Sontag's dictum is an eloquent summary: "The hallmark of Camp is the spirit of extravagance. Camp is a woman walking around in a dress made of three million feathers" (1983: 112).

If affectation and exaggeration were all that there were to camp, then one would not want to strain one's descriptive powers much beyond Dyer's "mincing and screaming" (1992: 135). But there is more to say on the matter of stylistics. Indeed that word is very apposite since camp is chiefly concerned with style:

> [Camp] is one way of seeing the world as an aesthetic phenomenon. That way ... is not in terms of beauty but in terms of the degree of artifice, of stylization ... To emphasize style is to slight content. (Sontag 1983: 106–107)[25]

Camp, then, concerns itself with surface, with frivolity. But the frivolity of camp is not all harmless fun. Camp is drawn to both bad taste and mockery. Christopher Isherwood's "swishy little boy" is a simple example of such bad taste:

> You thought it [viz. camp] a swishy little boy with peroxided hair, dressed in a picture hat and a feather boa, pretending to be Marlene Dietrich? Yes, in queer circles, they call *that* camping. It's all very well in its place, but it's an utterly debased form. (Isherwood 1954: 125; original emphasis)[26]

The remark is made by the character Kennedy, a homosexual doctor. The bad taste of the camp depicted in it is just as much a reflexion of Kennedy's snobbery as the boy's lack of discrimination. But bad taste can also take a more nuanced form, and this is a feature of camp that I bring to Ezekiel 23. It is that delight taken in something because of its poor quality. It is important to be clear here: camp in this case lies not in the object of the delight, but in the process of finding delight in it, and that process involves both an ironic detachment – a sense of superiority over the object – and a real enjoyment of it on its own terms. Sontag announced the "ultimate Camp statement: it's good because it's awful" (1983: 119), and Ross explored the cult of camp bad taste in popular culture (1989: 152–156).[27]

Nor is camp mockery any more principled. It may bite, but it dispenses with the underlying moral purpose of satire; no connoisseur of camp would claim to be driven, like Juvenal, by *indignatio*.[28] Even Dyer feels compelled to balance his claims for camp as an expression of gay solidarity with, rather prim, warnings about its corrosive dangers (1992: 136–137).

8.2.3 The Functions of Camp

This reference to the ambiguities of camp signals an opportune moment to ask what functions camp fulfils. Sontag denies any activist purpose: "Camp sensibility is disengaged, depoliticized – or at least apolitical" (1983: 117).

Yet even as she detaches same-sex desire from camp, she remarks that homosexuals use camp as a "moral solvent" to win acceptance into society; camp "neutralizes moral indignation, sponsors playfulness" (Sontag 1983: 118, n. 52). Esther Newton's camp is more positive and assertive: "by accepting his homosexuality and flaunting it, the camp undercuts all homosexuals who won't accept the stigmatized identity"

(1972: 111). Meyer argues for an intrinsically propagandist agenda: "I define Camp as the total body of performative practices and strategies used to enact a queer identity, with enactment defined as the production of social visibility" (1994: 5).

If Meyer's arguments for a camp's political purpose are less than persuasive, it is legitimate to explore camp's societal functionality, and how this can be exploited as a methodological tool. Meyer is helpful in one aspect of his statement, and that is his emphasis on *performance*. Dangerous though it is to make a general pronouncement on camp, it is nevertheless helpful to assert that camp is typically the performance of the ambiguities of gender, or at least it is one commonly found feature of camp that I wish to bring to my reading of Ezekiel 23.[29] Such performance is often described as parody, and here an important question immediately presents itself: who or what is the object of camp parody? Dyer (1992: 144–145) and, more forcefully, Leo Bersani (1988: 208) argue that it is women who are being parodied: camp is misogynistic.[30]

I shall discuss this crucial topic in the context of a distinction between public and private camp. By private camp I mean those situations where people use camp in their social interaction (and by "people" I am thinking mostly of gay men); this is in contrast to larger-scale public performances, as depicted in print, cinema or television. The telephone conversation described at the beginning of this chapter began as private camp, and although it is now entering a more public sphere, it retains the flavour of its private origins. Most writers on camp concentrate on its public manifestations, and it is rare to catch glimpses of its use in private. Dyer (1992) perhaps is talking mainly about the private sphere, although this is not made clear in his paper. Keith Harvey's article "Camp Talk and Citationality" (2002) purports to comment on the phenomenon, and indeed makes interesting observations about the common stock of cultural references used allusively by gay men in their private camp.[31] However the examples used by Harvey are all from literary sources, and he does not offer any evidence as to their accurate reflection of actual camp talk.

Given this virtual silence about private camp, it may be helpful to offer some tentative suggestions about its use of gender parody. The notion that gay men's camp is a means of promoting community identity has long been problematized. Cleto, for example, notes two opposing perceptions of pre-Stonewall camp:[32] on the one hand, it has been viewed as a flaunting of sexual dissidence, a means of defiantly, even stridently, declaring otherness – Quentin Crisp's autobiography (1985) can serve as a splendid example; on the other hand, it has been characterized as a means of discreetly communicating coded signals about one's desires. Cleto attempts to resolve this apparent contradiction by the use of the phrase "flaunting the closet": "the community-building survivalist dealing with the *signs* of a stigmatized (homosexual) identity" (1999: 90). Perhaps, rather, we should think of the process as *selective flaunting*, where one does indeed declare one's desires, but only to those "in the know", and where there is a frisson enjoyed in risking public hints about a forbidden secret – one recalls Sontag's remarks about "gestures full of duplicity, with a witty meaning for cognoscenti and another, more impersonal, for outsiders" (Sontag 1983: 110).

Post-Stonewall gay men's camp, however, can hardly act in this way: with the emergence of crossover camp, and a greater public awareness of gay behaviour, camp can no longer operate as a secret code. Yet it can still perform the rôle of acknowledging shared experience. The means whereby it does this is by performing femininity. Camp's representation of the feminine has attracted much attention. Indeed Bersani's comment that "[g]ay male camp is ... *largely* a parody of women" (1988: 208, emphasis added) would not raise many eyebrows. This parody has been both criticized as misogynistic and commended for its subversiveness. Bersani himself manages to combine blame and praise:

> The gay male parody of a certain femininity ... is both a way of giving vent to the hostility toward women that probably afflicts every male ... *and* could also paradoxically be thought of as helping to deconstruct that image for women themselves. (Bersani 1988: 208; original emphasis)

The "certain femininity", Bersani goes on to say, is of a type "glamorized by movie stars" and is revealed by the parodist as "mindless, asexual and hysterically bitchy" (1988: 208). While there may be a measure of truth in this interpretation, there is more to be said about such parody, especially in relation to private camp. For the two gay men whose telephone conversation prompted this discussion, and perhaps for many others, the central concern is not femininity *per se*. The parody of femininity is a means of negotiating their problematized masculinity, and this is where camp can be seen as very queer indeed. Queer theory insists that gender is performativity, a process fabricated and sustained by constant repetition. Most people, no doubt, put on a poor show. Gay men, however, even when they perform satisfactorily in speech, body language and other behaviours, will still always fail spectacularly because they break the taboo against same-sex desire. They find it harder than other men to avoid the label of femininity. Camp may act as a means of expressing this breakdown; gay performances of femininity can be used in a number of ways: as a way of sharing the experience of failure, for instance, as witty blame deflection or as defiance. And it is easy to spot failures around you, since performance breakdown is not a *rara avis*; masculinity, after all, is generally precarious. In 1972 Newton described a kind of drag[33] whose method "is to mix sex-role referents within the visible sartorial system": "This generally involves some 'outside' item from the feminine sartorial system such as earrings, lipstick, high-heeled shoes, a necklace, etc., worn with masculine clothing" (1972: 101). Although some of these feminine items are less unexpected thirty or forty years on when worn with men's clothing, nevertheless Newton's conclusion is worth bearing in mind:

> Even one feminine item ruins the integrity of the masculine system; the male loses his caste honor. The superordinate role in a hierarchy is more fragile than the subordinate. Manhood must be achieved, and once achieved, guarded and protected. (Newton 1972: 101, n. 3)

The thought of this fragility is something to take to the text of Ezekiel 23. Such concerns with masculinity may explain the ambivalence of camp's attitudes to femininity. The exaggeration with which the parody of femininity is performed has led to the conclusion that it is an attack on women generally. Whether the undermining of the feminine target is deliberate or simply an unintended side effect is very difficult to decide. Bersani (1988) and Sontag (1983a: 339) have argued that the parody has had a healthy result in that it has not targeted women in general, but has attempted to subvert a specific stereotype. But even if it is assumed that an element of malice can be detected in at least some camp parody, it also has to be recognized that there also exists a devotion to the icon of femininity, so that malice and love are often found together – one may echo Bersani and call it a "loving assassination" (1988: 208). The origins of this ambiguity of feeling towards femininity may very well lie in a complex of psycho-social factors outside the scope of my present enquiry, but I should put in a plea for them to be viewed against the background of troubled masculinity: for the developing homosexual consciousness, femininity may represent both an attractive escape from the demands of masculinity, and that which masculinity tells him to avoid at all costs.[34] Camp's ambiguous attitudes towards femininity, then, can be seen as an expression of a conflict caused by troubled masculinity. This ambiguity is something else that I should like to bring to Ezekiel 23.

But what sort of femininity? Would someone listening in to our telephone conversation have considered it feminine? Or perhaps effeminate? It may be helpful to recall at this point two different strands of camp. One is that of dandyism, the other is that fascination with, as Bersani puts it, "a type of femininity glamorized by movie stars" (1988: 208). I noted how Isherwood antithesized these two strands, by contrasting the camp that is "the whole emotional basis of Ballet, for example ..." with that of the "swishy little boy ... pretending to be Marlene Dietrich" (1954: 125). This binary, however, what one might characterize as a contrast between "high" and "low" camp is not as stable as Isherwood's words would suggest. I have already argued, for instance, that in the nineteenth century high camp was a parody of dominant bourgeois values, using the discourse of a declining aristocracy (Ross 1989: 147), but its exponents were not necessarily aristocratic themselves. Mark Booth says bluntly that "camp people have mostly been *arrivistes*" (1983: 83), and one of high camp's distinguishing features is that it maintains an air of superiority that is all too obviously contrived. From the point of view of social class, high camp is not that high. One might be tempted into making a geohistorical distinction: that high camp is something British of the nineteenth and early twentieth centuries, and low camp something to be found in the United States from the 1950s. The situation, however, is more complex than that; for instance, I have already noted how Ross talks of camp in the USA as an intellectual stratagem of revolt in the 1960s against traditional strongholds of cultural taste (1989: 147); this could be regarded as one adaptation in mid-twentieth century America of nineteenth century British high camp. If there is anything to distinguish high camp from low, it is that in accordance with its historical roots, high camp has a predilection for the effeminate rather than the feminine, its mannerisms more clearly a revolt from masculinity rather than a positive attraction towards femininity. In the following application of camp, I expect to jumble together high camp pretensions with low camp positive empathy with the feminine.

8.3 A Camp Application

8.3.1 Introduction
In the previous section I have attempted to highlight camp's hybrid, elusive origins, and its constantly changing networks of relationships. Like queer, it touches upon male/female, masculine/feminine, straight/

gay, private/public, complicit/subversive, serious/fun, bitter/benign. As though to demonstrate the aridity of binaries, camp both overrides and comprises them all. Perhaps it is this versatility (as well as its capacity for fun) that makes it the perfect weapon to apply to a set of texts that at first sight are far away from its accustomed stalking ground. As it happens, I am not entirely alone in choosing this perfect weapon: Stuart promotes camp "as a performance designed to subvert dominant readings and understandings" (2000: 28). She too sets her use of camp in the context of reader-response criticism and queer theory.[35] Moreover she aims to subvert an offensive text by mocking it.[36] Yet her view of camp is very different to mine. Over half of her brief paper is devoted to a discussion of the place of humour in Christian history and theology.[37] And she rules out of play less pleasant humour: "jokes against queers"; "humor directed against various groups within the queer community by other queers"; humour used "to ridicule the victims of social systems" (2000: 27). Camp based on such a benign view may possibly "disturb, disorder, and transform the straight church" (2000: 21), but it bears little resemblance to what I understand by camp, which for me is as vicious as it is loving and as complicit as it is fun. To take the example of her chosen biblical text, she maps the history of her own reception of Eph. 5:21–33: she was brought up to "read this text as a magnificent theology of marriage ..."; she moved on to "react to this text tragically as a heteropatriarchal and colonial manifesto for the ordering of male/female relationships"; and her "bodily" reactions "to hearing it read (often at weddings) were to wince or churn with anger but never with laughter" (2000: 32). She was persuaded to another reading by an unpublished paper by Loughlin who remarked that:

> [I]nsofar as women are members of the body, they too are called to be Christ to others; so that they too must also act as "groom"; and "husband"; to the "bride" and "wife" of the other, whether it be an actual man or woman. (quoted in Stuart 2000: 32)

Loughlin's reading of the text, with its subversion of heteronormativity certainly amounts to a queering of the text. And one can understand how a familiarity with his reading provokes laughter at the thought of this particular text's frequent recitation at weddings. But can this laughter be called camp? Without wishing to claim a monopoly for my understanding of camp, I miss in Stuart's understanding of camp those elements of performance, extravagance and complicity that makes it for me such an effective means of evoking new meanings from texts. This is not to say that I am dismissing the use of humour as an methodological approach to biblical texts. It can offer a means of seeing the Bible from a fresh vantage point, of defamiliarizing over-familiar texts.[38]

Stuart's ideas about camp have been taken up by Mona West for her chapter on Esther in *The Queer Bible Commentary*. Her concept of camp is perhaps more persuasive:

> Camp, drag and queer theory all use performativity to critique dominant conventions in a society or to sabotage binarisms such as male/female which are used to maintain a certain social order. (West 2006: 279)

Tactics used by camp, she continues, include "parody, exaggeration, boundary-crossing, occupying spaces, and miming privileges of normality" (2006: 279). She then offers examples of such features in the text of Esther; for instance, the exaggeration with which the various banqueting scenes are depicted. Her examples, however, do not quite carry conviction: exaggeration in itself does not automatically signal camp, and there may have to be a certain value-added ingredient in the commentator's presentation to help the reader see the point. The commentator has to perform to recreate the camp moment.

Roland Boer's chapter on Chronicles, also in *The Queer Bible Commentary* (2006), is more successful. He presents a concept of camp as a hermeneutic tool, a concept based in part on the utopian theory of Ernest Bloch:

> [C]amp is not merely an aspect of the interpretation of cultural products, a predilection for film and its stars, fashion and music, that is aesthetic rather than political. Rather, camp forward to a very different world – utopia if you like. (Boer 2006: 262)

It seems to me that the effectiveness of Boer's subsequent discussion of Chronicles lies not so much in his choice of examples but in the way that he transforms their impact upon the reader by the exuberance and the sense of wicked fun with which he presents them to us. And his conclusion resonates with my own belief about the hermeneutical possibility of camp:

> I don't want to suggest that camp detoxifies the misogyny of Chronicles ... [A] camp reading of Chronicles faces the negative – here the unremitting misogyny of the text – not in order to seek a dialectical resolution, nor to seek the redeeming elements that we can then appropriate for ourselves ... Rather, I have opened up the text in order to let it run away in different directions ... For it seems to me that the

cultic gravity and over-the-top masculinity of the text gives out to the playful overindulgence of camp. (Boer 2006: 267)

One lesson I draw from the previous sections is that to attempt my own definition of camp, at this point where it might be most expected, would be a fruitless exercise. Camp is too elusive and too polyvalent to be trapped in a sentence or two. It is tempting to leave further analysis aside and to make an immediate attempt to answer my original question of why two gay men should discover camp in Ezek. 23:11–21. Before giving way to such temptation, however, it may be helpful to make some preliminary remarks about such a reading.

8.3.2 'Reading' Ezekiel

There is an ambiguity about the word *reading* in the previous paragraph. In a literary context it could mean "interpretation". In one sense that meaning is apposite here. I am indeed going to discover a particular way of understanding Ezekiel. But "reading" also echoes the fact that my understanding stems from a specific occasion when an extract from Ezekiel was read aloud by one person to another. This is important because it recalls a recurring theme in what I have said about camp: it involves a performance, in one way or another, and my reading the text aloud was an example of a performance (there are other levels of performance in Ezekiel 23, which I shall discuss in due course).

A clearer understanding of the flavour of this performance may be gained by imagining the text declaimed by the late Kenneth Williams, not perhaps the Williams of the Julian and Sandy sketches from the 1960s *Round the Horne* radio comedy series, but the later Williams of chat shows and parlour games,[39] whose rather nasal actorly hauteur and cultural pretensions overlie petit-bourgeois London speech sounds. The delivery should be imagined as slow, serious and heavily committed to the text, and slyly shocked and emphatic at key points of outrage (for example on the repetitions of the words lust, whore and their compounds, and at verses 14–15 and 20). Why Kenneth Williams? Any conversation about camp, in a British context at any rate,[40] will, sooner or later, bring up his name. It is true that his considerable fame as a comic actor depended to a large extent upon the culturally meagre, if prolific, *Carry On* films, and perhaps, to a lesser extent, to his contributions to *Round the Horne*. But the ambiguities of his life and personality, well illustrated in his diaries and letters,[41] and the continuing interest in him over twenty years after his death,[42] make him a camp icon that is eminently fitted to my purposes. Williams, it should be added, was not only a supreme example of camp, but also a conscious fan: "Camp is a great *jewel*, 22 carats", he said in an interview.[43]

But how to tackle the text? Rather than proceed through it line by line, I shall pick out some broad themes suggested by a camp reading. These reflections will not entirely ignore past scholarship, but I shall at times cross-check them against what has been said by others. If what is said contradicts previous scholarly opinion, it is not intended as a systematic rebuttal of past scholarship, but as a reporting of personal impressions.

Notes

1. I am not the first to use camp in a theological setting; Stuart, for instance, has done so (2000), though, as I shall argue, in a very different way.
2. The initial capitalization of camp is employed by Sontag perhaps as a linguistic device to distinguish it from other meanings; Meyer's use of it (1994) seems to reflect the deeper significance he ascribes to the word.
3. The collection also offers an excellent 1000-item chronological bibliography (though one cannot help feeling that criteria for entry are generously elasticated).
4. The take-up of camp themes, often in a non-homosexual setting, in, for example, commercial popular music, cinema and television.
5. "Notes on Camp" first appeared in *Partisan Review*.
6. The title is part of a description of Noël Coward in Core's *Camp: The Lie That Tells the Truth* (Core 1984: 58).
7. Her other two sensibilities are high culture, based on morality, and avant-garde art, based on extreme sense of feeling (Sontag 1983: 115).
8. The readings edited by Cleto (1999), with their editorial introduction and comments, go some way to collect the raw material from which such a historical analysis of camp might be composed.
9. See above, p. 157.
10. This is the phenomenon of crossover camp (see note 4, above).
11. The actor is Kenneth Williams; for the part he plays in the next chapter, see Section 8.3.2.
12. This is the first incontrovertible published mention of camp. An earlier reference to camp can perhaps be demonstrated in a letter of 1869 from Frederick Park (*aka* Fanny) to his fellow experimenter in transvestism, Lord Arthur Clinton, "My campish undertakings are not at present meeting with the success they deserve. Whatever I do seems to get me into hot water somewhere" (quoted in Cleto 1999: 182).
13. I use *homosexuality* in this particular instance rather than an arguably more neutral term such as *same-sex desire*, on the grounds that the word shares a period flavour with Ware's dictionary.
14. It is interesting to note that the *Concise Oxford Dictionary* (10th edn, 1999) defines camp as "(of a man) ostentatiously and extravagantly effeminate";

there is no mention of homosexuality, not to mention various female versions of camp.

15. The four "iconic moments" with which Ross begins his essay (1989: 135–136) range in date from 1961 to 1969.
16. Their "iconic moment" was undoubtedly the Stonewall riots of 1969; the resistance to police riots on gay bars, and its effect upon the gay liberationist struggle is discussed by, amongst many others, Shilts (1999: 41–42), Weeks (1990: 188–189) and D'Emilio (1990: 466–468).
17. Dyer's article *It's Being So Camp As Keeps Us Going* was originally published in 1976 in the popular magazine *Playguy*. It bubbles with the ideas of an enthusiastic activist on the cusp of an optimistically liberationist wave. Dyer pays tribute to Sontag ("a marvellous essay on camp"), but it is significant that her "homosexual" has become "gay"; indeed the word homosexual appears only once in his article, and that in a footnote as part of the name of the organization The Campaign for Homosexual Equality (Dyer 1992: 146).
18. Like Dyer, Babuscio always uses the word gay – the five exceptions are in direct quotations of other authors.
19. I discuss high and low camp below.
20. I examine my own binary of public/private camp in the light of this objection in due course.
21. Sinfield (1994, especially pp 25–51).
22. This interpretation of manliness and effeminacy leaves unexplained the status of the rake's minion, who resembled a woman in that he performed the inferior rôle (it was often the case, as Sinfield pointed out, that he was inferior also in age, occupation or social status). Whether he was regarded as effeminate is not clear. This ambiguity is alluded to by Sinfield but not analysed. It may be accounted for as an example of masculinist narrative focus. The story is told, both in literary form and in life itself, entirely from the point of view of the man; the point of view of the mistress or of the minion (who by playing the rôle of a woman shares her invisibility) is of no importance. Whether or not the minion is effeminate is deemed to be of no interest to the reader or onlooker.
23. Cohen (1993) analysed the process whereby the press coverage of the trials synonymized Wilde and homosexuality. If Wilde embodied homosexuality, then Wilde's pre-trial public persona was drawn into the equation. And this is where at last the link with effeminacy becomes clear: "Wilde had adopted the manners and appearance of an effeminate aesthete in 1877; since 1882 he had presented himself as an effeminate dandy" (Sinfield 1994: 2).
24. On the one hand, camp for her is a perception, a way of seeing (a way of seeing Art Nouveau, for instance); on the other, there can be a camp object, deliberately created as such; Sontag offers the plays of Noël Coward as one example amongst a number. This form of camping (her verb), is in her view usually less successful because it lacks "failed seriousness", a quality born of naivety on the part of the creator.
25. The priorization of style over content is a recurring theme in Sontag (and most other writers on camp), for instance "Camp is the consistently aesthetic experience of the world. It incarnates a victory of 'style' over 'content'" (1983: 115), and succinctly, "Style is everything" (1983: 115).

26. Isherwood's comparison between the vulgarity of the boy and his claims for camp as "the whole emotional basis of the Ballet, for example, and of course of Baroque art" (1954: 125) highlight a tension between what one might call low and high camp, and may be the result of the encounter already described between camp's aristocratic roots and arriviste adaptations. Indeed Dyer makes a similar contrast in his juxtaposing the "mincing and screaming" mentioned earlier to "a certain taste in art and entertainment, a certain sensibility" (1992: 135).

27. This element of camp is perhaps the forerunner of what is often now popularly thought of as post-modern irony.

28. Juvenal *Satires*, I.79.

29. Compare Booth's description of camp as "an exhibition of stylised effeminacy" (1983: 18).

30. This is a continuing concern; see, for instance, Flinn (1999: 433–457).

31. Although the facility for quoting from a shared body of favoured cultural sources may well reflect what actually happens in private camp, one may observe that this is quite the opposite of what took place in the telephone conversation reported at the beginning of this chapter, in which a performance was created out of a text not hitherto remotely connected with camp.

32. For Stonewall, see note 16 above.

33. It should be stressed, however, that drag and camp, though overlapping, are not synonymous. Newton herself attempts to disentangle the two (1972: 101).

34. Masculinity in its turn may arouse similarly ambiguous feelings: both a threat and an object of desire.

35. She calls the result "queer-response criticism" (2000: 29–33).

36. Her chosen text is Eph. 5:21–33.

37. Indeed to judge from the subtitle of her paper ("Humor as a Hermeneutical Tool ..."), she seems to believe that humour is camp's chief ingredient.

38. One effective defamiliarizing exercise was offered by the recently published set of "virtual" letters from biblical characters (Davies 2004).

39. Illustrated, for example, by Williams (1997).

40. It may be noted, however, that many of the works about or by Williams, cited in the bibliography, appear in the United States and/or German versions of the online bookseller *Amazon*. Williams's appeal, then, may not be confined to the United Kingdom.

41. Williams (1994 and 1995).

42. A number of works, both by and about Williams, remain in print, including Williams (1994, 1995, 1997), and a new biography has appeared (Stevens 2010). A BBC Four *Kenneth Williams Night* on 13 March 2006 featured *Fantabulosa*, a drama based on his diaries, which, according to the web site *Stop Messin' About* "became the most-watched programme in the history of BBC Four ... netting nearly 1 million viewers" (http://www.stopmessinabout. co.uk/; viewed on 28/03/2006); a spin-off DVD is still available (2010).

43. Quoted by Cleto (1999:1; emphasis original, unsurprisingly).

Chapter 9

Queering Ezekiel, Part 2

It is natural that figures of speech that had the remotest connection with sex would be used most cautiously of God. (Holbrook 1984: 168)

9.1 Strange Flesh[1]

I shall begin by focusing on a particular verse, with the intention of extending the discussion from the particular to the general. It was verse 20 that produced the sharpest effect in our camp telephone performance of Ezek. 23:11–21:

> … and lusted after her paramours there [i.e. in Egypt], whose members were like those of donkeys, and whose emission was that like that of stallions. (NRSV)

I shall look first at the camp effects of the vocabulary used, then the semantic resonances and thirdly the context.

9.2 Dirty Words?

Well no, these words are not "dirty", to the extent that the words "members" and "emission" are not coarse in themselves. If by chance I had used the NEB, the effect would have been racier:

> … she was infatuated with their male prostitutes, whose members were like those of asses, and whose seed came in floods like those of horses. (NEB)

Male prostitutes and floods! The AV, on the other hand, retains the MT's repetitions and vocabulary:

> For she doted upon their paramours, whose flesh is as the flesh of asses, and whose issue is like the issue of horses.

If it were not for the words "donkeys" and "stallions" (and I shall return to those shortly), the tone of the NRSV's vocabulary might be thought of as seemly restraint, with its combination of the old-fashioned "paramours" and the neutral terms "members" and "emission". The meaning of the verse, if not well hidden, is at least decently clothed, and this image may remind us of remarks made by Brenner (1996; especially pages 78–82). She examines the vocabulary employed for "human erogenous zones" in biblical Hebrew, and makes an interesting comment:

> Biblical references to human erogenous zones ... are in general euphemistic. But over and above that (Jer. 5:8 and Ezek. 23:20 notwithstanding), the culture reflected in the Bible protects the penis and its physical environs with vigour ... This is surprising, because the society that created biblical literature is a phallic, phallocentric society. (Brenner 1996: 79–80)

I do not share Brenner's surprise: it is almost a psychoanalytical cliché to say that in a "phallocentric society" the phallus is concealed;[2] it is truer to say that actual penises must remain hidden, because it cannot be hoped that they can match up to the imagined promise of the phallus, the symbol of masculine power. Whatever the case, we can agree with Brenner that the penis rarely makes an appearance in the Hebrew Bible; where I am less in agreement with her is in her unequivocal exception of Jer. 5:8 and Ezek. 23:20. In Jer. 5:8 the penis hides behind expressions of male lust; but Brenner would be more surprised by my observation that in one sense Ezek. 23:20 confirms the notion of the hidden phallus: if the *sentiment* is blatant, the *names* given to the bodily parts and functions in this verse are as decently clad as the priest who obeys the rubric of Lev. 6:10.

The task I have set myself entails that I confine my remarks to a contemporary experience of reading Ezekiel. But it is still interesting to speculate the extent to which in Ezek. 23:20 the penis was hidden from a seventeenth-century reader of the AV. Was the meaning of the word "flesh" as clear as "member"? Certainly the word in this sense did not seem to enter the English vocabulary; according to the *Oxford English Dictionary*, the nearest the word flesh reached to a sexual meaning was the one at the head of section 9.1,[3] whereas other Biblical applications of the term (to blood relationship, for instance, or simply to people) did become established in English. And the meaning of the word "issue" may also have taken some time to be appreciated by the early readers of the AV. As for the Hebrew of the MT, it may well be that the originals of member and emission were just as decently clad as their English translations; the arguments to support this statement are set out in Excursus 1.

9.3 Monstrous Meanings

Clothing, of course, however apparently modest, can sometimes serve to emphasize what lies beneath, and it is my argument that there is in this verse a marked contrast between restrained vocabulary and outrageous meaning. This feature alone would produce at best an effect of archness, at worst, one of hypocrisy. Hypocrisy indeed would make the verse a candidate for camp scrutiny. What helps to ensure a successful candidature, however, is the presence of two seemingly innocent words: donkeys and stallions. The expression of penile size and seminal profusion in terms of quadrupeds seems oddly familiar, and not just to gay men. To enter the phrases "dick like a donkey" or "hung like a horse" into a Web search engine[4] will produce ample evidence that these animals are still appealed to as proverbial models of penile superabundance, and some experiment with the word "stallions" (particularly in combination with words to denote race) will demonstrate that they symbolize male virility. Moreover an interest in penile size, while by no means a monopoly of a gay male milieu, is frequently found there. At this point I should like to introduce a modern text to set against Ezekiel 23, and I have chosen for the purpose the monthly magazine *Gay Times*. It contains a regular section of "Escorts & Masseurs"; for edition No. 305 (February 2004, pp. 196–201), there are 123 advertisements, from whose details the most casual reader will infer that the services on offer are more intimate than suggested by the section title (indeed, one does not seem too far away from the sort of activity that the NEB thought was conveyed by the disputed word פִּלַגְשֵׁיהֶם in Ezek. 23:20). Twenty-nine of the advertisements make textual reference to penile size. In other words, more than 22% of the advertisers thought that they would attract custom more effectively by making this a feature of their self-description (the figure would be even higher if we added in those five or so advertisers whose photographs seemed to emphasize generously-proportioned genitals without any corresponding textual claims).

Although animal references are absent, the advertisers' language recalls that of Ezekiel. They manage to achieve semantic clarity without explicitness of vocabulary: large penises that we know they claim remain concealed. A favourite device is the abbreviation WE (well-endowed or well-equipped, with its own comparatives and superlatives – VWE,

XVWE and XXVWE). There are several reference to "equipment"; e.g. "Sexy Andrew" boasts "stunning, thick equipment". In two cases, size has crept into the *nom de plume* (BRUNO XVWE and HUNG HUGE), so that the advertiser is defined by his penile size. In both Ezek. 23:20 and this section from *Gay Times*, the penis remains unmentioned specifically, but we are left in no doubt of its underlying presence, and its use – the bigger the better – as a means of sexual allure.

So far I have said little about Ezek. 23:20b. For me it is a highly suggestive verse, and in discussing it I shall have to repair one important omission in my remarks on penile size. I have argued that a camp view of verse 20a finds an excitatory intention in the reference to penile size. What I have not done is to compare such a finding to the traditional interpretation or to that of feminist commentators. I hope that such a comparison will be possible in the discussion of verse 20b, that it will help to clarify what I see as a camp position, and that it will pave the way to a broader discussion of verses 11–21.

Where they discuss verse 20b at all, non-feminist commentators assume that the intention of the verse is to emphasize the lustfulness of the Egyptians. Greenberg is typical:

> The oversize genitals of Egyptians figure as well in 16:26 (evidently a commonplace), expressing a popular notion of their lewdness, and are here compared in size and seminal discharge to those of equines, proverbially lascivious. (Greenberg 1997: 480)

But why is it necessary to stress the lasciviousness of the *Egyptians*? Surely it is *Oholibah's* lasciviousness that is under discussion, unless it is assumed that the details about the Egyptians, "evidently a commonplace", are added simply to underline the general tone of immorality? A gay male camp reading would understand that the reference to ejaculation, like that to large penises, emphasizes not the desires of the Egyptians, but those of Oholibah: she is depicted as sexually attracted to their large penises and copious ejaculation. My comparison with gay advertisements demonstrates that penile size can be sexually alluring, but what of ejaculation?

Claims of ejaculatory prowess are absent in the advertisements examined above, but that this is due more to such other factors as editorial policy rather than to their lack of sexual appeal will borne out by another look at the Web. Despite nearly two decades of warnings about the medical dangers lurking in semen, its (profuse) production is regularly invoked as alluring. The phrase "cum shots" typed in a Google search will find well over a million results (alternatively the word "cumshots" will find over seven million[5]). But here a warning note must be sounded, which will not only fulfil the promise made earlier to compare traditional non-feminist interpretations of Ezek. 23:20 with feminist and camp counterparts, but will also shed a clearer light on my previous remarks on penile size. It is not my intention to offer a detailed critique of Internet pornography, but some important distinctions must be made. The addition of the word "gay" to the Google search on "cum shots" found just over 700,000 results (out of the original million); and a similar addition to the word "cumshots" found nearly two million results (out of the original seven million). Even if allowance is made for the fact that not all online depictions of ejaculation aimed at a male same-sex market will mention the word gay, it is still clear that a considerable proportion of the original results are aimed at a heterosexual market (in the case of the word "cumshot", indeed, the ratio of cross-sex to same-sex is 2:1). If the consumers of heterosexual pornography are assumed to be mainly men, then the inclusion of ejaculation scenes may present a puzzle, until a mere glance at some of them will reveal their purpose: in heterosexual pornography, ejaculation symbolizes the display of virility, all too often indeed that of power over, and, in many cases, humiliation of, the female sexual partner. Ejaculation is excitatory not *per se*, but for what it symbolizes. It is this abusive aspect of pornography that has been the object of feminist attack for the last 30 years, and justifiably so; and it is the perception that it is present in Ezekiel 23 (and, of course, in the other prophetic passages that I have been discussing) that has attracted the feminist label of pornoprophetics.

While not denying the force of this analysis (for, after all, the situation in Ezekiel 23 is supposedly cross-sex), a gay male camp point of view may see things slightly differently. In male same-sex pornography, the symbolism of dominance is sometimes found as in heterosexual pornography, but just as often (in the depiction of solo masturbation scenes, for instance), ejaculation is portrayed as arousing in itself, a symbol not of power but of pleasure.

A piece of corroborative evidence can be found in a letter in the *Gay Times* agony column "Ask Jack" (No. 306, March 2004, p. 100); there the writer asks, "How can I increase the amount of semen I produce?". The reply includes the reassurance that "we've all seen porn stars shoot gallons [of semen], but … this is often 'stunt cum' made from strained chicken soup, and ejected from a pump container attached to his cock." This curious insight into the technicalities of pornographic film-making demonstrates that ejaculatory prowess, or at least a pretence of it, seems to be a *sine qua non* of a porn star's skills; it is in itself an excitatory phenomenon. The ejaculatory process is emphasized as an intrinsic part of the actor's appeal, not as a means of humiliating his partner.[6]

This brief return visit to the Web, then, has highlighted the resonances involved when I argue that, from a gay male point of view, Ezek. 23:20 reads as a depiction of penile size and ejaculatory profusion in terms of sexual allure.

9.4 Drastic Metaphor[7]: Big Dicks in the Bible?

But just because two gay men have found in Ezek. 23:20 a portrayal of sexual arousal, does this make it camp? I have already argued that there is something camp in the contrast between the vocabulary and the meaning; I described the effect of this contrast as arch or even hypocritical. But it may be better to apply the Sontagian label of failed seriousness to this effect. The language aims at seriousness though it dithers between the poetic sonority of "paramours" and the similes, and the prosaic neutrality of "members" and "emission"; but it is cut down in its flight by its own outrageous meaning.

Another obvious feature, unmentioned so far, makes the verse even more appealing to camp taste. Interpretative mechanisms to explain the use of exaggeration are familiar to the reader of the Hebrew Bible. Methuselah and his fellow super-ancients, for instance, present few problems. So the rhetoric that compares Egyptian penises and ejaculation to those of quadrupeds will unnerve no one except the most literal biblical interpreter. But exaggeration lies at the heart of camp practice. As I have already pointed out, it appeared in Ware's 1909 definition of camp: "Actions and gestures of an exaggerated emphasis" (1909: 61), and takes a bow in most of the succeeding literature on camp; Sontag, for instance, in a phrase that could have been written for this verse in Ezekiel, talks of camp "relish for the *exaggeration of personal characteristics* and personality mannerisms" (1983: 109; emphasis added). And camp talk, no less than actions, gestures, characteristics and mannerisms, is prone to hyperbole. Consider the well-worn gay witticism: "My dear, without us there would be no Theatre, no Church of England, and Harrods would be self-service".[8] Camp delights in saying that something is Huge, Enooormous, and so on when both the speaker and the listener know that such is not *quite* the case.

But the most telling reason why this verse appeals to camp taste is its contextual outrageousness. Large penises and superabundant ejaculation are not what one expects to find in the Bible, unless perhaps one is a scholar of the ancient Near East. They are not only splendidly exaggerated, they are also a magnificent example of incongruity, another staple ingredient of camp. Of course, they do not exactly match the classic expression of incongruity in camp, that is, the parade of feminine characteristics in a man, but the contrast of opposites is as shocking: classic camp confronts the onlooker with woman in a man, Ezekiel with gross profanity in a sacred text, though, as I hope to show, a man/woman ambiguity is embedded in Ezekiel too.

9.5 Broadening Out

Before turning to verses 11–21 as a whole, I shall attempt to take stock of my observations so far. By now it should be apparent that the traditional interpreter of Ezekiel – let me call him Walter, since he usually is masculine – no longer has sole control over the text: a doughty campaign against his autocracy has been waged for some time by a feminist insurgent – let me call her Erika, since she is nearly always a woman. And I have had the pleasure of introducing to you a newcomer – let me call him Evelyn, since in this case he is a man, though not necessarily masculine. How do Walter, Erika and Evelyn differ in their interpretation of Ezek. 23:11–21?

There are two distinctive features of Walter's interpretative stance that are problematized by Erika and Evelyn. First, Walter subscribes to the world of the narrator; he may distrust the present state of the *text*, but he knows that somewhere within it he can discover the genuine words of the narrator, and can (re)discover the original, authentic meaning. Second, he prioritizes the tenor of the metaphor over the vehicle. By this I mean that he concentrates on the religio-historical situation of the ancient Israelites, and in consequence fails to recognize the reflexive nature of metaphor for the reader: that is, to take the example of the present metaphor, if you say that Israel is the adulterous wife of Yhwh, you not only say something about the historical relationship between Israel and Yhwh, but also are ensuring that what you say about the divine-human relationship leaves its mark on the reader's subsequent perception of male-female human relationships in general. Indeed it is difficult to decide whether it is this general vehicular indifference of Walter or his embarrassment about the details in this particular example that is the more responsible for the capriciousness with which chapter 23 has been dealt with by Walter and his colleagues.

The Babylonian Talmud sets the pace: Zimmerli says of two references in Berakoth that 'what here [i.e. Ezekiel 23] denotes the coarse sensuality of the Egyptians is expanded in *b.Berakoth* 25b and 58a to all non-Jews' (1979: 487). In fact 'coarse sensuality' is not the point of either passage. Rather, what they discuss is whether the comparison with asses implies that the Egyptians are less than fully human, though Zimmerli is right, in the case of 25b at least, to say that the debate is extended to all non-Israelites. The point is that all sexual details are ignored, just as they are in the third Talmudic reference to the verse: in *b.'Arakin 19b* the reference to asses is used for, in Zimmerli's words, 'a peculiar process of reckoning in affirming a vow' (1979: 487)! Modern commentators are less wayward than their early predecessors, but they still exhibit a tendency to shy away from the sexual details of verse 20. W. F. Lofthouse may serve as a type. 'The flesh of asses' prompts the comment: 'Ezekiel here uses proverbial phrases to express his contemptuous loathing' (1913: 196); sex disappears into folklore. Even Zimmerli and Greenberg, commendably frank about the details, turn their discussion to other concerns, in Zimmerli's case into the question 'how far ... we are to find any evaluation of national character' (1979: 487), and in Greenberg's that of popular proverbs (1997: 480).

If Walter trusts the narrator and prioritizes the tenor, Erika does the opposite. She points to the danger of a metaphorical vehicle that not only reinscribes the male-female power hierarchy but that also promotes violence against women, and that does so in pornographic terms. In her view the narrator serves to give divine sanction to such attitudes. She has little interest in the historical context; her concern is the effect of the text on the readers of her own time. Greenberg, in a succinct account of 'The Feminist Critique of Ezekiel 23', declares that 'Van Dijk-Hemmes would presumably not be consoled by evidence that the women of Ezekiel's audience were persuaded by his rhetoric and identified with his pillorying of the wanton sisters' (1997: 494). He is quite right, and not only because no such evidence is forthcoming (who would bother to ask them anyway?).

But what of Evelyn? His position is much more ambiguous than Erika's. He shares her predilection for a reader-response approach to the text; in his case he enjoys features in the text that recall those of twentieth- and early twenty-first century camp. And the word enjoyment is significant here, because unlike Erika, he does not condemn the text. Although like her he concentrates on the vehicle of the metaphor, this is because he is uninterested in deeper meanings, in what others see as serious. He revels in the lurid details of the metaphor, and pretends rather than feels outrage. Like Erika, he distrusts the narrator, but it is a distrust that expresses itself in poking fun, and at seeing in the narrator the rather tawdry desires and attitudes that are common to all human beings.

I must eventually discuss whether there is anything valuable for biblical hermeneutics in this pricking of pretensions, but first I shall return to the reading of verses 11–21.

In discussing verse 20, I noted the incongruity of encountering such a verse in the Bible. Although it is conspicuously outrageous, it does not sit uncomfortably in the section as a whole, where the overheated desire of Oholibah is explored in graphic detail. But the incongruity is made all the sharper when the reader begins to wonder who the narrator is, the narrator, that is, who insists on reminding the reader of himself: he relates that he witnessed Oholibah's defilement (verse 13); that he turned from her in disgust; and it is the narrator who breaks off his narration in order to address Oholibah direct in verse 21. Imagine the surprise when, trespassing a little outside this text, the narrator of these outrageous statements turns out to be not a human prophet, but God himself (e.g. verses 1 and 22).

9.6 First Performance: Sex Addicted

The text of verses 11–21 is no mere static list of rude words, nor even just a story. The writer has presented here a performance, and camp is well-qualified to aid an appreciation of this. For performance is at the heart of camp, from Isherwood's 'swishy little boy … pretending to be Marlene Dietrich' (Isherwood 1954: 125) to, say, the Batman television series of the 1960s (see Torres 1999); and one can very well understand Babuscio's claim for 'theatricality' to be considered one of the staple ingredients of camp.

I hope to use the telephone narration of verses 11–21, itself a performance, as a means of eliciting from the text those elements of performance that most excite the camp gaze: the interlocking features of flamboyance and exaggeration, artificiality and artifice, and the relationship between performer and performed.

Performance involves pretence. In the formal situation of a theatrical or filmed performance, the pretence is conventionalized as rôle; but in an informal situation, it may go undetected by onlookers or even by its practitioner. I should like to begin this exploration of performance by invoking the aid of the telephone conversation and with another intertextual reading of my travelling companion *Gay Times* in order to discover in the text a particular sort of pretence – its delightful hypocrisy. To the aficionado of camp, hypocrisy is always a pleasure, but especially so when its practitioner is unconscious of the crime, but to link those two words *delightful* and *hypocrisy* reveals the chasm between Evelyn and his predecessors.

Something else that delights the aficionado of camp is, as I have already pointed out, the detailed description of Oholibah's sexual career. But apart from the obvious attractions of the overheated language, not to mention the even more overheated camp performance, what – to my surprise – the performance accentuates is a certain rhythm in the description: there is a careful, almost formal and certainly effective structure in these verses. The scene is set in verse 11, where Oholibah is described as worse than her sister in her lust and whoring. This distinction between desire and enactment provides a pattern for what follows. She is described as having lusted after the Assyrians (verse 12), and as then having acted out her desire (verse 13). The pattern is repeated with the Chaldeans – lust (verses 14–15) followed by enactment (verses 16–17), and, in what the critic of a film performance would call a flashback, with the Egyptians – lust (verse 20) followed by enactment (verse 21). The details, it is interesting to note, cluster around the desire rather than its enactment, and this is a feature to which I shall return.

There is another structural feature in these verses accentuated by the camp performance: the relationship between these descriptions of sexual desire/enactment and the interspersed expressions of condemnation – and, as an aside, whatever else might be said about (or against) Ezekiel, the more I read, the more I am impressed by his technical skill. The vividness of the descriptive detail is remarkable, going far beyond anything in the versions of the *marriage metaphor* in Jeremiah or Hosea. Ezekiel's amplification of earlier themes has long been recognized; Zimmerli, for instance, talks of his 'preference for a broad elaboration of particular themes which earlier prophets touch upon' (1979: 20), and mentions as examples not only chapters 16 and 23, but also the Last Day (chapter 7) and the Shepherd (chapter 34). The interspersed condemnatory expressions register the disgust of the narrator at verse 11, 13, and 18, and of Oholibah herself at verse 17. One supposes that the function of this reiterated disgust is to underline the horror of the sexual details. Certainly the effect is one of crescendo; the disgust marks stage after stage in the accumulating charges against the accused. So, the relationship between details and disgust is causative, or, diagrammatically speaking:

Details → Disgust

But my naughty camp reading of the text, with its exaggerated emphasis on both the details and the condemnation leads to the suspicion of a different relationship between the two. The details are so fascinating, indeed so titillating in themselves, that they begin to contrast with and even undermine the expressions of disgust. The relationship begins to look more like

Details versus Disgust

I could, I suppose, illustrate this disjuncture between expressions of disgust and a suspicious lingering upon salacious detail by pointing to any number of '*exposés*' of scandals reported in the popular Sunday press. But I happened to be in the middle of writing this section when I chanced upon an article in *Gay Times* for April 2004 (No. 307). 'My Name Is … ', a serious, if brief, piece on the problem of sex addiction, written by 'a private registered GP and director of Freedom Health' (Cummings 2004), curiously echoes the tension between the details of Oholibah's sexual desire/behaviour and the declarations of her, and the narrator's, disgust. Sean Cummings relates how casual gay sex is easier than ever to come by with the advent of Internet websites such as *Gaydar*. He informs us that participants on the websites can manipulate the digital photographs of themselves: "You can take your kit off, snap a few digital photos of yourself, *exaggerate your genital size by an inch or three* and put your profile on the set" (Cummings 2004, emphasis added).

It is not only the reference to genital size that sounds familiar. The depiction of Oholibah running amok in the ancient Near East is not too far away from: "The result will be astounding – scores and scores of men nearby who want to meet briefly for sex at all hours of the day and night" (Cummings 2004). But there is a cost, which Cummings spells out:

> The individual will … engage in sex he doesn't really want, and then beats himself up about it over the days that follow. This *self-loathing* goes on until the next episode, when he loses control again. (Cummings 2004, emphasis added)

So here in Cummings' article there are references to penis size, serial sex and self-disgust, all three key elements in verses 11–21.[9] But I also said of verses 11–21 that the camp reading had pointed to a tension between the lingering over salacious details and the expressions of disgust. This is not exactly paralleled in Cummings' article, where, despite its relaxed style, the content maintains an air of sobriety. But the tone of concern is amusingly, perhaps unconsciously, undermined by Cummings' (or his editor's) choice of illustration. In the photograph that accompanies the article (Figure 9.1), a svelte young man, clad only in briefs, lounges on a sofa, languidly tapping away at a keyboard balanced between his open thighs. He smiles. What he sees on the PC's (out-of-camera) monitor seems to please him in a dreamy sort of way, or perhaps he is just pleased by his reader's attention. He certainly shows no distress at his overwhelming addiction, by his 'long-lasting and severe loss of self-esteem and confidence' (Cummings 2004). One might have expected some little sign of tension on his tanned brow. Instead the reader is left admiring his good looks and his apparent, if rather soppy, pleasure. The photograph does not underscore the message that sex can do you harm.

Figure 9.1: Photograph that accompanies Cummings (2004)

And this apparent undermining of Cummings' message is intensified if the reader's eye strays across to the adjacent page, which is taken up with four advertisements for sex-related products: one for books and videos, another for rubber and leather gear; a third promotes a gym, where, to judge from the photograph, the clientele sport bare over-developed chests, fashionable hairstyles and rubber trousers. The fourth advertisement is a delight (Figure 9.2): it features "an all natural semen volumiser created to increase your Semen production by an average of 300%" – surely stallion levels?

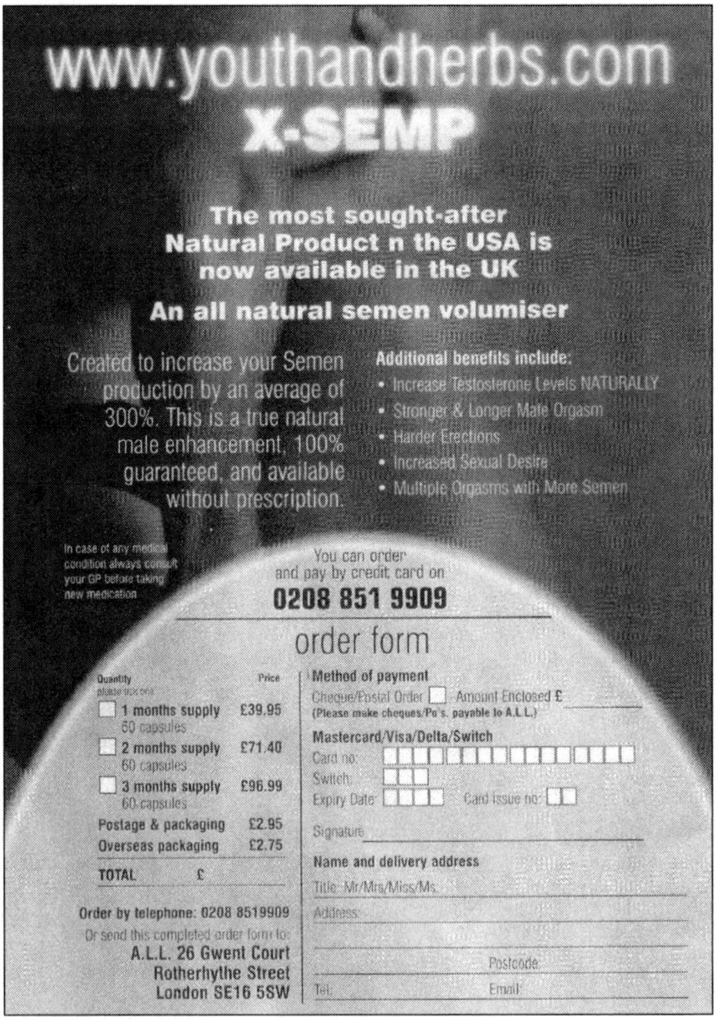

Figure 9.2: "Semen Volumiser": advertisement from *Gay Times* April 2004, p. 114

If you read beyond Cummings' article you will find the next page taken up entirely by Dickie Collier (his *real* "Christian" name?) (Figure 9.3), who introduces you to "some of this month's hardcore hits", the film this month being one in which:

> Finger tips caress and tongues trace erotic designs on eager flesh; these two studs work each other into a frenzy of sexual adoration, devoted cock-sucking, and powerful fucking. (Collier 2004)

No worries here, then, about sex addiction. And if the language offends you (*devoted* cock-sucking?), is it any worse than Ezek. 23:21?

Figure 9.3: Dickie Collier's Hardcore Review, from *Gay Times* April 2004, p. 116

Cummings' warnings about sex addiction are undermined by the element of sexual titillation both in the photograph that accompanies his article and by the content of the surrounding pages. Ezekiel's (or Yhwh's) exclamations of disgust are undermined by the lingering attention to the details of Oholibah's desires. Both these texts, then, are marked by an embedded hypocrisy, but with one crucial difference. In the case of the *Gay Times* article, one suspects that Cummings may not be responsible for the hypocrisy; he may be the victim of his editors; but in the case of Ezekiel 23, the reader is left with the question, who is the real sex addict, Oholibah or the narrator?

9.7 Second Performance: He Knows the Secrets of the Heart[10]

The Williamsesqe performance, in which a lubricious lingering over the details of Oholibah's sexual career is set against the mock horror with which the expressions of disgust are invested, has helped to detect in verses 11–21 the presence of hypocrisy: the narrator is giving his own performance in which he expresses disapproval of something that secretly fascinates him. But camp can promote appreciation of another aspect of performance in these verses. For they provide a supposedly male narrator who if not exactly taking on a female persona – the classic gay male camp stance – at least comes oddly close to doing so.

To begin a justification of this claim, I should like to revisit verse 20. I argued earlier that this verse treats big penises and copious ejaculations as sexually attractive. But it is worth emphasizing that the person to whom they are alluring is Oholibah, a woman. It may be that Greenberg is right to describe this reference to Egyptian sexual endowments as "evidently a commonplace, expressing a popular notion of their lewdness" (1997: 480). Zimmerli is more circumspect, and the biblical evidence for assuming that such a commonplace existed is skimpy.[11] The writer's model for comparing human sexual endowments to those of animals may have been Jer. 5:8, and there it is clear that the main emphasis is on male lasciviousness (this time, that of the children of Judah). What is striking in Ezekiel, both here and in 16:26, is that, in contrast to Jer. 5:8, the emphasis is not on the men; in these two passages, the men are mere toy boys, mentioned only in order to say something about the woman. It is *her* desire that preoccupies the narrator.

I observed earlier that the main descriptive effort in these verses is focused on Oholibah's desire rather than its enactment. And it is here where the male narrator seems to assume a female persona; he puts himself into the mind of a woman. If these verses are compared to a passage that I have already mentioned, the attempted seduction of Joseph by Potiphar's wife, their writer's stance will be easily seen to be very distinctive. The reason why Potiphar's wife desires Joseph is straightforwardly described in Gen. 39:6b and 7a – he is handsome, she "casts her eye on him". At a stretch, one might say that this factual account of the reason for desire is a little like Ezek. 23:20, though without the outrageous anatomical details – she desired the Egyptians because they had large penises, etc. But in all other ways, Ezekiel's portrayal of desire is entirely different. Potiphar's wife voices her desire in verse 7b, and again in verse 12; and then her frustrated desire turns to vengeance. Oholibah, on the other hand, is silent. Instead, there are striking descriptions of the progress of her desires, descriptions unique to Ezekiel. Certainly nothing in Jeremiah or Hosea prepares the reader for this; in their accounts the evidence for female desire is presented in terms of female action. The nearest approximation to Ezekiel's description is Jer. 2:23–24 and 3:10, or Hos. 2:5b, but these are either flat allusions to a state of mind, or, in the case of the last passage, a speech put in the mouth of the woman that does not state desire but describes the economic motivation for the return to her first lover/husband.

The descriptions in Ezekiel are not only intrinsically vivid, they also add to the sense of crescendo in the passage as a whole; for they portray a woman whose cycle of desire intensifies in such a way that it takes decreasingly direct sexual associations to get it inflamed. In verse 12, the desire is incited by *direct sight* of a group of young, handsome Assyrians; in verse 14 simply by *depictions* of the Babylonians; by verse 20 simply Egyptian *reputation* for being well-endowed. In arguing for this sequence, I agree with Greenberg's comment on these verses:

> Apparently the prophet escalates his wanton's lewdness: if at first she lusted for the Assyrians in the flesh, the next stage of her degeneracy is conceiving a passion for the Babylonians from mere pictures of them. (Greenberg 1997: 478)

I suggest that it is possible to go one step beyond Greenberg and to consider verse 20 as a third "stage of degeneracy"; unless it is thought that her desire is for a return match with the Egyptians, in which case she can account for their physical endowments by personal experience, *reputation* is the only conceivable means whereby their endowments would be known to her.

The description of Oholibah's desire enflamed by pictures or statues of the Babylonians is as psychologically telling as her subsequent disgust. Greenberg calls it a "bizarre scene" (1997: 478); and perhaps its inspiration can be seen in the tenor of the *marriage metaphor* – disgust at the unedifying foreign idolatry creeping into Israelite religion (one might compare Ezek. 8:10), and suggested by the Babylonian portraiture described by Greenberg (1997: 478). But the *result* is not only convincing in terms of the vehicle of the *marriage metaphor*; but is also hauntingly evocative of our own time, as described by Cummings; here is an ancient Israelite version of *Gaydar*, where someone scans the profiles and arranges for sex to be delivered to their door.

The imaging of female desire by a male narrator is so intense that one has to ask, how does the narrator know? Does one picture him as a voyeur, observing the woman covertly while she gazes on the assembled Assyrians, or peeping, perhaps from behind a curtain, as she studies the Babylonians' portraits? Of course the observant reader will have noticed that there is actually no explicit textual allusion to the narrator's gender in verses 11–21, and it was perhaps naughty of me to assume that it is a man who speaks. If one steps outside the confines of verses 11–21, one learns that the narrator is well placed to know all about the secrets of Oholibah's heart. In verses 1 and 22 the narrator is revealed to be none other than God himself. It is God who takes this interest in Oholibah's desires, and thus the mystery of the narrator's knowledge is solved.

But this discovery does not resolve all the issues. To begin with I have said that the description of female desire is vivid. I have even said that some of the psychological insight is telling (verses 14–17), and I have praised the technical skill with which the passage in general is constructed. But is the portrayal of female sexual desire *authentic*? Because, of course, if it is God who is describing it, it really ought to be.

At this point I should like to invoke the Sontagian concept of failed seriousness, and suggest that the reason why this performance appeals so much to camp taste is that it has made an unparalleled (in biblical terms) and serious attempt to portray female desire, but like the female impersonator whose extravagant couture cannot quite divert attention from one or two little tell-tale signs of maleness (or perhaps the very extravagance is a clue) it has failed to convince the reader of its authenticity. The little tell-tale signs of maleness obtrude. Female animals may act strangely when on heat, but has anyone really come across a woman driven mad with desire at the thought of big penises and copious ejaculations? The narrator has presented a male version of female desire, as authentic as those depictions of "lesbian" sex in pornography aimed at a male heterosexual audience. The one more likely to be enflamed with lust is the male narrator rather than the female subject. And it is this male obtrusion that has justified my assuming that the narrator is masculine. Oholibah is bad drag, and all the more fun for being so. And my incontrovertible piece of evidence for this judgement is my sensational discovery of a portrait of Oholibah, which shows how unreal a woman she really is (Figure 9.4).

Figure 9.4: Ezekiel's Oholibah, or Mae West (1892–1980). American actress. In the role of Diamond Lil.
Topfoto/The Granger Collection

Of course, readers conversant with the history of the cinema, may find the portrait strangely familiar, and I must admit to a little deceit. For it dawned on me that Oholibah is, though certainly not in every detail, none other than the Mae West of the Hebrew Bible.

It seems that nobody has been able to bury the real Mae West. In recent years she has staged a comeback as the heroine of feminist camp, and several books have appeared that celebrate her transgressive career as a sexual outlaw. But West has always been a camp icon, in classic gay male terms. She wrote two plays about male homosexuals, which, according to Lillian Schlissel, she "staged with gay actors playing themselves" (2002: 72; Schlissel's article is a useful short account of West's connexions with male homosexuality). She partly modelled her stage persona on homosexual camp performers; her loyalty to her homosexual actors is well attested, and she herself summed up her easy relations with them: "She brought them home to meet her mother. 'They'd do her hair and nails, and she'd have a great time'" (Schlissel 2002: 81, quoting West's own words).

One might profitably read this cosy, if unorthodox, domestic scene against the verdict meted out to her by the Hearst newspapers: "a menace to the Sacred Institution of the American Family" (quoted in Schlissel 2002: 82; capital letters original). Her persona, just like Oholibah's, was unrelenting in its sexual appetite and entirely unrepentant; she was regularly attacked in the press for her lack of moral taste, and the two homosexual plays mentioned above were closed down by the police. Reading about her career as an actress, playwright and film star or watching her hard, brash cinema persona one can easily understand how she became a camp icon in her lifetime. As noted in the preceding chapter, Ross discusses the camp admiration for the independent woman of cinema. With women like Bette Davis in mind he comments:

> [G]ay camp looks forward to later appraisals of the "independent" women of Hollywood, who fought for their own roles, either against the studios themselves, or in the highly mannered ways in which they acted out, acted around, or acted against the grain of the sexually circumscribed stereotypes they were contracted to dramatize. (Ross 1989: 159)

But how does this comparison between Oholibah and Mae West fit in with my other characterization of Oholibah as "bad drag"? To answer this, I must ask another question: was Mae West really real? The answer is: not really, at least her persona had something very artificial about it. Ross says of it:

> But Mae West is the star who most professionally exploits the ironies of *artifice* when, like a female drag queen, she represents a woman who parodies a burlesque woman, and then seems to take on the role for real, as a way of successfully fielding every kind of masculine response known to woman. West pioneered a new, bold, no-nonsense, no-romance relation with sex. (Ross 1989: 160; emphasis original)

Schlissel considers that a key tactic in her performance was her speech (West's notorious one-liners are, of course, her most enduring legacy):

> [W]hile she was always regarded as a "dangerous woman", the danger she posed was not her flagrant physicality, or her harlot's disguise. It was the language with which she turned sex into comedy. (Schlissel 2002: 73–74)

In other words, West exuded sexuality, but actually only talked about sex; and by means of her mastery of innuendo "turned sex into comedy". Ross and Schlissel were by no means the first to notice the element of artifice, of exaggeration and of drag in her act. George West, writing in *Vanity Fair* in 1936, famously rhapsodized, "I love you, Miss West, because YOU are the greatest female impersonator of all time".

Oholibah and Mae West, then, have much in common. But there is also a key difference between them. West is deliberate camp. She knew what she was doing, she meant to overplay her role, and the fact that she had a large homosexual following seems to disprove Sontag's rule that self-aware camp necessarily fails in its effect. Moreover, although one may well suspect that there is a serious purpose underlying her persona (that of female survival in a harsh world), she plays the rôle for laughs. Again, she is a woman playing a woman, and the female persona, though a product of artifice, has enough reality in it to convince the reader/ viewer of a certain foolish authenticity. West manages the difficult feat of being both good drag and good camp. Oholibah, on the other hand, is naïve camp. It is a rôle played with complete earnestness, but because it is a woman played unconvincingly by a man, it amply fulfils the criteria necessary to be classed as Sontagian failed seriousness. It is bad drag, but very good camp.

9.8 Conclusions

The camp performance of verses 11–21 has offered particular views of Ezekiel's/Yhwh's account of Oholibah. To a limited extent these views overlap those already pointed out by past feminist scholarship, particularly the observation that the verses portray a male version of female sexuality. But the camp version of this observation has striking differences from those of earlier interpreters. For one thing it is unabashedly ambiguous, for I have suggested that *two* contrasting pictures of Oholibah emerge from the camp performance. One is very much indebted to the masculinist bias of the narrator; Oholibah is pathologized as helplessly sex-addicted, disgusting even to herself. But struggling to emerge from this Oholibah is a very different figure, splendidly outrageous, the Mae West of her day, who pursues her long sexual career with unswerving zeal. The more the narrator disapproves, the more she defies him "openly, flaunting her nakedness". He tries to keep her silent; there are no direct words from her, unlike the wantons of Jeremiah and Hosea (for example, at Jer. 2:25 and Hos. 2:5), but one can catch just the echo of her voice in verse 18, where, confident in her charms and imperious in her manner, she summons the distant objects of her fancy to her bed. And they obey her. As if to reiterate the importance of this event, there is another version of it at verses 40–42. This Oholibah is a camp heroine, inauthentic as a woman, but magnificent as a personification of unrestrained desire.

Oholibah, then – yes, even the sad, sex-addicted Oholibah – is a camp heroine because she reveals in an outrageous fashion not so much her own sexual problems as those of her narrator. The description of her sexual career in the middle of the Hebrew Bible has all the outrageousness of a *Carry-On* comedy filmed on Mount Athos. But what is one to make of this frivolity? Does it have any value other than that of transient entertainment? I was going to remark that there is a vast difference between making fun of the Bible and making the Bible fun,[12] but I am conscious that it is difficult to make a clear distinction between these two activities. Perhaps the answer lies in the fact that the fun in camp has a hard edge. As I suggested at the beginning of this chapter, gay male camp is an expression of failures in masculinity; knowledge of one's own failures makes one efficient at spotting identical or similar failures in others and ruthless in drawing attention to them. As it happens, the narrator's masculinity in this text does not so much fail as succeed too well; it attempts a performance of female impersonation, but cannot bring it off because the audience spots the man beneath the wig. Oholibah is not the woman he wants us to see. Nor is the narrator, that dodgy narrator who so loudly disapproves of what secretly fascinates him, nor is he what God is really like. The truth lurking in this text is a picture of what God is not.

And it then may follow that once the reader has seen how funny this narrator is, how improbable a reflection of God, then the threats uttered by him in the rest of the chapter, which have alarmed and disgusted readers, will carry no more conviction than the camp horror movies of the late twentieth century.

A different kind of fun, one unanticipated by me at least, emerged from the camp reading; this was the gradual discovery of the underlying skill with which the writer structured the text, a skill that runs counter to the failed seriousness that I observed in the text's surface. And this is not the only ambiguity: that a camp reading should allow a sight of the text's handsome skeleton, when it is supposed to confine its gaze to the text's complexion is all the more surprising: one expects camp to be more beautician than radiologist.

I readily admit that camp is not the only possible route to these insights. But it was the route that worked for me, and it may work for others. I should argue two particular benefits of using camp, first that it is enjoyable, and second that because camp is at home with ambiguity, it is good at spotting ambiguity in others; the two contrasting Oholibah's that have emerged from Ezekiel 23 leave Evelyn quite unfazed.

Finally, I should readily concede that camp is not a universal tool, but a specialist application. One can easily demonstrate this by turning back, true to my previous practice, to Jeremiah and Hosea. I challenge the reader to attempt a Williamsesque performance of, say, Hosea 2. It is a tribute to Ezekiel's idiosyncrasy, as well as an acknowledgement that opportunities for camp readings in biblical studies are not omnipresent, that Hosea's and Jeremiah's pictures of the treacherous wife of Yhwh are unattractive to a camp aficionado. Faced with little in the way of florid language, less exaggeration and no (fe)male impersonation of female desire, there is nothing left for Evelyn to do but take a bow and glide away in search of more alluring prospects.

Appendix

9.9 Excursus One: The Hidden Penis

It is not part of reader-response practice to take any notice of earlier (let alone early) reaction to the text, particularly when the original is in a different language. Yet the language of Ezek. 23:20 in the MT throws some entertaining light upon Brenner's assertion that that verse is an exception to the general rule that the penis remains hidden in the Hebrew Bible. It is true that the verse alludes to penile size, but the terms in which it does so are themselves obscure. בָּשָׂר presents the translator with a problem. The standard interpretation is that it is a euphemism for penis (see, for instance, Greenberg on the related 16:26 (1983: 283)). Translations have adopted a variety of solutions. AV retains the literal meaning of בָּשָׂר, flesh, and I have already discussed to what extent this has enlightened the understanding of seventeenth-century readers, but it may be fair to conclude that AV prioritized decorum over intelligibility. Modern English translations try to maintain both. NEB and NRSV use the word "members", and one might feel that this is an effective solution were it not for the suspicion that בָּשָׂר was less familiar to its readers as a euphemism for penis than member is to the English-speaking reader. Unambiguous evidence for such a usage is hard to find. The only other clear case, cited by *TDOT*, seems to be Lev. 15:2–7.[13] Other cases are more ambiguous. Some seem to refer more vaguely to the genital area, e.g. Exod. 28:42; Lev. 6:10 and 16:4. Where בָּשָׂר occurs with reference to circumcision as in the phrase בְּשַׂר עָרְלַתְכֶם (for example, Gen. 17:11) it is reasonable to construe it literally ("the flesh of your foreskin"). It is unnecessary to assume with Greenberg (1983: 283) that בָּשָׂר in Gen. 17:13 means "penis". It certainly does seem to be picking up the phrase בְּשַׂר עָרְלַתְכֶם nearby and could be viewed simply as hendiadys for the whole phrase (as indeed elsewhere in Ezekiel, at 44:7 and 9), or, more generally, retaining its literal meaning. So vaguely focused is this "euphemistic" use of בָּשָׂר that *TDOT* even argues for the meaning of "vagina" at Lev. 15:19, although there again it could be interpreted in a more general sense.[14]

One fares little better when looking at the ancient versions for help. For MT's repetition of בָּשָׂר at 23:20, LXX has the plural αἱ σάρκες, and *TDNT* comments that "the LXX shows no inclination to link σάρξ esp. with sexuality, but rather avoids this issue";[15] and in a note adds "Only in Ezek. 23:20 (cf. 16:26) is there reference to the sexual member' (vol. 12, p. 108); all of which does make one wonder whether αἱ σάρκες should be taken as "the sexual member" at all. Targum Jonathan renders the verse sexually innocuous, as does the Vulgate.

One is saved from the surmise that בָּשָׂר should be interpreted literally and that Oholibah is pictured as a fan of Egyptian muscularity only by the context: donkeys are not a byword for muscular bulk. And the word זִרְמָה is also supposed to help to reinforce the penile interpretation. "Issue", i.e. "ejaculation of semen" seems to be the unequivocal meaning here. But the case is not helped by the fact that the word is a *hapax legomenon*, and that an alternative interpretation that suggests that the word may mean "penis" is examined by Greenberg (1997: 480) and Zimmerli (1979: 475). Whatever the case, the penis, while not as shy about revealing itself here as in the rest of the Hebrew Bible, does not do so with quite the *élan* suggested by modern English translations.

9.10 Excursus Two: Oholibah's Disgust

What disgusts Oholibah? Ezekiel 23:17 contains a striking and, as it turns out, characteristic image. I have characterized וַתֵּקַע נַפְשָׁה מֵהֶם perhaps rather rashly as describing Oholibah's *self*-disgust, and have compared it to Cummings's description of the sex addict's "self-loathing". Certainly NRSV is not as rash when it translates the phrase as "... she turned from them in disgust".

The *qal* of the verb יָקַע is rare; its use in Gen. 32:26 (MT) relates to the dislocation of Jacob's hip in his tussle with the angel:

וַתֵּקַע כַּף־יֶרֶךְ יַעֲקֹב בְּהֵאָבְקוֹ עִמּוֹ

In the present passage and in 23:18, Ezekiel may well have in mind Jer. 6:8, where the same subject (נֶפֶשׁ – mind, soul) is used; there Yhwh threatens to turn away from Jerusalem because of her wickedness. If I am right in seeing Ezekiel's inspiration in Jeremiah, then I can say that he follows it closely in 23:18, where Yhwh recoils from the wicked Oholibah, just as he recoiled from her wicked sister. But in 23:17, Ezekiel goes beyond his model by adding a twist. Rather than the "innocent" male party, it is the wicked Oholibah who does the recoiling. It seems to me a psychologically telling stroke, and one that is confirmed by the experience of Cummings's sex addict, who despite his self-loathing, is still caught up in his cycle of addictive sexual behaviour. Is the NRSV justified in using the word disgust? And if so, what disgusts Oholibah? The *qal* of the verb, especially if the Genesis passage is borne in mind, implies a sharp, even violent reversal. Greenberg, keeping the tenor of the *marriage metaphor* in the forefront of his attention, compares the verb to its Arabic equivalent, which can mean to "deviate from", and sees the reference of the verse in "Judah's change of policy from alliance with Babylonia ... to rebellion against it" (1997: 479). He then, very interestingly from my present point of view, adds the comment that this historical event "is metaphorized as the wanton's disgust with herself projected against her lovers" (1997: 479). Ezekiel, of course, is less precise about Oholibah's state of mind, but it seems fair to say that the NRSV's phrase "she turned from them in disgust" is not too bold a translation, and that it is fair to think of that disgust, in part at least, as directed against herself.

Notes

1. The *Oxford English Dictionary* defines one meaning of flesh as "*to go after* or *follow strange flesh*: a Biblical expression referring to unnatural crime", and quotes the 1382 Wycliffe translation of Jude 1:7 "Sodom and Gomor ... goyng aftir other flesch".
2. One is reminded of Butler's comment on the Lacanian distinction between men "having" the phallus and women "being" the Phallus: "men are said to 'have' the Phallus yet never to 'be' it, in the sense that the penis is not equivalent to that Law and can never fully symbolize that Law" (Butler 1990: 199).
3. "Flesh" at Jude 1:7, a translation of σαρκὸς, evidently refers not so much to penis in particular as sexual or sinful nature in general. Wycliffe's translation is followed by AV.
4. The search engine Google will do as well as any, particularly if the phrases are enclosed in double quotation marks, and as long as no filter against pornography is employed.
5. These were the results of searches made in 2006; in 2010, the figures were, respectively, 3.8 and 18.9 million (the phrase "cum shots" was searched with the "..." limiter). I should hazard a guess that the phrase "cum shot" (or in its equivalent word "cumshot") means an "image of ejaculation", using "shot" in the photographic sense, rather than in the sense of "ejaculated". It is an irony that the ambiguity about the word recalls that of the Hebrew זִרְמָה in 23:20b. Jennings makes a similar comparison between these verses and online pornography, though he sees the reason for such scenes in pornography ("money shots") as the way in which "the viewer received visual proof of 'real sex'" (2005: 162). Jennings may be right in terms of heterosexual pornography (which he sees as the main arena for "money shots"), but in terms of homosexual pornography allure seems to me just as much a reason for the phenomenon.
6. For another reference to ejaculatory prowess as possibly excitatory, see Figure 9.2.
7. The phrase "drastic metaphor" derives from Zimmerli's note to vv. 19–20 in which he talks of "the exaggerated language which sets out in drastic metaphors the power of Egyptian political conspiracy" (Zimmerli 1979: 487).

8. The source is unknown; the words must be spoken in an appropriately exaggerated high-class accent, à la Noël Coward.
9. For a further comment on Oholibah's disgust, see Excursus 2.
10. Psalm 44:21.
11. Zimmerli can mention only Gen. 12:11–12, where Abram is concerned about Sarai's vulnerability to Egyptian attentions; but the vulnerability is based on her beauty rather than their hypersexuality; Gen. 39:6–12 is even less convincing: it is Potiphar's wife rather than any Egyptian male who is the problem, and once again it is because of Israelite beauty, in this case, that of Joseph.
12. Compare Isherwood's remark, noted in the historiography above, that "[camp] always has an underlying seriousness. You can't camp about something you don't take seriously. You're not making fun of it; you're making fun out of it" (Isherwood 1954: 125).
13. Botterweck and Ringgren (1974/1993, s.v. בָּשָׂר, vol. 2, p. 319).
14. Botterweck and Ringgren (1974/2003, s.v. בָּשָׂר, vol. 2, p. 319).
15. Kittel, G. (1964/1976, s.v. σάρξ, vol. 7, p. 108).

Chapter 10

Conclusions

10.1 Introduction

It is an oddity for someone working within so fluid a model as queer theory – "necessarily indeterminate" as Jagose calls it (1996: 99) – to follow the conventional pattern of presenting the reader with a set of "conclusions". But unease provoked by a sense of the finality conveyed by that word is to some extent offset by that other convention which expects suggestions for further research to be undertaken on the subject. These closing remarks, then, are not a closure; they represent, rather, a drawing together of some threads, in the spirit of the self-reflection which I invoked at the end of chapter 2, and have set out to exercise at key points in subsequent chapters. This concern for self-reflection has gone hand-in-hand with a further concern for the transparency of the research process. So chapters 5–7 and 9 are presented as they were first written, except for minor alterations and corrections. Prioritizing in this way transparency over seamlessness, the text tells of the development of a research idea, from the implications of the abrupt changes of grammatical gender in the *marriage metaphor* in Jeremiah until its eventual transmogrification into Ezekiel's Mae West. This transition from ך to camp may not strike the reader at first as inexorably smooth. But part of its unity depends on its being a story, a narration of how ideas develop over a long period of gestation. I do not imply by "development" a modernist concept of progress, an ascent from a primitive past to a perfect end; rather, development here should be thought of as a succession of ideas, each new one suggested by its predecessor, and each, in turn, having some new light to cast on what was said before. Moreover the process of development was furthered, conventionally enough, by reading, thinking and debate, but it was also my experience, as discussed in Entr'Acte,[1] that "thought happened in the writing",[2] and I have endeavoured to leave the process as visible as possible.

The story began, then, with an encounter between, on the one hand, the fact that biblical Hebrew distinguishes gender in the second person of verbal and pronominal forms, and, on the other, a queer view of metaphorical theory. That queer view places the signification of metaphor not entirely under the control of either the author or the reader/listener. Instead, metaphor may be considered as one way in which performativity operates; it has an ideological function. The theme of the *marriage metaphor* may be the relationship between Yhwh and Israel,[3] but the metaphor also acts to reinforce, by bestowing divine sanction upon, a patriarchal and heteronormative lesson on how human sexual life should be lived. It is this ideological function of the metaphor that has disturbed and enraged a succession of feminist critics, and it is to this corpus of writings that I happily acknowledge a heavy debt. Where exactly I stand, however, in relation to their readings is not always easy to pinpoint. Certainly it is a long way from Carroll, who, though rejecting Ezekiel 16 and 23 on moral grounds, insists that "serious scholarship has to move beyond outrage to rational discourse" (Carroll 1996: 78). My own position is that I do not dismiss outrage as incompatible with "serious scholarship"; I accept many of the insights offered by feminist biblical commentary on the *marriage metaphor*, but I argue that there is room to offer *another* view to set beside that of feminist scholarship (not to replace it), that adds a different perspective. This can be illustrated by returning to the ideological function of the metaphor and demonstrating that there is a hitch in it.

10.2 Gender Slippages in Jeremiah

The ideology of the metaphor ought to involve a neat interrelationship between the vehicle of a loving husband and adulterous wife and the tenor of a loving Yhwh and faithless Israel. But if the argument of chapter 4 is accepted, that is that the Israelites are male, then the heteronormative message is threatened by the logic of the metaphorical structure in which the faithless wife is equated with the male citizenry of Israel. One could argue that this in itself is sufficient to excite queer interest. But at this point a phenomenon comes into play that may be characterized as a form of naturalization, that process described by Butler whereby performativity masks its own operation so that its result appears to be entirely natural.[4] The queer logic I have described in the marriage metaphor is ignored by nearly all commentators, including most feminists. They either fail to notice it, or they negate its force by arguing that there is a device in the text whereby a strict segregation of the genders is maintained: in the text of Jeremiah, female Jerusalem is used when the text refers to the faithless wife of the vehicle, and male Israel is used when it refers to the male citizens of the tenor. My response, therefore, is to offer a more rigorous demonstration of the marriage metaphor's queer potential, by responding to the segregationists. By means of an anti-schema, which maps the grammatical genders used in the text, I demonstrate breakdowns in this alleged gender segregation, and thereby argue that the oddity of equating a faithless wife with male citizens cannot be easily ignored.

Such breaches are real challenges to heteronormativity, but they are also, like many queer insights, fragile and fleeting. I may compare this fragility by recalling Schori's remark ("Our mother Jesus gives birth to a new creation, and you and I are his children")[5] and how its ascription of gender ambiguity to Jesus, fascinating as it is, risks extinction in the simple process of translation.[6] In the case of Jeremiah's anti-schema, fragility is demonstrated by the failure to replicate it in Hosea (even though there *is* a gender breakdown in Hosea – which the anti-schema fails to pick up).[7] I have turned instead to two other literary indications of breakdown within the text. In fact both of these queer insights had their origin in the text of Jeremiah.

10.3 The Prophets Unmanned

I chose to end chapter 5 with an almost incidental comment that linked Yhwh's marriage veto (16.2) and Jeremiah's protest against Yhwh's seduction of him (20.7). But the full significance of these texts is fully appreciable only by a comparison with Yhwh's instruction to Hosea to marry an אֵשֶׁת זְנוּנִים (1:2). In chapter 6 I argued that this extraordinary command is an extreme symbolic act in reaction to Israel's extreme act of abandonment. However one reads the structural place of the command in the *marriage metaphor* (I read it as having no direct structural rôle), it demands attention if only because of its intrinsic oddity. Read alongside Jeremiah's marriage veto, it becomes evident that Yhwh is refusing both Jeremiah and Hosea the opportunity of fulfilling two basic criteria of Jewish manhood, that is marriage itself in the case of Jeremiah, and, in the case of Hosea, control over his wife's sexuality and the security of his patrilinear succession. This leaves doubt about the maleness of Yhwh himself. He is the one who brings about these two episodes of prophetic unmanning. Moreover in his rôle as divine husband he is associated with Hosea whose manliness he has just compromised with such emphasis at the beginning of the book. As for Jeremiah, he believes that Yhwh has seduced him![8]

10.4 The Third Movement

Of those feminist biblical scholars who have recognized the oddity of equating faithless wife with male citizenry,[9] all except Leith (1989: 104) have focused upon the negative implications (men imaged as *bad* women). But the *marriage metaphor* has, either implicit or explicit, three elements or "Movements".[10] The first is the early golden age of the relationship, the second the period of the wife's betrayal and the third the promised reconciliation. To focus on the third, or even to identify it at all, is a dangerous manoeuvre. One runs the risk of being labelled recuperative, of playing down the abusive ugliness of the second movement. Moreover, at first sight the manoeuvre has no obvious relevance to an application of queer theory – except that it might feed those feminist suspicions of queer theory as a conservative, masculinist project. Yet there can be little doubt that the third Movement is present in all three books, even if in Jeremiah it is long delayed (31:3b–5a), and in Ezekiel expressed in less than loving terms (16:60–63). The case of Hosea is particularly interesting. Where it is mentioned at all by feminist biblical scholars it is dismissed – "sinister", according to Connolly (1998: 62), "a patriarchal fantasy" in the words of Sherwood (1996: 309). Yet, as I argue, it is expressed in terms of unconditional forgiveness, of fulfilled sexual intimacy and, moreover, at a cosmic level with solemn divine asseveration. And to appreciate the queer significance of the third Movement it only has to be asked who the referent is of this cosmic marriage. Whose heart is Yhwh about to win over? Whose body is he about to enjoy? One of the queerest features of the *marriage metaphor* in Hosea is that it is the male Israelites who are the recipients of this sexual fervour.

10.5 The Anti-Schema and Ezekiel: M for F Forms

I argue, then, that an application of queer theory to the texts of Jeremiah and Hosea reveals inherent breakdowns in terms of gender and desire. The *marriage metaphor* ought to be prescriptive of patriarchy and heteronormativity, but in both its structure and expression it presents slippages, the presence of which calls its ideological function into question.

The linguistic method of finding breakdowns in the heteronormative function of the *marriage metaphor* works wells with Jeremiah, but less so with Hosea. The fact that I have sought other literary clues to breakdowns in gender performativity is an acknowledgement of the anti-schema's limitations. But this is not to say that by the end of chapter 6 I have exhausted its potential for uncovering such breakdowns in the *marriage metaphor*. In chapter 7 the application of the anti-schema to Ezekiel 16 and 23 has uncovered little of significance in chapter 16, but in chapter 23 has drawn attention in verses 36–49 to the use of the masculine pronominal suffix in place of the feminine – which I have labelled *m for f form(s)*. This has led me to offer a new theory of the use of such forms in Ezekiel in general, and in chapter 23 in particular. I challenge the view put forward by Rooker (1990) that these and examples elsewhere are necessarily a mere linguistic feature of late Hebrew without semantic significance. Supported by an analysis of four groups of these forms in chapter 23 and elsewhere in Ezekiel, I have argued that their presence indicates not a linguistic tic, but a literary device. In verses 36–39, for instance, they are associated with references to the conceptual masculine gender of the tenor of the metaphor – the cultic shortcomings of the Israelites – and are carefully segregated from the female vehicle – the sinful wife or wives. But in verses 45–47, there is a regular patterning of masculine and feminine genders, whereby the writer exploits the opportunity presented by *m for f forms* to play gender games; the result is a breakdown of gender norms caused by the conflation of female vehicle and masculine tenor. The anti-schema, then, has drawn attention to the phenomenon of *m for f forms* and has led me to suggest with support from examples of these forms elsewhere in Ezekiel that, particularly when they occur in groups, they can be viewed as a literary device, the effect of which in chapter 23 is to undermine the gender separation of tenor and vehicle in the *marriage metaphor*, an effect they share with those other features that I have identified in Jeremiah.

The process of self reflection announced in chapter 2, actively pursued in the concluding sections of chapter 5–7 and 9, and referred to at the beginning of this chapter is an enactment of the principle that there is always something more to say. Even the fact that by the end of chapter 7 I called a halt to searching within the text for breakdowns in the heteronormative performativity of the *marriage metaphor*, there is scope for further exploration of biblical texts using this methodology.

I should like to take the principle of the anti-schema, for instance, and test whether an application of it to other gendered texts in the Hebrew Bible produces interesting results, perhaps to the Song of Songs. And, finally, despite the very different grammatical structure of Greek, I am interested in putting texts from the Septuagint to the same test.

10.6 The Significance of the Subverted Metaphor

To leave the question of breakdowns at this point might suggest that what I have offered is an academic exercise with no application for questions on the reading of biblical texts. It is evident that the *marriage metaphor* remains a potent device for both interpreting the human relationship with the divine, and for maintaining adherence to a heteronormative understanding of gender and desire. In the Introduction, I observed in Ortlund's panegyric on conventional marriage a divinizing effect of the *marriage metaphor*.[11] Anderson's criticism of Schori's maternal imagery of Jesus offers further evidence of the need to subvert the *marriage metaphor*; in a public interview he speculated on the implications of such imagery for the metaphor of the Church as the Bride of Christ: "it would suggest that somehow this is a lesbian relationship".[12] That "somehow" is eloquent of the inconceivability of such a proposition for someone with Anderson's conservative worldview. He takes it for granted that a cross-sex relationship is the only interpretative option on offer. It is vital to demonstrate, as I have set out to do, that a direct forebear of the Bride of Christ metaphor, that is, the *marriage metaphor* of the Hebrew Bible, is structured and expressed in terms that undermine the "normal" ordering of gender and desire. A lesbian understanding of Jesus and "his" bride may shock Anderson, but it should not surprise anyone who has read Section II of this book.

10.7 Ezekiel, Camp and Mae West

And yet the naturalizing process of performativity is so powerful, that, as the history of biblical scholarship demonstrates, hardly any reader of the *marriage metaphor* has even noticed its inherent breakdowns, let alone thought through their implications. In order to interrupt this indifference it may be necessary to employ shock tactics. This is the aim of Section III. I turn from searching for breakdowns *within* the text and step *outside* it. The strategy involves the tactic of adopting the feminist use of reader-response criticism as a means of uncovering dominant ideologies. Another tactic is the use of autobiographical criticism, a positionality that adds self-revelation to self-reflection; it shows me, the writer reporting and reflecting on a personal encounter with the biblical text. That personal encounter took the form of a camp performance of Ezek. 23:11–21. Camp is not an obvious methodological companion to biblical texts. Chapter 8 is a discussion of its potential as a queer methodological tool: it performs the fragility of the boundaries of gender and desire, and, in a gay male context in particular, is used to express and seek consolation for impaired masculinity. It is this awareness of self-failure that enables the camp performance both to highlight mercilessly gender dysfunction in others, but also to do so with a sense of complicity. I have found camp, therefore, a valuable means of highlighting the narrator's lubricious descriptions of Oholibah's overheated sexual desires, in hypocritical contrast to his horror at her behaviour. It has also enabled an ambiguous portrait of Oholibah to emerge: one, the creation of the narrator, is a helpless sex-addict, repulsive even to herself, the other, the assertively outrageous Mae West character, sweeps into view despite the narrator. Moreover I have deliberately underscored the narrator's lubricity and cant by an intertextual reading of Ezekiel 23 with elements of gay online pornography and with contact advertisements and articles from *Gay Times*.

The images I use, both verbal and visual, are graphic to the point of obscenity. They are there to parallel and underscore the language and imagery of the biblical text. If Section II has concentrated on exposing breakdowns within the text, Section III breaks down the text by matching the sexual violence of its language with a counter-violence. The camp attack creates a tension between *outrage* (Yhwh's outrage at the lewd woman; *our* outrage as readers at his treatment of her) and *outrageousness* (the effrontery of intertextualizing biblical texts and gay contact advertisements). One or two readers commented that I should "tone down" some of the language, imagery and sexual allusions of chapter 9. For my part, I wonder whether the writer of Ezekiel was ever asked to do the same. One element that my examination of Ezekiel 23 exposed, but did not comment upon, was the question of ethnicity.[13] Oholibah's lovers obviously owe their racial origins to the tenor of the metaphor; but it would be of interest to explore further in a queer theoretical context the part played by the racial allusions in the tenor of the *marriage metaphor*.

As for camp as a methodological approach to biblical texts, I am very reluctant to wave farewell to such an entertaining and enlightening companion. I have often wondered, for instance, about David as dancer (2 Sam. 6:14-16). So has Jennings (2005: 38–45); but whereas he ponders on the homoerotic overtones of the episode, a camp treatment might see something more nuanced and altogether odder about such a performance. Song of Songs, also, might yield some strange secrets under camp's quizzical gaze. Camp may prove to be a powerful addiction.

Notes

1. Above, pages 157–164.
2. Richardson and Adams St Pierre (2005: 968–969).
3. I use "Israel" here to stand for Israel/Jerusalem/Judah.
4. Butler 1990; see above, Section 1.3.2.
5. See above, page 5.
6. See above, page 5, n. 8.
7. See above, Section 6.2.
8. See above, Section 5.5.
9. For example, Bird (1989), Bauer (1999); compare Patton (2000).
10. I have argued that all three movements are present in Jeremiah, movements two and three in Hosea, and one and two (and, briefly, three) in Ezekiel.
11. Ortlund (1996:173); see also above, page 4.
12. See above, page 12.
13. Liew (2001, especially pages 186–190) complains of a similar omission in Stone (2001).

Schedule of Antischemas

Anti-schema 1: Jeremiah 2-3

Section	Addressee/Subject	Singular or Plural?	Male or Female?	Marriage Metaphor Present?	Apostasy Theme explicit?
2: 1-2	Jerusalem	S	F	Yes	?Yes
2: 3	Israel	S	M	No	?Yes
2: 4-6	1: House of Jacob, and all the families of the house of God	P	M	No	(Yes)
	2: Fathers of 1.	P	M	Hints?: divorce theme in 5; and use of וְשִׁלְּחָהּ	Yes
2: 7-10	As 4-6 but with no subsidiary	P	M	No	Yes
2: 11	My people	S	M	No	Yes
2: 12-13	1: Heavens	P	M	No	Yes
	2: My people	S	M		
	3: They (sc. "My people")	P	M		
2: 14-15	1: Heavens still?	(P)	(M)	No	Yes
	2: Israel	S	M		
2: 16-25	Jerusalem?	S	F	Yes	Yes
2: 26-27	House of Israel (expanded into kings, princes, etc.)	P	M	No	Yes
2: 28	Judah	S	M (except for לְךָ)	No	Yes
2: 29-32	?Inhabitants of Judah	P	M	Yes	Yes
2: 33-37	?Jerusalem	S	F	Yes	Yes

Anti-schema 1 (continued)

Section	Addressee/Subject	Singular or Plural?	Male or Female?	Marriage Metaphor Present?	Apostasy Theme explicit?
3: 1-5	?Jerusalem	S	F	Yes	No
3: 6-11	1: Israel	S	F	Yes	Yes
	2: Judah	S	F		
3:12	Israel	S → P	M	No	Yes
3:13	?Israel	S → P	F → M	Yes	No
3: 14-18	1: Children	P	M	No	Yes
	2: Future generations	P	P		
3:19	?Israel/Jerusalem	S	F	No but hints of female ownership of land?	?Yes
3: 20	House of Israel	S	M	Yes (via simile)	Yes
3: 21-25	Children	P	M	No	Yes

Anti-schema 2: Hosea 1

Verses	Addressee/Subject	Singular/ Plural?	Male/ Female?	Marriage Metaphor Present?	Apostasy Theme explicit?
1:1	Title				
1:2	Yhwh: Hosea	S	M	Yes?	No
1:3	1: Hosea	S	M	Yes?	Yes?
	2: Gomer	S	M		
1:4-5	1: Yhwh: Hosea: 1st son	S	M	Yes?	Yes
	2: [Yhwh]: Israel*	S	M		
1:6	1: Gomer	S	F	Yes?	No
	2: [Yhwh]: [Hosea]: daughter	S	F	Yes?	Yes?
	3: [Yhwh]: [Hosea]: Israel	M → P	M	No	Yes?
1:7	[Yhwh]: Judah	P	M	No	Yes
1:8	Gomer: daughter	S	F	Yes?	No
	Gomer: 2nd son				
1:9	1: [Yhwh]: [Hosea]: 2nd son	S	M	Yes?	Yes?
	2: [Yhwh]: Israel	P	P	No	

* Actually, the "house of Israel" (בֵּית יִשְׂרָאֵל) a grammatically singular phrase, which is followed, as often, by masculine plural pronominal suffixes. The same remark applies to Judah in verse 7.

Anti-schema 3: Hosea 2-3

Verses	Addressee/Subject	Singular/Plural?	Male/Female?	Marriage Metaphor Present?	Apostasy Theme explicit?
2:1-2	[Yhwh]: [Hosea]: Israel	P	M	No	Yes
2:3	[Yhwh?]: [Israel?]	P	M	No	Yes
2:4	[Yhwh?]: [Israel?]: mother	P	M	No?	Yes?
	[Yhwh?]: (not-) wife	S	F	No?	Yes?
2:5	[Yhwh?]: (not-) wife	S	F	Yes?	Yes?
2:6	[Yhwh?]: children	P	M	Yes?	Yes?
2:7-19*	[Yhwh?]: (not-) wife	S	F	Yes?	Yes?
2:20	[Yhwh?]: [Israelites?]	P	M	No?	Yes?
2:21-22	[Yhwh?]: (not-) wife?	S	F	Yes?	No?
2:23-24	[Yhwh?]: heavens etc.	P	M	No?	Yes?
2:25	[Yhwh?]: (not-) wife?	S	F	Yes?	No?
	[Yhwh?]: [Israel?]	P	M	No?	Yes?
3:1	Yhwh: Hosea: woman	S	M → F	Yes?	No?
	Yhwh: children of Israel	P	M	Yes?	Yes
3:2-3	Hosea: woman	S	M → F	Yes?	No?
3:4-5	Children of Israel	P	M	No?	Yes

*These verses contain both 3rd person assertions about the (not-) wife and, in verses 8 and 18, direct address to her

Antischema 4: Ezekiel 16 & 23

Verses	Addressee/Subject	Singular/ Plural?	Male/ Female?	Marriage Metaphor Present?	Apostasy Theme explicit? Yes? (אֶתַזְנוּתֵךְ)
16. 1-2	Prophet - Jerusalem	S	M → F	No?	Yes? (אֶתַזְנוּתֵךְ)
3-58	Jerusalem	S	F	Yes	No
59-63	Jerusalem	S	F	No	Yes
23: 1-4	Jerusalem (Oholibah) & Samaria (Oholah)	P	F	Yes	No
5-10	Oholah	S	F	Yes	No
11-35	Oholibah	S	F	Yes	No
36-38	Oholah and Oholibah	P	F	Yes?	Yes?
39	Oholah and Oholibah	P	M	Yes?	Yes?
40-44	Oholah and Oholibah	P → S	F	Yes	Yes?
45	Oholah and Oholibah	P	M → F	Yes	No?
46	Oholah and Oholibah	P	M → F	Yes	No?
47	Oholah and Oholibah	P	M → F → M	Yes	No?
48	Oholibah?	S	F	Yes	No?
49	Oholah and Oholibah	P	F	Yes	No?

Bibliography

Andersen, Francis T. and Freedman, David N. (1980) *Hosea: A New Translation with Introduction and Commentary.* (AB) Garden City, NY: Doubleday.

Anderson, Janice Capel and Staley, Jeffrey L. (eds) (1995) *Taking it Personally: Autobiographical Biblical Criticism.* (Semeia; 72) Atlanta, GA: Scholars Press.

Atwood, Margaret (2001) *The Blind Assassin.* London: Virago.

Austin, J. L. (1962) *How to Do Things with Words.* Oxford: Oxford University Press.

Babuscio, Jack (1977) "Camp and the gay sensibility". In Richard Dyer (ed.), *Gays and Film,* 40–57. London: British Film Institute.

Bach, Alice (1993) "Reading allowed: Feminist biblical criticism approaching the millennium". *Currents in Biblical Research,* 1: 191–215.

Bachofen, J. (1897) *Das Mutterrecht: Eine Untersuchung über die Gynaikokratie der alten Welt nach ihrer Religiösen und Rechtlichen Natur.* Basel: Schwabe.

Bakon, Shimon (1988) "For I am God and not man", *Dor Le Dor,* 17: 243–249.

Balz-Cochois, Helgard (1982) "Gomer oder die Macht der Astarte: Versuch einer feministischen Interpretation von Hos 1–4", *EvT,* 42: 37–65.

Bauer, Angela (1999) *Gender in the Book of Jeremiah: A Feminist-Literary Reading.* New York: Lang.

Baumann, Gerlinde (2003) *Love and Violence: Marriage as Metaphor for the Relationship between YHWH and Israel in the Prophetic Books.* Collegeville, PA: Liturgical Press.

Bell, Diane and Klein, Renate (eds) (1996) *Radically Speaking: Feminism Reclaimed.* London: Zed Books.

Berlant, Lauren and Warner, Michael (1995) "What does queer theory teach us about X", in *PMLA,* 110 (3): 343–349.

Bersani, Leo (1988) "Is the Rectum a Grave". In Douglas Crimp (ed.) *AIDS: Cultural Analysis, Cultural Activism,* 197–222. London: MIT Press.

Bersani, Leo (1995) *Homos.* Cambridge, MA and London: Harvard University Press.

Bible and Culture Collective (1995) *The Postmodern Bible.* New Haven, CT and London: Yale University Press.

Bird, Phyllis (1989) "To play the harlot: An inquiry into an Old Testament metaphor". In Peggy Day (ed.) *Gender and Difference in Ancient Israel,* 75–94. Minneapolis, MN: Fortress Press.

Black, Max (1962) *Models and Metaphors: Studies in Language and Philosophy.* Ithaca, NY: Cornell University Press.

Black, Max (1979) "More about metaphor". In Andrew Ortony (ed.) *Metaphor and Thought*, 19–43. Cambridge: Cambridge University Press.

Block, Daniel I. (1997) *The Book of Ezekiel: Chapters 1 to 24*. (The New International Commentary on the Old Testament) Grand Rapids, MI: Eerdmans.

Block, Daniel I. (1998) *The Book of Ezekiel: Chapters 25 to 48*. (The New International Commentary on the Old Testament) Grand Rapids, MI: Eerdmans.

Boer, Roland (2006) "1 and 2 Chronicles". In Deryn Guest, Robert E. Goss, Mona West and Thomas Bohache (eds) *The Queer Bible Commentary*, 251–267. London: SCM.

Booth, Mark (1983) *Camp*. London: Quartet Books.

Boswell, John (1980) *Christianity, Social Tolerance and Homosexuality: Gay People in Western Europe from the Beginning of the Christian Era to the Fourteenth Century*. Chicago, IL and London: University of Chicago Press.

Botterweck, G. Johannes and Ringgren, Helmer (1974/1993) *Theological Dictionary of the Old Testament* (trans. John. T. Willis) 14 vols. Grand Rapids, MI: Eerdmans.

Bozak, Barbara A. (1991) *Life "Anew": A Literary-Theological Study of Jer. 30–31*. Rome: Biblical Institute Press.

Bray, Alan (1982) *Homosexuality in Renaissance England*. London: Gay Men's Press.

Brenner, Athalya (1995a) "Introduction". In Athalya Brenner (ed.) *A Feminist Companion to the Latter Prophets*, 21–37. Sheffield: Sheffield Academic Press.

Brenner, Athalya (1995b) "On prophetic propaganda and the politics of 'Love': The case of Jeremiah". In Athalya Brenner (ed.) *A Feminist Companion to the Latter Prophets*, 256–274. Sheffield: Sheffield Academic Press.

Brenner, Athalya (1996) "Pornoprophetics revisited: Some additional reflections". *Journal for the Study of the Old Testament*, 70: 63–86.

Brenner, Athalya and Dijk-Hemmes, Fokkelien van (1996) "On 'Jeremiah' and the Poetics of (Prophetic?) Texts". In Athalya Brenner and Fokkelien van Dijk-Hemmes (eds) *On Gendering Texts: Female and Male Voices in the Hebrew Bible*, 177–193. Leiden: Brill.

Bright, John (1986) *Jeremiah: Introduction, Translation and Notes*. (Anchor Bible) Garden City, NY: Doubleday.

Brownstein, Rachel M. (1996) "Interrupted reading: Personal criticism in the present time". In H. Aram Veeser (ed.) *Confessions of the Critics*, 29–39. New York; London: Routledge.

Budd, Philip J. (1984) *Numbers*. (WBC) Waco, TX: World Books.

Buss, M. J. (1969) *The Prophetic World of Hosea: A Morphological Study*. Berlin: Alfred Töpelmann.

Butler, Judith (1990) *Gender Trouble: Feminism and the Subversion of Identity*. 1999 reprint with rev. preface. London: Routledge.

Butler, Judith (1993) *Bodies That Matter: On the Discursive Limits of "Sex"*. New York: Routledge.

Camp, Claudia V. (1997) "Feminist theological hermeneutics: Canon and Christian identity". In Elisabeth Schussler Fiorenza (ed.) *Searching the Scriptures: Vol. 1: A Feminist Introduction*, 154–171. London: SCM.

Carden, Michael (2007) *Sodomy: A History of a Christian Biblical Myth*. London: Equinox.

Carroll, Robert P. (1986) *Jeremiah: A Commentary*. (OTL) London: SCM.

Carroll, Robert P. (1995) "Desire under the terebinths: On pornographic representation in the prophets – a response". In Athalya Brenner (ed.) *A Feminist Companion to the Bible*, 275–307. Sheffield: Sheffield Academic Press.

Carroll, Robert P. (1996) "Whorusalamin: A tale of three cities as three sisters". In Bob Becking and Meindert Dijkstra (eds) *On Reading Prophetic Texts: Gender-Specific and Related Studies in Memory of Fokkelien van Dijk Hemmes*, 67–82. Leiden: Brill.

Chase, Susan E. (2005) "Narrative inquiry: Multiple lenses, approaches, voices". In Norman K. Denzin and Yvonna S. Lincoln (eds) *The Sage Handbook of Qualitative Research*, 651–679, 3rd edn. Thousand Oaks, CA and London: Sage.

Cleto, Fabio (ed.) (1999) *Camp: Queer Aesthetics and the Performing Subject: A Reader*. Ann Arbor, MI: University of Michigan Press.

Clines, D. (1979) "Hosea 2: Structure and interpretation", *Studia Biblica*, 1: 83–103.

Cohen, Cathy (1997) "Punks, bulldaggers and welfare queens: The real radical potential of queer politics?", *Gay and Lesbian Quarterly* 3: 437–465.

Cohen, Ed (1993) *Talk on the Wilde Side: Toward a Genealogy of a Discourse on Male Sexualities*. London: Routledge.

Colette (1966) *The Pure and the Impure* (trans. Herma Briffault). New York: Farrar, Straus and Ciroux.

Collier, Dickie (2004) "Hotshots", *Gay Times*, no. 307 (April), p. 116.

Connolly, Tristanne J. (1998) "Metaphor and abuse in Hosea", *Feminist Theology*, 18: 55–66.

Core, Philip (1984) *Camp: The Lie That Tells the Truth*. London: Plexus.

Crisp, Quentin (1985) *The Naked Civil Servant*. London: Fontana (first published London: Cape, 1968).

Cummings, Sean (2004) "My name is ...", *Gay Times*, no. 307 (April), p. 113.

Darr, Katheryn Pfisterer (1992a) "Ezekiel". In Carol A. Newsom and Sharon H. Ringe (eds) *The Women's Bible Commentary*, 183–190. London: SPCK.

Darr, Katheryn Pfisterer (1992b) "Ezekiel's justification of God: Teaching troubled texts", *Journal for the Study of the Old Testament*, 55: 97–117.

Davies, Graham I. (1993) *Hosea*. (OTG) Sheffield: JSOT.

Davies, Philip R. (2004) *Yours Faithfully: Virtual Letters from the Bible*. London: Equinox.

Davis, John (1977) *People of the Mediterranean: An Essay in Comparative Social Anthropology*. London: Routledge & Kegan Paul.

Day, John (2004) "Does the Old Testament refer to sacred prostitution and did it actually exist in Ancient Israel?". In Carmel McCarthy and John F. Healey (eds) *Biblical and Near Eastern Essays: Studies in Honour of Kevin J. Cathcart*, 2–31 (JSOTSupp; 375). London: T&T Clark.

Day, Linda (2000) "Rhetoric and domestic violence in Ezekiel 16", *Biblical Interpretation: A Journal of Contemporary Approaches*, 8 (3): 205–230.

Day, Peggy L. (2000a) "Adulterous Jerusalem's imagined demise: Death of a metaphor in Ezekiel XVI", *Vetus Testamentum*, 50(3): 285–309.

Day, Peggy L. (2000b) "The bitch had it coming to her: Rhetoric and interpretation in Ezekiel 16", *Biblical Interpretation: A Journal of Contemporary Approaches*, 8 (3): 231–254.

Dearman, Andrew (1999) "YHWH's house: Gender roles and metaphors for Israel in Hosea", *Journal of Northwest Semitic Languages*, 25 (1): 99–108.

De Beauvoir, Simone (1959) *The Second Sex.* New York: Bantam. (Originally published 1949.)

D'Emilio, John (1990) "Gay politics and community in San Francisco since World War II". In Martin Duberman, Martha Vicinus and George Chauncey (eds) *Hidden from History: Reclaiming the Gay & Lesbian Past.* New York: Meridian.

Dempsey, Carol J. (1998) "The 'Whore' of Ezekiel 16: The impact and ramifications of gender-specific metaphors in light of biblical law and divine judgment". In Victor H. Matthews, Bernard M. Levinson and Tika Frymer-Kensky (eds) *Gender and Law in the Hebrew Bible and the Ancient Near East,* 57–78 (JSOTSupp; 262). Sheffield: Sheffield Academic Press.

Denzin, Norman K. and Lincoln, Yvonna S. (eds) (2005) *The Sage Handbook of Qualitative Research,* 3rd edn. Thousand Oaks, CA and London: Sage.

Dever, W. G. (2005) *Did God have a Wife?: Archaeology and Folk Religion in Ancient Israel.* Cambridge: Eerdmans.

Diamond, A. R. Pete (1999) "Introduction". In A. R. Pete Diamond, Kathleen M. O'Connor and Louis Stillman (eds) *Troubling Jeremiah,* 15–32 (JSOTSupp; 260). Sheffield: Sheffield Academic Press.

Diamond, A. R. Pete and O'Connor, Kathleen M. (1996) "Unfaithful passions: Coding women coding men in Jeremiah 2–3 (4:2*)", Biblical Interpretation: A Journal of Contemporary Approaches,* 4 (3): 288–310.

Dijk-Hemmes, Fokkelien van (1989) "The imagination of power and the power of imagination: An intertextual analysis of two biblical love songs, The Song of Songs and Hosea 2", *Journal for the Study of the Old Testament,* 44: 75–88.

Dijk-Hemmes, Fokkelien van (1993) "The metaphorization of woman in prophetic speech: An analysis of Ezekiel XXIII". In Athalya Brenner and Fokkelien van Dijk-Hemmes (eds) *On Gendering Texts: Female & Male Voices in the Hebrew Bible,* 167–176. Leiden: Brill; an expanded version of an article first published in *Vetus Testamentum,* 1993, 43 (2): 162–169.

Dollimore, Jonathan (1991) *Sexual Dissidence: Augustine To Wilde, Freud to Foucault.* Oxford: Clarendon.

Donne, John (1967) *Complete Poetry and Selected Prose* (ed. John Hayward). London: Nonesuch.

Douglas, Mary (1969) *Purity and Danger.* London: Routledge and Kegan Paul.

Dyer, Richard (1992) "It's being so camp as keeps us going". In *Only Entertainment,* 135–147. London: Routledge. Originally published in 1977 in *Body Politic,* 10: 11–13 and in 1976 in *Playguy.*

Dynes, W. R. (1990) "Camp". In *Encyclopedia of Homosexuality,* vol. 1: 189–190. London: Garland.

Eidevall, Göran (1996) *Grapes in the Desert: Metaphors, Models and Themes in Hosea 4–14.* Stockholm: Almqvist & Wicksell.

Eilberg-Schwartz, Howard (1990) *The Savage in Judaism: An Anthropology of Israelite Religion and Ancient Judaism.* Bloomington, IN: Indiana University Press.

Eilberg-Schwartz, Howard (1994) *God's Phallus: and Other Problems for Men and Monotheism.* Boston, MA: Beacon Press.

Emmerson, Grace I. (1984) *Hosea.* (JSOT Supp) Sheffield: JSOT Press.

Escoffier, J. (1990) "Inside the ivory closet: The challenges facing lesbian and gay studies", *Out/Look: National Lesbian and Gay Quarterly,* 10: 40–48.

Exum, J. Cheryl (1993) *Fragmented Women: Feminist (Sub)Versions of Biblical Narrative.* Valley Forge, PA: Trinity Press International.

Exum, J. Cheryl (1995) "The ethics of biblical violence against women". In John W. Rogerson, Mark Daniel Carroll and Margaret Davies (eds) *The Bible in Ethics: The Second Sheffield Colloquium*, 248–271. Sheffield: Sheffield Academic Press.

Exum, J. Cheryl (1996) "Prophetic pornography". In J. Cheryl Exum *Plotted, Shot and Painted: Cultural Representation of Biblical Women*, 101–128. Sheffield: Sheffield Academic Press.

Fensham, F. C. (1984) "The marriage metaphor in Hosea for the covenant relationship between the Lord and His people (Hos. 1: 2–9)", *Journal of North West Semitic Languages* , 13: 71–86.

Fetterley, Judith (1978) *The Resisting Reader: A Feminist Approach to American Fiction*. Bloomington, IN: Indiana University Press.

Fewell, Danna Nolan (1987) "Feminist readings of the Hebrew Bible: Affirmation, resistance and transformation", *Journal for the Study of the Old Testament*, 39: 77–87.

Fisch, S. (1950) *Ezekiel: Hebrew Text & English Translation with an Introduction and Commentary*. (Soncino Books of the Bible) London: Soncino.

Fish, Stanley E. (1980) *Is there a Text in the Class?: The Authority of the Interpretive Community*. Cambridge, MA: Harvard University Press.

Fitzgerald, Aloysius (1972) "The Mythological Background for the Presentation of Jerusalem as a Queen and False Worship as Adultery in the OT", *Catholic Biblical Quarterly*, 34: 403–416.

Fitzgerald, Aloysius (1975) "BTWLT and BT as titles for capital cities", *Catholic Biblical Quarterly*, 37: 167–183.

Flinn, Caryl (1999) "The deaths of camp". In Fabio Cleto (ed.) *Camp: Queer Aesthetics and the Performing Subject: A Reader*, 433–457. Ann Arbor, MI: University of Michigan Press.

Fohrer, G. (1968) *Introduction to the Old Testament*. Nashville, TN: Abingdon.

Fontaine, Carole R. (1995a) "Hosea". In Athalya Brenner (ed.) *A Feminist Companion to the Latter Prophets*, 40–59. Sheffield: Sheffield Academic Press.

Fontaine, Carole R. (1995b) "A Response to 'Hosea'". In Athalya Brenner (ed.) *A Feminist Companion to the Bible*, 60–69. Sheffield: Sheffield Academic Press.

Foucault, Michel (1977) *Discipline and Punish: The Birth of the Prison* (ed. Alan Sheridan). New York: Vintage. Translated from the French 1975.

Foucault, Michel. (1990) *The History of Sexuality: Volume 1: An Introduction* (ed. Robert Hurley). New York: Vintage. Translated from the French 1976.

Fowler, Robert M. (1995) "Taking it personally: A personal response". In Janice Capel Anderson and Jeffrey L. Staley (eds) *Taking it Personally: Autobiographical Biblical Criticism*, 231–239. (Semeia; 72) Atlanta, GA: Scholars Press.

Frantzen, Allen J. (1996) "Between the lines: Queer theory, the history of homosexuality, and Anglo-Saxon penitentials", *Journal of Medieval and Early Modern Studies*, 26 (2): 255–296.

Freedman, Diane P., Frey, Olivia and Zauhar, Frances Murphy (eds) (1993) *The Intimate Critique: Autobiographical Literary Criticism*. Durham, NC: Duke University Press.

Freedman, Diane P. (1996) "Autobiographical literary criticism as the new Belletrism: Personal experience". In H. Aram Veeser (ed.) *Confessions of the Critics*, 3–16. New York and London: Routledge.

Friedman, M. A. (1980) "Israel's response in Hosea 2.17b: 'You are my husband'", *Journal of Biblical Literature*, 99 (2): 199–204.

Frymer-Kensky, Tikva (1998) "Virginity in the Bible". In Victor H. Matthews, Bernard M. Levinson and Tika Frymer-Kensky (eds) *Gender and Law in the Hebrew Bible and the Ancient Near East*, 79–96. (JSOTSupp; 262) Sheffield: Sheffield Academic Press.

Fuchs, Esther (1997) "God's phallus and other problems for men and monotheism [review of Eilberg-Schwartz:1994]", *Journal of the Amerixan Academy of Religion*, 65 (1): 199–201.

Galambush, Julie (1992) *Jerusalem in the Book of Ezekiel: the City as Yahweh's Wife*. Atlanta, GA: Scholars Press.

Gilmore, David (ed) (1987) *Honor and Shame and the Unity of the Mediterranean*. Washington, DC: American Anthropological Association.

Goldingay, John (1995) "Hosea 1–3, Genesis 1–4 and masculinist interpretation". In Athalya Brenner (ed.) *A Feminist Companion to the Latter Prophets*, 161–168. Sheffield: Sheffield Academic Press.

Goldman, M. D. (1952) "Was Jeremiah married?", *Australian Biblical Review* 2 (1–2): 42–47.

Good, Edwin M. (1970) "Ezekiel's ship: Some extended metaphors in the Old Testament", *Semitics*, 1: 79–103.

Gordis, Robert (1954) "Hosea's marriage and message: A new approach", *HUCA*, 25: 9–35.

Gordon, Pamela and Washington, Harold C. (1995) "Rape as a military metaphor in the Hebrew Bible". In Athalya Brenner (ed.) *A Feminist Companion to the Latter Prophets*, 308–325. Sheffield: Sheffield Academic Press.

Goss, Robert E. (2002) *Queering Christ: Beyond Jesus Acted Up*. Cleveland, OH: Pilgrim Press.

Goss, Robert E. and West, Mona (eds) (2000) *Take Back the Word: A Queer Reading of the Bible*. Cleveland, OH: Pilgrim Press.

Gottwald, Norman K. (1991) "From tribal existence to empire: The socio-historical context for the rise of the Hebrew prophets". In J. M. Thomas and V. Visick (eds) *God and Capitalism: A Prophetic Critique of Market Society*, 11–29. Madison, WI: AR Editions.

Graetz, Naomi (1995) "God is to Israel as husband is to wife: The metaphoric battering of Hosea's wife". In Athalya Brenner (ed.) *A Feminist Companion to the Latter Prophets*, 126–145. Sheffield: Sheffield Academic Press.

Greenberg, Moshe (1983) *Ezekiel 1–20: A New Translation with Introduction and Commentary*. (AB) Garden City, NY: Doubleday.

Greenberg, Moshe. (1997) *Ezekiel 21–37: A New Translation with Introduction and Commentary*. (AB) Garden City, NY: Doubleday.

Guest, Deryn (2005) *When Deborah Met Jael: Lesbian Biblical Hermeneutics*. London: SCM.

Guest, Deryn, Robert E. Goss, Mona West and Thomas Bohache (eds) (2006) *The Queer Bible Commentary*. London: SCM.

Hackett, J.R. (1989) "Can a sexist model liberate us?: Ancient Near Eastern fertility goddesses", *Journal of Feminist Studies in religion*, 5 (1): 65–76.

Hadley, Judith M. (2000) *The Cult of Asherah in Ancient Israel and Judah: Evidence for a Hebrew Goddess*. Cambridge: Cambridge University Press.

Hall, Gary (1982) "Origin of the Marriage Metaphor", *Hebrew Studies*, 23: 169–171.

Halperin, David J. (1993) *Seeking Ezekiel: Text and Psychology*. University Park, PA: Pennsylvania University Press.

Halperin, David M. (1989) *One Hundred Years of Homosexuality*. New York: Routledge.

Halperin, David M. (1995) *Saint Foucault: Towards a Gay Hagiography*. New York and Oxford: Oxford University Press.

Halperin, David M. (2002) *How to do the History of Homosexuality*. Chicago, IL and London: University of Chicago Press.

Harvey, Graham. (1995) "God's phallus and other problems for men and monotheism [review of Eilberg-Schwartz:1994', *JJS*, 46 (1–2): 348.

Harvey, Keith (2002) "Camp talk and citationality: A queer take on 'authentic' and 'represented' utterance", *Journal of Pragmatics*, 34 (9): 1145–1165.

Hendel, Robert S. (1995) "God's phallus and other problems for men and monotheism [review of Eilberg-Schwartz:1994]", *BRev*, 11: 15.

Hinkle, Christopher (2007) "Love's urgent longings: St John of the Cross". In Gerard Loughlin (ed.) *Queer Theology: Rethinking the Western Body*. Malden, MA and Oxford: Blackwell.

Holbrook, Clyde A. (1984) *The Iconoclastic Deity: Biblical Images of God*. Lewisburg: Bucknell University Press.

Holladay, William L. (1986) *Jeremiah 1: A Commentary on the Book of the Prophet Jeremiah, Chapters 1–25*. (Herm) Philadelphia, PA: Fortress.

Holladay, William L. (1989) *Jeremiah 2: A Commentary on the Book of the Prophet Jeremiah, Chapters 26–52*. (Herm) Philadelphia, PA: Fortress.

Hopkins, David C. (1983) "The dynamics of agriculture in monarchical Israel", *Society of Biblical Literature Seminar Papers*, 22: 177–202.

Hopkins, Gerard Manley (1953) *Poems and Prose*; selected and edited by W. H. Gardner. Harmondsworth: Penguin.

Hornsby, Teresa J. (1999) "Israel has become a worthless thing: re-reading Gomer in Hosea 1–3", *Journal for the Study of the Old Testament*, 12: 115–128.

Houtman, C. (1996) *Exodus*. Vol. 2. (Historical Commentary on the Old Testament) Kampen: Kok.

Huffer, Lynne (2001) "'There is no Gomorrah': Narrative ethics in feminist and queer theory", *differences: A Journal of Feminist Cultural Studies*, 12 (3): 1–32.

Iser, Wolfgang (1974) *The Implied Reader: Patterns of Communication in Prose Fiction from Bunyan to Beckett*. Baltimore, MD: Johns Hopkins University Press.

Iser, Wolfgang (1978) *The Act of Reading: A Theory of Aesthetic Response*. Baltimore, MD: Johns Hopkins University Press.

Isherwood, Christopher (1954) *The World in the Afternoon*. London: Methuen.

Jagose, Annamarie (1996) *Queer Theory: An Introduction*. New York: New York University Press.

Jameson, Frederic (1988) "Metacommentary". In Frederick Jameson *The Ideologies of Theory. I. Situations of Theory, Essays 1971–1986*, 3–16. London: Routledge.

Jansen, S. C. and Sabo, D. (1994) "The sport war metaphor: Hegemonic masculinity, the Persian Gulf war, and the New World Order", *Sociology of Sport* 11 (1): 1–17.

Jeffreys, Sheila (1994) "The queer disappearance of lesbians: Sexuality in the academy", *Women's Studies International Forum*, 17 (5): 459–472.

Jennings, Theodore W. (2005) *Jacob's Wound: Homoerotic Narrative in the Literature of Ancient Israel*. New York; London: Continuum.

Johnson, Barbara (1987) "Deconstruction, feminism and pedagogy". In Barbara Johnson *A World of Difference*, 42–46. Baltimore: Johns Hopkins University Press.

Jones, Stacy Holman (2005) "Autoethnography: Making the personal political". In Norman K. Denzin and Yvonna S. Lincoln (eds) *The Sage Handbook of Qualitative Research*, 763–791, 3rd edn. Thousand Oaks, CA and London: Sage.

Keefe, Alice A. (1995) "The female body, the body politic and the land: A socio-political reading of Hosea 1–2". In Athalya Brenner (ed.) *A Feminist Companion to the Latter Prophets*, 70–100. Sheffield: Sheffield Academic Press.

Keefe, Alice A. (2001) *Woman's Body and the Social Body in Hosea*. London: Sheffield Academic Press.

Kennedy, Liam (1995) *Susan Sontag: Mind As Passion*. Manchester: Manchester University Press.

Kittel, Gerhard (1964/1976) *Theological Dictionary of the New Testament* (trans. Geoffrey W. Bromiley), 10 vols. Grand Rapids, MI: Eerdmans.

Kleinhans, Chuck (1994) "Taking out the trash: Camp and the politics of parody". In Moe Meyer (ed.) *The Politics and Poetics of Camp*. London: Routledge.

Koch, Timothy R. (2001) "Cruising as methodology: Homoeroticism and the scriptures". In Ken Stone (ed.) *Queer Commentary and the Hebrew Bible*, 169–180. London: Sheffield Academic Press.

Koehler, Ludwig (1956) *Hebrew Man: Lectures Delivered at the Invitation of the University of Tübingen, December 1–16, 1952* (trans. Peter R. Ackroyd). London: SCM.

Koehler, Ludwig and Baumgartner, Walter (1994) *Hebrew and Aramaic Lexicon of the Old Testament* (trans. M. E. J. Richardson) 5 vols. Leiden: Brill.

Kristeva, Julia (1980) *Desire in Language: A Semiotic Approach to Literature and Art*. New York: Columbia University Press.

Kristeva, Julia (1984) *Revolution in Poetic Language*. New York: Columbia University Press. Originally published in 1974.

Lacan, Jacques (1985) "The meaning of the phallus". In Juliet Mitchell and Jacqueline Rose (eds) *Feminine Sexuality: Jacques Lacan and the École Freudienne*, 83–85. New York: Norton.

Lakoff, George and Johnson, Mark (1980) *Metaphors We Live By*. Chicago, IL: University of Chicago Press.

Landy, Francis (1995) 'Fantasy and the displacement of pleasure: Hosea 2.4–17'. In Athalya Brenner (ed.) *A Feminist Companion to the Latter Prophets*, 146–160. Sheffield: Sheffield Academic Press.

Landy, Francis (1995a) *Hosea* (Readings: A New Biblical Commentary). Sheffield: Sheffield Academic Press.

Leith, Mary Joan Winn (1989) "Verse and reverse: The transformation of the woman, Israel, in Hosea 1–3". In Peggy L. Day (ed.) *Gender and Difference in Ancient Israel*, 95–108. Minneapolis, MN: Fortress Press.

Lemche, Niels Peter (1992) "The God of Hosea". In Eugene Ulrich (ed.) *Priests, Prophets and Scribes: Essays on the Formation and Heritage of Second Temple Judaism in Honour of Joseph Blenkinsopp*, 241–257. Sheffield: JSOT Press.

Lévi-Strauss, Claude (1963) *Totemism*. Boston, MA: Beacon Press.

Lévi-Strauss, Claude (1969) *The Element Structures of Kinship*. Boston, MA: Beacon Press.

Lewy, Julius (1944) "The old west semitic sun-god Hammu", *HUCA*, 18: 429–488.

Liew, Tat-Siong Benny (2001) "(Cor)responding: A letter to the editor". In Ken Stone (ed.) *Queer Commentary and the Hebrew Bible*, 182–192. London: Sheffield Academic Press.

Lofthouse, W. F. (1913) *Ezekiel: Introduction, Revised Version with Notes and Index.* (CB) Edinburgh: T. C. & E. C. Jack.

Loughlin, Gerard (ed.) (2007) *Queer Theology: Rethinking the Western Body.* Malden, MA; Oxford: Blackwell.

Lundbom, Jack R. (1999) *Jeremiah 1–2: A New Translation with Introduction and Commentary.* (AB) New York, etc.: Doubleday.

McDonald, J. R. B. (1964) "The marriage of Hosea", *Theology*, 67(526): 149–156.

McFague, Sallie (1983) *Metaphorical Theology: Models of God in Religious Language.* London: SCM.

Macintosh, A. A. (1997) *A Critical and Exegetical Commentary on Hosea.* (ICC) Edinburgh: T&T Clark.

McIntosh, Mary (1968) "The homosexual role", *Social Problems*, 16 (2): 182–192.

Macky, Peter W. (1990) *The Centrality of Metaphors to Biblical Thought: A Method for Interpreting the Bible.* (Studies in the Bible and Early Christianity; 19) Lewiston, NY: Edwin Mellen.

McNeill, John J. (1993) *The Church and the Homosexual*, 4th edn. Boston, MA: Beacon Press. First edn published 1976.

Macwilliam, Stuart (2002) "Queering Jeremiah", *Biblical Interpretation: A Journal of Contemporary Approaches*, 10 (4): 384–404.

Magdalene, F. Rachel (1995) "Ancient Near Eastern treaty-curses and the ultimate texts of terror: A study of the language of divine sexual abuse in the prophetic corpus". In Athalya Brenner (ed.) *A Feminist Companion to the Latter Prophets*, 326–352. Sheffield: Sheffield Academic Press.

Malinowitz, Harriet (1993) "Queer theory: Whose theory?", *Frontiers*, 13: 168–184.

Mays, James L. (1969) *Hosea: A Commentary.* (OTL) Philadelphia, PA: Westminster Press.

Meyer, Moe (ed.) (1994) *The Politics and Poetics of Camp.* London: Routledge.

Miller, Nancy K. (1991) *Getting Personal: Feminist Occasions and Other Biographical Acts.* London: Routledge.

Moore, Stephen D. (1986) "Negative hermeneutics, insubstantial texts: Stanley Fish and the biblical interpreter", *Journal of the American Academy of Religion*, 54 (4): 707–719.

Moore, Stephen D. (1989) *Literary Criticism and the Gospels: The Theoretical Challenge.* New Haven, CT and London: Yale University Press.

Moore, Stephen D. (1989a) "The 'Post-'age stamp: Does it stick?: Biblical studies and the postmodernism debate", *Journal of the American Academy of Religion*, 57 (3): 543–559.

Moore, Stephen D. (1995) "True confessions and weird obsessions: Autobiographical interventions in literary and biblical studies". In Janice Capel Anderson and Jeffrey L. Staley (eds) *Taking it Personally: Autobiographical Biblical Criticism*, 19–50. (Sem; 72) Atlanta, GA: Scholars Press.

Moughtin-Mumby, Sharon (2008) *Sexual and Marital Metaphors in Hosea, Jeremiah, Isaiah, and Ezekiel.* Oxford: Oxford University Press.

Newsom, Carol A. (1987) "A maker of metaphors: Ezekiel's oracles against Tyre". In J. L. Mays and P. J. Achtemeier (eds) *Interpreting the Prophets*, 188–199. Philadelphia, PA: Fortress.

Newton, Esther (1972) *Mother Camp: Female Impersonators in America*. Chicago, IL and London: University of Chicago Press (1979 reprint).

Nussbaum, Martha C. (1999) "The professor of parody: The hip defeatism of Judith Butler", *The New Republic*, 22 February: 37–45.

O'Brien, Julia M. (1995) "On saying 'No' to a prophet". In Janice Capel Anderson and Jeffrey L. Staley (eds) *Taking it Personally: Autobiographical Biblical Criticism*, 111–124. (Sem; 72) Atlanta, GA: Scholars Press.

O'Connor, Kathleen (1992) "Jeremiah". In Carol A. Newsom and Sharon H. Ringe (eds) *The Women's Bible Commentary*, 169–177. London: SPCK.

Odell, Margaret S. (1992) "The inversion of shame and forgiveness in Ezekiel 16.59–63", *Journal for the Study of the Old Testament*, 56: 101–112.

Ortlund, Raymond C. (1996) *Whoredom: God's Unfaithful Wife in Biblical Theology*. Leicester: Apollos.

Pardes, Ilana (1992) *Countertraditions in the Bible: A Feminist Approach*. Cambridge, MA: Harvard University Press.

Parmenides (1984) *Fragments: A Text and Translation* (trans. and ed. David Gallop). Toronto: University of Toronto Press.

Patton, Corrine L. (2000) "'Should our sister be treated as a whore?': A response to feminist critiques of Ezekiel". In Margaret S. Odell and John T. Strong (eds) *The Book of Ezekiel: Theological and Anthropological Perspectives*, 221–238. Atlanta, GA: Society of Biblical Literature.

Piggford, George (1999) "'Who's that girl?': Annie Lennox, Woolf's *Orlando*, and female camp androgyny". In Fabio Cleto (ed.) *Camp: Queer Aesthetics and the Performing Subject: A Reader*. Ann Arbor, MI: University of Michigan Press.

Plaskow, Judith (1999) "Transforming the nature of community: Towards a feminist people of Israel". In Alice Bach (ed.) *Women in the Hebrew Bible: A Reader*, 403–418. New York and London: Sage.

Pollock, Donald (1985) "Food and sexual identity among the Culina", *Food and Foodways*, 1: 25–42.

Premnath, D. N. (1988) "Latifundialization and Isaiah 5.8–10", *Journal for the Study of the Old Testament*, 40: 49–60.

Richards, I. A. (1936) *The Philosophy of Rhetoric*. London: Oxford University Press.

Richardson, Laurel and Adams St Pierre, Elizabeth (2005) "Writing: A method of inquiry". In Norman K. Denzin and Yvonna S. Lincoln (eds) *The Sage Handbook of Qualitative Research*, 3rd edn, 959–978. Thousand Oaks, CA and London: Sage.

Ricoeur, Paul (1978) *The Rule of Metaphor: Multi-Disciplinary Studies of the Creation of Meaning in Language*. London: Routledge & Kegan Paul.

Ringgren, Helmer (1987) "The marriage motif in Israelite religion". In Patrick D. Miller, Paul D. Hanson and S. Dean McBride (eds) *Ancient Israelite Religion*. Philadelphia, PA: Fortress Press.

Riviere, Joan (1929) "Womanliness as a masquerade", *The International Journal of Psychoanalysis*, 10: 303–313.

Rooker, Mark F. (1990) *Biblical Hebrew in Transition: The Language of the Book of Ezekiel*. (JSOTSupp; 90) Sheffield: JSOT Press.

Ross, Andrew (1989) "Uses of camp". In Andrew Ross *No Respect: Intellectuals and Popular Culture*, 135–170. London: Routledge.

Rowley, H. H. (1956/7) "The marriage of Hosea", *Bulletin of the John Rylands Library*, 39: 200–233.

Salih, Sara (2003) "Judith Butler and the ethics of 'difficulty'", *Critical Commentary*, 45 (3): 42–51.

Schlissel, L. (2002) "Mae West and the 'Queer plays'", *Women's History Review*, 11 (1): 71–88.

Schmitt, John J. (1983) "The gender of Ancient Israel", *Journal for the Study of the Old Testament*, 26: 115–125.

Schmitt, John J. (1989) "The wife of God in Hosea 2", *Biblical Research*, 24: 5–18.

Schmitt, John J. (1991) "Israel and Zion – two gendered images: Biblical speech traditions and their contemporary neglect", *Horizons*, 18 (1): 18–32.

Schmitt, John J. (1995) "Yahweh's divorce in Hosea 2 – who is that woman?", *Scandinavian Journal of the Old Testament*, 9 (1): 119–132.

Schüngel-Straumann, Helen (1995) "God as mother in Hosea 11". In Athalya Brenner (ed.) *A Feminist Companion to the Latter Prophets*, 194–218. Sheffield: Sheffield Academic Press.

Sedgwick, Eve Kosofsky (1993) "Queer performativity: Henry James's *The Art of the Novel*", *GLQ*, 1: 1–16.

Sedgwick, Eve Kosofsky (1994) *Epistemology of the Closet*. London: Penguin. Originally published 1991.

Seidman, Steven (1993) "Identity and politics in a 'postmodern' gay culture: Some historical and conceptual notes". In Michael Warner (ed.) *Fear of a Queer Planet*, 105–142. Minneapolis, MN and London: University of Minnesota Press.

Seidman, Steven (ed.) (1996) *Queer Theory/Sociology*. Cambridge, MA and Oxford: Blackwell.

Setel, T. Drorah (1985) "Prophets and pornography: Female sexual imagery in Hosea". In Letty M. Russell (ed.) *Feminist Interpretation of the Bible*, 86–95. Philadelphia, PA: Westminster Press.

Sherwood, Yvonne (1995) "Boxing Gomer: Controlling the deviant woman in Hosea 1–3". In Athalya Brenner (ed.) *A Feminist Companion to the Latter Prophets*, 101–125. Sheffield: Sheffield Academic Press.

Sherwood, Yvonne (1996) *The Prostitute and the Prophet: Hosea's Marriage in Literary-Theoretical Perspective*. Sheffield: Sheffield Academic Press.

Sherwood, Yvonne (2004) *Derrida's Bible: Reading a Page of Scripture with a little Help from Derrida*. New York and Basingstoke: Palgrave Macmillan.

Shields, Mary E. (1998) "Multiple exposures: Body rhetoric and gender characterization in Ezekiel 16", *Journal of Feminist Studies in Religion*, 14 (1): 5–18.

Shilts, Randy (1993) *The Mayor of Castro Street: The Life and Times of Harvey Milk*. London: Penguin. Originally published 1982.

Simpson, Mark (1994) *Male Impersonators: Men Performing Masculinity*. London: Cassell.

Simpson, Mark (ed.) (1996) *Anti-Gay*. London: Freedom Editions.

Sinfield, Alan (1994) *The Wilde Century: Effeminacy, Oscar Wilde and the Queer Movement*. London: Cassell.

Sinfield, Alan (1998) *Gay and After*. London: Serpent's Tail.

Slonim, Mayer G. (1939) "The substitution of the masculine for the feminine Hebrew pronominal suffixes to express reverence", *The Jewish Quarterly Review*, New Series 29 (4): 397–403.

Slonim, Mayer G. (1941) "The deliberate substitution of the masculine for the feminine pronominal suffixes in the Hebrew Bible", *The Jewish Quarterly Review*, New Series 32 (2): 139–158.

Slonim, Mayer G. (1944) "Masculine predicates with feminine subjects in the Hebrew Bible", *Journal of Biblical Literature*, 63 (3): 297–302.

Sontag, Susan (1983) "Notes on camp". In *A Susan Sontag Reader*, 105–119. Harmondsworth: Penguin. Originally published 1964.

Sontag, Susan (1983a) "The 'Salmagundi' interview". In *A Susan Sontag Reader*, 105–119. Harmondsworth: Penguin. Originally published in *Salmagundi*, no. 31–32, Fall 1975–Winter 1976.

Sontag, Susan (1991) *Illness as Metaphor, and Aids and its Metaphors.* London: Penguin. *Illness as Metaphor* first published 1979; *Aids and its Metaphors* first published 1989.

Soskice, Janet Martin (1985) *Metaphor and Religious Language.* Oxford: Clarendon Press.

Spargo, Tamsin (1999) *Foucault and Queer Theory.* Duxford: Icon Books.

Spencer, Daniel T. (2001) "A gay male ethicist's response to queer readings of the Bible". In Ken Stone (ed.) *Queer Commentary and the Hebrew Bible*, 193–209. London: Sheffield Academic Press.

Sperber, Alexander (ed.) (1962) *The Bible in Aramaic, v.3: The Latter Prophets According to Targum Jonathan.* Leiden: Brill.

Stein, Arlene and Plummer, Ken (1996) "'I can't even think straight': 'Queer' theory and the missing sexual revolution". In Steven Seidman (ed.) *Queer Theory/ Sociology*, 129–144. Cambridge, MA and Oxford: Blackwell.

Stevens, Christopher (2010) *Kenneth Williams: Born Brilliant.* London: John Murray.

Stienstra, Nellie (1993) *YHWH is the Husband of His People: Analysis of a Biblical Metaphor with Special Reference to Translation.* Kampen: Kok Pharos.

Stigliano, Tony (1985) "Remarks on C. A. Bowers's 'Curriculum as reproduction: an examination of metaphor as a carrier of ideology'", *Teachers College Record*, 83 (2): 285–291.

Stone, Ken (ed.) (2001) *Queer Commentary and the Hebrew Bible.* London: Sheffield Academic Press.

Stone, Ken (2001a) "Queer commentary and biblical interpretation: An introduction". In Ken Stone (ed.) *Queer Commentary and the Hebrew Bible*, 11–34. London: Sheffield Academic Press.

Stone, Ken (2001b) "Lovers and raisin cakes: Food, sex and divine insecurity in Hosea". In Ken Stone (ed.) *Queer Commentary and the Hebrew Bible*, 116–139. London: Sheffield Academic Press.

Streete, G. C. (1996) "God's phallus and other problems for men and monotheism [review of Eilberg-Schwartz:1994]", *Journal of the History of Sexuality*, 6 (3): 461–463.

Stuart, Elizabeth (2000) "Camping around the canon: Humor as a hermeneutical tool in queer readings of biblical texts". In Robert E. Goss and Mona West (eds)

Take Back the Word: A Queer Reading of the Bible, 23–24. Cleveland, OH: Pilgrim Press.

Sullivan, Nikki (2003) *A Critical Introduction to Queer Theory.* Edinburgh: Edinburgh University Press.

Swanepoel, M. G. (1993) "Ezekiel 16: Abandoned child, bride adorned or unfaithful wife?". In Philip R. Davies and David J. Clines (eds) *Among the Prophets: Language, Image and Structure in the Prophetic Writings*, 84–104. (JSOTSup; 144) Sheffield: JSOT Press.

Tompkins, Jane (1993) "Me and my shadow". In Diane P. Freedman, Olivia Frey and Frances Murphy Zauhar (eds) *The Intimate Critique: Autobiographical Literary Criticism*, 23–40. Durham, NC: Duke University Press.

Torres, Sasha (1999) "The caped crusader of camp: Pop, camp and the *Batman* television series". In Fabio Cleto (ed.) *Camp: Queer Aesthetics and the Performing Subject: A Reader*, 330–343. Ann Arbor, MI: University of Michigan Press.

Tyler, Carole-Anne (1999) "Boys will be girls: Drag and transvestic fetishism". In Fabio Cleto (ed.) *Camp: Queer Aesthetics and the Performing Subject: A Reader*, 369–392. Ann Arbor, MI: University of Michigan Press.

Ullendorf, Edward (1979) "The bawdy Bible", *Bulletin of the School of Oriental and African Studies, University of London*, 42 (3): 425–456.

Van Selms, A. (1964) "Hosea and Canticles", *Ou Testamentiese Werkgemeenskap Suid Afrika*, 7 (8): 85–89.

Veeser, H. Aram (ed.) (1996) *Confessions of the Critics.* New York; London: Routledge

Vogels, Walter (1998) "Hosea's gift to Gomer (Hos. 3,2)", *Biblica*, 69 (3): 412–421.

Wacker, Marie-Theres (1987) "Frau-Sexus-Macht: Eine feministische Relecture des Hosea Buches". In *Der Gott der Männer und der Frauen*, 101–125. (Theologie zur Zeit; 2) Düsseldorf: Patmos.

Wakeman, Mary K. (1982) "Sacred Marriage", *Journal for the Study of the Old Testament*, 22: 21–31.

Ware, J. Redding (1909) *Passing English of the Victorian Era: A Dictionary of Heterodox English, Slang, and Phrase.* London: Routledge.

Warner, Michael (ed.) (1993) *Fear of a Queer Planet: Queer Politics and Social Theory.* Minneapolis, MN: University of Minnesota Press.

Watney, Simon (1992) "Homosexual, gay or queer? Activism, outing and the politics of sexual identities", *Outrage*, April: 18–22.

Weeks, Jeffrey (1990) *Coming Out: Homosexual Politics in Britain from the Nineteenth Century to the Present.* Rev. edn. London: Quartet Books.

Weems, Renita J. (1989) "Gomer: Victim of violence or victim of metaphor", *Semeia*, 47: 87–104.

Weems, Renita J. (1995) *Battered Love: Marriage, Sex and Violence in the Hebrew Prophets.* Minneapolis, MN: Fortress Press.

Wenham, Gordon J. (1979) *The Book of Leviticus.* Grand Rapids, MI: Eerdmans.

West, Mona (2001) "The gift of voice, the gift of tears: A queer reading of Lamentations in the context of AIDS". In Ken Stone (ed.) *Queer Commentary and the Hebrew Bible*, 140–151. London: Sheffield Academic Press.

West, Mona (2006) "Esther". In Deryn Guest, Robert E. Goss, Mona West and Thomas Bohache (eds) *The Queer Bible Commentary*, 278–285. London: SCM.

Westbrook, R. (1990) "Adultery in ancient Near East law", *Revue Biblique*, 97(4): 542–580.

Wilchins, Riki (2004) *Queer Theory, Gender Theory*. Los Angeles, CA: Alyson Books.

Williams, Kenneth (1994) *The Kenneth Williams Diaries*. London: HarperCollins.

Williams, Kenneth (1995) *The Kenneth Williams Letters*. London: HarperCollins.

Williams, Kenneth (1997) *An Audience with Kenneth Williams*. London: Music Collection International. (Audiocassette).

Wittig, Monique (1992) *The Straight Mind and Other Essays*. Boston, MA: Beacon Press.

Wolff, H. W. (1974) *Hosea: A Commentary on the Book of the Prophet Hosea*, Paul D. Hanson (ed.). (Herm.) Philadelphia, PA: Fortress Press.

Yee, Gale A. (1987) *Composition and Tradition in the Book of Hosea: A Redaction Critical Investigation*. Atlanta, GA: Scholars Press.

Yee, Gale A. (1992) "Hosea". In Carol A. Newsom and Sharon H. Ringe (eds) *The Woman's Bible Commentary*. London: SPCK.

Yee, Gale A. (2001) "'She is not my wife and I am not her husband': A materialist analysis of Hosea 1–2", *Biblical Interpretation: A Journal of Contemporary Approaches*, 9 (4): 345–383.

Zimmerli, Walther (1979) *Ezekiel 1: A Commentary on the Book of the Prophet Ezekiel Chapters 1–24*. Translation of the 1969 German edn by Frank Moore Cross and Klaus Baltzer. (Herm) Philadelphia, PA: Fortress.

Zimmerli, Walther (1983) *Ezekiel 2: A Commentary on the Book of the Prophet Ezekiel Chapters 25–48*. Translation of the German edn by Paul D. Hanson with Leonard Jay Greenspoon. (Herm) Philadelphia, PA: Fortress.

INDEX OF BIBLICAL REFERENCES

Hebrew Bible

(Verse numbering is in accordance with the Masoretic Text; variants in the English versions are indicated in brackets; 'n' = note.)

Genesis		8:1	106	Numbers	
1:46	142	10:2	123	1	83 n.19
1:28	112, 132	12:2	123	1:2-3	80
	n.24, 142	12:3	81	5:28	124
2:18-20	132 n.24	12:37-38	82 n.3	9:19	81
8:17	112	13:18	79	14:2-3	76
9:1	112	14:4	123	14:28-35	76
9:7	112	14:19	80	25:1	83 n.12
12:11-12	209 n.11	19:14-15	75	26:2-51	81
17:5	109	20:2	123	31:17	122
17:11	206	20:14(17)	81		
17:13	206	20:17	81	Deuteronomy	
17:15	109	20:19(22)	76	7:12	77
19	46–47, 57	22-23(23-24)	75	10:12	77
	n.33, 58	28:42	206	10:22	73
	n.45	32:2-3	72–73	13:6(7)	76–77
19:8	122	34:15-16	106	17:2-17	73–74, 76
22:17	132 n.24	35:4-5	73	21	73
32:26	207	35:20-22	73	22	73
32:28	109	35:29	73	22:13-21	133 n.26
34:3	133, n.36			27:1	74
35:10	109	Leviticus		28:11	77
39:6-7	198	6:10	185, 206	28:18	77
39:6-12	209 n.11	15:2-7	206	28:30	77
39:7	199	15:19	206	28:53	77
39:12	199	16:4	206	28:54-57	74
46:8-27	83 n.19	18	76	29	75
		18:22	40	29:1	74
Exodus		19:20	76	29:9-10(10-11)	74
6:2	123	20:13	40	30:9	77
6:7	106				

Joshua		2:7	114	50:18-45	118
5:6	82 n.11	2:23-24	199	51:36-52	118
10:24	82 n.6	2:25	204		
		3	152–153	Ezekiel	
Judges		3:6-11	90–92	1:5-26	139–142
3:5-6	77	3:10	199	1:9	149
11:39	122	3:12-14	114–115	1:19	149
19	46–47, 57	4:19-21	38	1:24	137
	n.33	5:8	185, 198	3:3	77
19:2	133 n.36	6:8	207	3:13	137
21:12	122	6:11-15	78	5:6	138
		6:15-21	117	5:7-11	118
1 Samuel		7:16-20	39	7	193
4:1-11	80	8:10-11	78	8:7-12	41
15:29	100	14:16	78	8:10	199
15:29-35	131 n.3	15:7-8	78	8:16	41
		15:17	112	8:23	41
2 Samuel		16:1	112	10:2	139
6:14-16	217	16:2	96, 212	13:20	137
6:19-20	75	17:2	39	16	1, 41, 57
19:7	133 n.36	18:19-23	75		n.21, 69
24:1-9	81	19	132 n.23		n.3, 135,
		20:7	38, 96,		224
2 Kings			121, 212	16:26	187, 198,
1:2-8	49	27	132 n.23		206
		29.1	79	16:39	56 n.11
Isaiah		29:6	79	16:40	42
1:21	5 n.1	30:6	38	16:45-55	136,
13:16	83 n.13	30:11	115		147–148
23:17	132 n.15	30:15	115	16:60-63	213
49:15	82 n.4	30:24	115	18:12	156 n.2
50:1	5 n.1	30-31	56 n.18	18:19	138
54:1-6	5 n.1	31:3	39	18:26	137
57:6-13	5 n.1	31:3-5	94–95,	20:16	138
62:4-5	5 n.1		213	20:37	138
		31:4-6	124	22:11	156 n.2
Jeremiah		31:18	115	23	1, 33, 41,
2	150–152	31:27-34	130		54, 57
2-3	1, 39,	37:12	112		n.21
	84–96,	38:19	115	23:11-21	157, 167,
	129–131,	44:15-25	73		169, 172,
	211–212,	44:15-19	39, 58		180–181,
	220–221		n.39		184–209,
2:1-3	35	44:19	73		216
2:1-16	85–90	44:20	74	23:17	207–208
2:2	70, 114	44:24-25	74	23:18	207
2:2-3	133 n.32	44:25	39	23:20	189–190,
2:2-39	117–118	49:2-26	118		206–207

23:21	197	2-3:	223	78:87-93	133 n.32
23:36-49	146–150,	2:5(3)	199, 204	105:39-43	133 n.32
	213–214	2:7(5)	48, 49	106:3-33	133 n.32
23:39-47	135–156	2:10(8)-11(9)	48, 49	127:35	132 n.24
23:40-42	204	2:13(11)	73	128:1-4	78
23:45	42	2:14(12)	48	128:3-4	132 n.24
23:46-47	42	2:16(14)	31, 96	132:11	77
24:15-27	41		n.12, 108		
25:4-16	118	2:17(15)	48	Job	
32:24	79	2:20(18)	106	19:17	77
32:26	79	2:22(20)	121		
33:18-19	137	2:24(22)-25(23)	48, 108	Ruth	
34:1-31	139,	2:25(23)	123	2:13	133 n.36
	142–144,	3	32, 56		
	155, 193		n.5, 154	Lamentations	2
34:6	149	3:1-2	48		
36:3-7	118	3:1-4	99	Ezra	
37:1-14	139,	4:13-14	82 n.1	2:2-67	81
	145–146,	4:14	37	9:1-2	77–78
	155	8:2	133 n.39	10:9-12	78
40:38	138	9:10	132 n.20		
40:44	138	9:11-12	49	Nehemiah	
42:4-5	138	10:4	106	4:8(14)	80
42:11	138	11:1	132 n.20	7:7-69	81
42:4-11	156 n.3	11:1-9	100		
44:7	206	11:9	131 n.3	1 Chronicles	179–180
44:9	206	12:2	106		
46:19-23	138	13:3	101	2 Chronicles	179–180
		13:8	101	20:13	77
Hosea		14:16	49	30:22	133 n.36
1	154, 222			32:6	133 n.36
1-2	33	Amos			
1-3	1, 48,	5:11-16	118	New Testament	
	97–134				
1:2	212	Micah		Ephesians	
1:3-2.3(2.1)	107	1:7	132 n.15	5:21-33	178
1:4-9	123	6:7	77		
1:9	106			Jude	
2	40,	Psalms		1:7	208 n.1,
	153–154,	33:5	39		208 n.3
	205	44:21	209 n.10		

Index of Modern Authors

('n' = note)

Adams St Pierre, E. 163
Andersen, F.T. 100, 103–104, 108,
  111–112, 116–117, 119–120, 121,
  122, 131 n.5, 132 n.11, 153, 156 n.12
Anderson, J.C. 161
Atwood, M. 56 n.12
Austin, J.L. 17–18

Babuscio, J. 170, 182 n.18, 192
Bach, A. 50
Bakon, S. 100
Balz-Cochois, H. 32, 105
Bauer, A. 34, 38–39
Baumann, G. 5 n.2, 5 n.6, 39–40, 55 n.1
Baumgartner, W. 78, 83 n.15
Berlant, L. 27
Bersani, L. 38, 51–52, 59 n.47, 174–177
Bible & Culture Collective 158–159
Bird, P. 32, 37, 57 n.24, 82 n.1, 113
Black, M. 5 n.9, 65–66
Block, D. 136, 144, 156 n.7 & 10
Boer, R. 179–180
Booth, M. 168, 177, 183 n.29
Boswell, J. 46–47
Botterweck, G. 78, 81, 83 n.16, 105, 132
  n.15, 206
Bozak, B. 56 n.18
Bray, A. 12
Brenner, A. 29, 31, 40, 56 n.4, 56 n.11,
  125, 185, 206
Brownstein, R.M. 160, 164 n.9 & 14
Budd, P.J. 80–81
Butler, J. 9, 10, 13–24, 36, 43, 68,
  158–159, 161, 168, 208 n.2

Carden, M. 5 n.5
Carroll, R.P. 41, 57 n.21, 66, 89, 96 n.6,
  211
Chase, S.E. 164 n.13
Cleto, F. 168, 170–171, 174–175, 181
  n.8, 9 & 12, 183 n.43
Clines, D. 117
Cohen, C. 52
Cohen, E. 182 n.23
Colette 58 n.45
Collier, D. 197
Collins, A.E. 113, 132 n.25
Connolly, T.J. 31, 56 n.4, 125–128, 213
Core, P. 168, 181 n.6
Crisp, Q. 174–175
Cummings, S. 194, 200, 207

Davies, G.I. 102, 104, 109, 122, 132
  n.20, 133 n.39
Davies, P.R. 183 n.38
Davis, J. 58 n.37
Day, J. 132 n.16
D'Emilio, J. 182 n.16
Dempsey, C.J. 56 n.4
Denzin, N.K. 161–163, 164 n.12
Dever, W.G. 69 n.6
Diamond, A.R.P. 28–29, 34–35, 86,
  88–89, 92–93, 96 n.7 & 9, 98
Dijk-Hemmes, F.V. 30, 35, 56 n.4, 105,
  191
Dollimore, J. 168
Donne, J. 38, 56 n.17
Douglas, M. 17

Dyer, R. 170, 172–174, 182 n.17 & 18, 183 n.26

Eilberg-Schwartz, H. 42–45, 57 n.19, 57 n.24, 65
Emmerson, G.I. 119, 122, 125, 133 n.38, 134 n.43
Escoffier, J. 53
Exum, J.C. 31, 84–85, 92–93

Fensham, F.C. 106–107
Fetterley, J. 159
Fish, S.E. 158–160, 164 n.3
Fitzgerald, A. 64, 69 n.4
Flinn, C. 183 n.30
Fontaine, C.R. 55 n.2, 56 n.4
Foucault, M. 10–12, 15–17
Fowler, R.M. 160
Freedman, D.N. 100, 103–104, 108, 111–112, 116–117, 119–120, 121, 122, 131 n.5, 132 n.11, 153, 156 n.12
Freedman, D.P. 160, 164 n.7 & 8
Frymer-Kensky, T. 132 n.25
Fuchs, E. 57 n.25

Galambush, J. 55 n.2, 63–64, 71, 85, 93, 96 n.3
Gilmore, D. 58 n.37
Goldingay, J. 40–41
Goldman, M.D. 112
Gordis, R. 109
Gordon, P. 39, 129
Goss, R.E. 45–47, 57 n.26 & 28
Gottwald, N.K. 33
Graetz, N. 31
Greenberg, M. 27, 28, 35–36, 41, 56 n.9, 66, 136–137, 140, 142–146, 149, 187, 191, 198, 199, 206, 207
Guest, D. 14, 45, 50, 52–53, 164 n.10

Hackett, J.R. 32, 106, 132 n.16
Hadley, J.M. 69 n.6
Halperin, D.J. 41–42, 57 n.23
Halperin, D.M. 12, 24 n.1
Harvey, G. 57 n.25
Harvey, K. 174

Hendel, R.S. 57 n.25
Hinkle, C. 54
Holbrook, C.A. 184
Holladay, W.L. 90–91, 96 n.5, 112
Hopkins, D.C. 33
Hopkins, G.M. 56 n.17
Hornsby, T.J. 32, 132 n.17
Houtman, C. 81
Huffer, L. 51–53

Iser, W. 158, 164 n.4
Isherwood, C. 173, 177, 183 n.26, 192, 209 n.12

Jagose, A. 9, 23, 24 n.1 & 3, 50, 57 n.27, 210
Jameson, F. 101
Jansen, S.C. 68
Jeffreys, S. 23, 51, 53
Jennings, T.W. 46–48, 208 n.5, 217
Johnson, B. 162
Johnson, M. 64, 67, 69 n.5
Jones, S.H. 162

Keefe, A.A. 33–34, 48, 56 n.5, 104, 105–106, 109, 113, 132 n.15 & 16, 133 n.27
Kittel, G. 206
Kleinhans, C. 168
Koch, T.R. 49–50
Koehler, L. 78, 83 n.15, 112
Kristeva, J. 15–16

Lacan, J. 15–16
Lakoff, G. 64, 67, 69 n.5
Landy, F. 40, 104, 132 n.13
Leith, M.J.W. 33, 37–39, 57 n.24, 70–71, 213
Lemche, N.P. 105–106
Lévi-Strauss, C. 15–16, 58 n.37
Lewy, J. 69 n.4
Liew, T.B. 217 n.13
Lincoln, Y.S. 161–163, 164 n.12
Lofthouse, W.F. 191
Loughlin, G. 45, 178
Lundbom, J.R. 88, 112

McFague, S. 63–66, 69 n.1, 7 & 9
Macintosh, A.A. 104, 116, 120, 122–124, 133 n.35
McNeill, J.J. 46–47
Macwilliam, S. 96 n.1
Malinowitz, H. 53
Mays, J.L. 122, 133 n.32, 33 & 37
Meyer, M. 170, 174, 181 n.2
Miller, N.K. 161–162, 164 n.8
Moore, S.D. 158–161, 164 n.3, 7 & 15
Moughtin-Mumby, S. 1, 55 n.2, 69 n.3, 132 n.18
Murray, D. 82 n.6, 133 n.32

Newton, E. 14, 173, 176, 183 n.33
Nussbaum, M.C. 14, 20–21

O'Brien, J.M. 157
O'Connor, K. 30, 34–35, 56 n.4 & 8, 86, 88–89, 92–93, 96 n.7 & 9, 98
Odell, M.S. 55 n.2
Ortlund, R.C. 4, 5 n.10, 215

Patton, C.L. 29, 33, 39, 129
Plaskow, J. 70
Plummer, K. 9
Pollock, D. 58 n.37
Premnath, D.N. 33

Richards, I.A. 65
Richardson, L. 163
Ricoeur, P. 63
Ringgren, J. 78, 81, 83 n.16, 105, 132 n.15, 206
Riviere, J. 15, 56 n.14
Rooker, M.F. 136–138, 142, 145, 156 n.5, 214
Ross, A. 164 n.1, 169, 171, 173, 177, 182 n.15, 202
Rowley, H.H. 55 n.1, 103, 107, 110, 131 n.6, 9 & 10

Sabo, D. 68
Salih, S. 25 n.19
Schlissel, L. 202–203
Schmitt, J.J. 86–88, 90–91, 131 n.7
Schüngel-Straumann, H. 100–102, 131 n.5

Sedgwick, E.K. 9–12, 23–24, 24 n.10, 160, 168
Seidman, S. 23, 24 n.3
Setel, T. D. 29–30, 105, 125
Sherwood, Y. 28, 31–32, 35–36, 37, 38, 50, 55 n.1, 56 n.3, 66, 101, 107, 109, 121, 123, 128, 132 n.21, 213
Shibles, W. 69 n.1
Shields, M.E. 56 n.4
Shilts, R. 182 n.16
Simpson, M. 9
Sinfield, A. 171–172, 182 n.21, 22 & 23
Slonim, M.G. 156 n.4
Sontag, S. 67–68, 168–173, 175–176, 181 n.2, 5, 7, 17, 24 & 25, 189, 203
Soskice, J.M. 63–64, 66–67
Spargo, T. 10, 24 n.3
Spencer, D.T. 49
Sperber, A. 112
Staley, J.L. 161
Stein, A. 9
Stevens, C. 183 n.42
Stienstra, N. 63, 86
Stigliano, T. 67
Stone, K. 1–2, 5 n.3 & 4, 27–28, 34, 45, 48–50, 53, 54, 56 n.5, 133 n.25 & 26
Streete, G.C. 57 n.25
Stuart, E. 45, 178, 181 n.1
Sullivan, N. 9, 24 n.3

Tompkins, J. 160
Torres, S. 192
Tyler, C. 56 n.14

Ullendorf, E. 133 n.40, 164 n.2

Veeser, H.A. 160, 164 n.8

Wacker, M. 30, 37, 100
Wakeman, M.K. 69 n.4
Ware, J.R. 169–172, 181 n.13, 189
Warner, M. 24 n.3 & 4, 27
Washington, H.C. 39, 129
Watney, S. 58 n.43
Weeks, J. 25 n.13 & 14, 182 n.16
Weems, R.J. 30, 31, 125
Wenham, G.J. 81
West, M. 2, 45, 57 n.28, 179

Williams, K. 169, 180–181
Wittig, M. 15–16
Wolff, H.W. 100, 104, 105, 108, 110,
117, 118, 119, 121–122, 123, 133
n.34, 37 & 41

Yee, G.A. 31, 33

Zimmerli, W. 136, 138, 142–149, 156
n.7 & 11, 191, 193, 198, 207, 208 n.7,
209 n.11

Subject Index

('n' = note)

Antischemata
    Ezekiel 135–136, 224
    Hosea 98–99, 222–223
    Jeremiah 88–91, 220–221
Asherah 32, 39–40
autobiographical criticism 160–164

Binaries 2, 10–12, 171
body 16–18

Camp 157–158, 167–183
    crossover 168, 169–172
    dandyism 171
    definition 168, 169, 171
    effeminacy 170, 171
    exaggeration 169, 172, 189–190
    Ezekiel 184–209
    failed seriousness 182 n.24,
        200–203
    femininity 175–177
    functions 173–177, 178, 179–180,
        192–193
    gay 169–172, 174–177
    high/low 169–172, 172–173, 177
    hypocrisy 186, 192–198
    mockery 173
    misogyny 175
    public/private 174–175
    stylistics 172–173
chiasms
    Jeremiah 86–88
Crisp, Quentin 174–175
cultic prostitution 32

Drag 14–22, 176

Ejaculation 187–189

Failures
    see necessary failures
feminist biblical scholars
    see marriage metaphor: feminist
    scholars

Gay Times 186–187, 188–189,
    194–198
gender identity
    see identity
gender performativity
    see performativity

Homosexualities 10–12, 55

Identity 13–18
inception criticism 29, 31–34
indecency 158
interrogative shift 36–40
Israel/Israelites
    assumed to be male 70–72, 86–87
    as wives of Yhwh 92–94
    censuses 80–81
    gender inclusivity 72–75
    gender exclusivity 75–79

Marriage metaphor
    addressees 92–93
    as dead metaphor 84

as three movement suite 94–95,
114–125, 127–129, 213
feminist criticism 28–34, 125–126

definition 1
Ezekiel 135–156, 184–209
Hosea 98–134, 153–154
Jeremiah 84–96, 130–131,
150–153
queer criticism 45–55
referential intrusion 136–137,
142–143, 147–156
see also metaphor
masculine for feminine forms 136–150
masculist criticism 40–41
metaphor
definition 63–65
ideology 67–68
interaction of tenor/vehicle 4, 5
n.9, 65–66
origins 64–65
necessary failure 68
scientific thought 66–67
see also marriage metaphor

Naturalness, naturalization 2, 13,
15–18
necessary failures 18–20, 91–92, 161

Penis
hidden 206–207
size 185–190
performativity 13–22
pornophophetics 31
prostitution
see cultic prostitution

psychoanalysis 41–42

Qualitative research 161–163
queer
'holdall' view 45
inward/outward 2, 45–50
history 11–12
terminology 1–3, 55
queer theory 9–26
biblical criticism
see marriage metaphor: queer
criticism
definitions 9
ethics 20–22, 49–50, 50–55
resistance 18–22
self reflexion 51, 129–131,
150–156, 157–164, 205
theorists 9–10

Reader-response criticism 28,
158–160
reception criticism 2, 29–31

Self disgust 193–194, 207–208
Self-reflection 51, 29–131, 150–154,
157–158, 161
Sex addiction 192–198

West, Mae 201–203
Wilde, Oscar 169
Williams, Kenneth 169, 180–181
writing as methodology 163–164

Yhwh
maternal imagery 100–102

9 781845 536732